M

Work Out

English

GCSE

The titles in this series

For examinations at 16+

Accounting
Biology
Chemistry
Computer Studies
Economics
English
French
German

Human Biology
Mathematics
Numeracy
Physics
Sociology
Spanish
Statistics

For examinations at 'A' level

Applied Mathematics
Biology
Chemistry
English Literature

Physics
Pure Mathematics
Statistics

For examinations at college level

Dynamics
Elements of Banking
Mathematics for Economists

Operational Research
Engineering Thermodynamics

MACMILLAN
WORK OUT
SERIES

Work Out

English

GCSE

S. H. Burton

MACMILLAN

First published 1986
Reprinted with corrections 1986
This edition 1987

Published by
MACMILLAN EDUCATION LTD
Houndmills, Basingstoke, Hampshire RG21 2XS
and London
Companies and representatives
throughout the world

Typeset by TecSet Ltd,
Wallington, Surrey
Printed in Great Britain at The Bath Press, Avon

British Library Cataloguing in Publication Data
Burton, S. H.
Work out English GCSE. —2nd ed. —
(Macmillan work out series)
1. English language — Grammar — 1950–
I. Title   II. Burton, S. H. Work out English
Language 'O' level & GCSE
428   PE1112
ISBN 0-333-44003-X
ISBN 0-333-43452-8 export

Contents

Acknowledgements

The author and publishers wish to thank the following who have kindly given permission for the use of copyright material:

Jack Cross for an extract from his article 'Money matters', published in *The Guardian* (April 3, 1984).

A. M. Heath and Company Ltd on behalf of the Estate of the late **Sonia Brownell Orwell** and **Martin Secker and Warburg Ltd** for an extract from the *Collected Essays, Journalism and Speeches of George Orwell*, Vol. 4.

A. P. Watt Ltd on behalf of **Robert Langley** for extracts from his published work.

London and East Anglian Group for GCSE for permission to use the specimen paper 'English Paper 2: Understanding and response'.

Every effort has been made to trace all the copyright holders, but if any have been inadvertently overlooked, the publishers will be pleased to make the necessary arrangements at the first opportunity.

Organisations Responsible for GCSE Examinations

In the United Kingdom, examinations are administered by the following organisations. Syllabuses and examination papers can be ordered from the addresses given here:

Northern Examining Association (NEA)

Joint Matriculation Board (JMB)
Publications available from:
John Sherratt & Son Ltd
78 Park Road, Altrincham
Cheshire WA14 5QQ

North Regional Examinations Board
Wheatfield Road
Westerhope
Newcastle upon Tyne NE5 5JZ

Yorkshire and Humberside Regional Examinations Board (YREB)
Scarsdale House
136 Derbyside Lane
Sheffield S8 8SE

Associated Lancashire Schools Examining Board
12 Harter Street
Manchester M1 6HL

North West Regional Examinations Board (NWREB)
Orbit House, Albert Street
Eccles, Manchester M30 0WL

Midland Examining Group (MEG)

**University of Cambridge Local
 Examinations Syndicate (UCLES)**
Syndicate Buildings, Hills Road
Cambridge CB1 2EU

**Oxford and Cambridge Schools
 Examination Board (O & C)**
10 Trumpington Street
Cambridge CB2 1QB

Southern Universities' Joint Board (SUJB)
Cotham Road
Bristol BS6 6DD

**East Midland Regional Examinations
 Board (EMREB)**
Robins Wood House, Robins Wood Road
Aspley, Nottingham NG8 3NR

**West Midlands Examinations Board
 (WMEB)**
Norfolk House, Smallbrook
Queensway, Birmingham B5 4NJ

London and East Anglian Group (LEAG)

**University of London School
 Examinations Board (L)**
University of London Publications Office
52 Gordon Square
London WC1E 6EE

**London Regional Examining Board
 (LREB)**
Lyon House
104 Wandsworth High Street
London SW18 4LF

East Anglian Examinations Board (EAEB)
The Lindens, Lexden Road
Colchester, Essex CO3 3RL

Southern Examining Group (SEG)

The Associated Examining Board (AEB)
Stag Hill House
Guildford, Surrey GU2 5XJ

**University of Oxford Delegacy of
 Local Examinations (OLE)**
Ewert Place, Banbury Road
Summertown, Oxford OX2 7BZ

**Southern Regional Examinations
 Board (SREB)**
Avondale House, 33 Carlton Crescent
Southampton, Hants SO9 4YL

**South-East Regional Examinations
 Board (SEREB)**
Beloe House, 2–10 Mount Ephraim Road
Royal Tunbridge Wells, Kent TN1 1EU

Scottish Examination Board (SEB)

Publications available from:
Robert Gibson and Sons (Glasgow) Ltd
17 Fitzroy Place, Glasgow G3 7SF

Welsh Joint Education Committee (WJEC)

245 Western Avenue
Cardiff CF5 2YX

Northern Ireland Schools Examinations
Council (NISEC)

Examinations Office
Beechill House, Beechill Road
Belfast BT8 4RS

Introduction

How to Use This Book

As its title tells you, it is a *work* book. It gives you jobs to do, explaining their various purposes and suggesting ways of tackling them. Then, when you have worked through them (sometimes, *while* you are working through them), it shows you how to judge your performance and how to improve it. By getting down to these jobs you will take an active part in a variety of experiences and learn from them how to use language effectively in different situations, for different purposes and in different forms.

That is what 'being good at English' means. That is what the GCSE examination expects of you. That is what this book will help you to do if you follow the work outs step by step and then apply their lessons to the practice material.

Problems are approached methodically, so you must be prepared to apply yourself closely to detailed explanations and demonstrations. General advice — 'write clearly', 'organise your answer', 'choose your words carefully' — is easy to give, but not helpful to receive. That is why the work outs occupy a lot of space. You will have to spend time on them, but it will be time well spent.

In the examination the various pieces of work you submit (either assessed coursework or examination papers) are given different 'job descriptions'. For example, some work is classified as 'Expression', some as 'Understanding and Response', and so on. Each kind of work in which you will be examined is explained (and what it requires of you is demonstrated) in a separate chapter. Inevitably, there is some overlap. Neither this book nor the examination can (or attempts to) isolate one 'part' of English from the rest. The book starts with 'Expression', but there is a very real sense in which all English is 'expression'. For example, your answers in 'Understanding and Response' are 'expression' — they express your understanding and response! Similarly, there is common ground in 'Practical Writing' and 'Directed Writing', as Chapters 2 and 5 make clear.

However, it *is* true that each particular kind of question (and, of course, each 'work area') has its own particular 'target'. That 'target', which determines the kind of answer required, is implicit in the wording of the question. Chapters 1–5 provide detailed demonstrations of successful methods of 'target recognition'. They show you how to discover the full implications of a question and how to ensure that your answer is relevant in its contents and appropriate in its language.

Two parts of the book may seem at first sight to be less firmly linked than the others to the examined uses of English as described in your syllabus. Chapter 4 teaches you how to summarise, and it may well be that your examining board does not set questions which *directly* test that skill. Do not be tempted to skip Chapter 4. As you will see, the ability to summarise is crucial to a good performance in 'Understanding' and 'Directed Writing'.

Chapters 6–10 deal with the basic skills of written English. The examiners do not set separate questions testing vocabulary, grammar, punctuation and spelling, but your standards in all those matters play a large part in determining the grade you get. It is not much good having lots of interesting things to write about an 'Expression' topic if your written English is ungrammatical, badly punctuated and misspelt. You are unlikely to write a good 'Understanding' answer if your vocabulary is so limited that you cannot understand key words and expressions in the passage on which you are working.

So do not fail to use those chapters to improve your basic skills, referring to them for guidance whenever you need help with your written English. (If you find the first two sections of Chapter 8 heavy going at first, don't worry. They set out the basic grammar underlying the ground rules applied for practical purposes in Sections 8.3–8.5. Those sections provide the help you need to write well-constructed sentences and to avoid common blunders. Having proved for yourself how useful the ground rules are, you will probably return to Sections 8.1 and 8.2 with renewed interest.)

Fully worked-out answers to the test papers and examination questions come at the end of the book. Do *not* look at my answers until you have written your own. Then make a careful comparison between them. Do not accept my answers uncritically. I have done my best to make a good job of them, but you may think yours are better — or, at least, better in places. Think hard. Try to find out exactly *why* yours are better (or, of course, why mine are). You will learn a lot by making detailed critical comparisons.

Preparation

In books designed to help examination candidates it is a time-honoured custom to offer some hints on revision, but I would argue that 'revision' is not an appropriate term to apply to any stage of your preparation for GCSE English. Some of the coursework you submit for assessment may have been written quite early in your final year. In any case, learning to use English is a continuous (indeed, a life-long) process of growth. You — and I — are for ever trying to find better ways of using language as we encounter new experience.

That is why I am suggesting fruitful ways of preparing rather than attempting to offer you advice on late-stage cramming. It wouldn't do you any good. GCSE English tests all the English skills you have learnt ever since you started to talk.

Even so, while acquiring new skills, you have to consolidate those you learnt earlier. One of the best ways of at once enlarging and reinforcing your command of language is by reading. Make time for reading — all kinds of reading: novels, short stories, biographies, newspapers, magazines, 'specialist' writing (about your leisure interests and hobbies, for instance). Read in the careful, *comprehending* way described in Chapters 3 and 4. Read critically, with an eye to the style as well as the content. Try to be discriminating. Use your dictionary and build up your word stock.

Talk about your reading, too, with anybody you can find who shares your interests. Only don't just ramble on. Try to say something! (People often talk a lot without saying anything.) That advice goes for all your talking about all your interests. Cut out the *ums* and *ers*. Try to be clear and crisp. Arrange your ideas so that one follows another sensibly. Good talking improves your writing. Good writing improves your talking.

Study your examination syllabus and specimen papers. The syllabus explains the objectives of the examination and what is expected of you. It also explains the options open to you — subject to the advice of your teachers, who are responsible for the framework within which you are working.

Both the syllabus and the specimen papers will give you ideas for coursework and provide you with extra practice material to use when you have completed all the work in this book. You cannot have too much practice. Experiment as you write. There is always more than one way of tackling a piece of writing. Try out different openings and overall structures. Be adventurous with words and vary your sentences. See what you can do.

The Examination

Many of the most important features of GCSE English have been touched on earlier in this Introduction. The examination is a test of all your English skills — in talking and listening, in writing and reading. It gives you scope to exercise your own talents by using language in a variety of situations and in a variety of forms.

The part played by assessed coursework (for which *at least* 20 per cent of your marks will be awarded) ensures that you will be graded on your own best efforts. As this book and your syllabus and specimen papers will show, both in coursework and in work done under examination conditions, GCSE English encourages — and rewards — a personal response to tests which, without 'tricks' and 'traps', put you on your mettle.

The situations in which the examiners require you to use language vary from the strictly practical to the creative, but they are all intended to interest you and to draw out the best that you can do. The practical situations are such as you may well become involved in (probably have been involved in) in 'real life'. The opportunities to use your imagination are so varied that you can hardly fail to find at least one subject that gets you going.

GCSE English tests your ability to get through to other people — to *communicate*, orally and in writing. It gives you opportunities to show what *you* know, what *you* understand, and what *you* can do. I hope this book will help you to make the most of those opportunities in *all* your written English — in coursework, in examination papers, and in the English of your daily life.

S. H. Burton

1 Expression

1.1 Definition and Description

(a) The Meaning of 'Expression'

The term 'Expression' is applied to writing assignments and questions that test your ability to write at some length on a variety of subjects and in different forms. The different kinds of subjects set in these assignments and questions and the different forms of writing that you have to be able to use are explained in this chapter and the next.

- The *sustained pieces of writing* on which you will be graded according to your ability to write clearly, correctly and imaginatively are tests of 'Expression'.

(b) 'Composition Writing' and 'Practical Writing'

All assignments and questions in 'Expression' can be classified as being tests of your ability *either* to write a 'composition' *or* to carry out a 'practical' writing task. The instructions make it clear which you are being asked to do. All the examining boards require you to provide examples of both kinds of writing. In assessed coursework the emphasis is on compositions, but some practical writing must be included. In examination papers the emphasis is on practical writing, but some 'compositional' writing may be asked for as well. You must be aware of the distinctive features of each kind of writing, and you must practise both kinds as you prepare for the examination.

(c) The Differences between Composition Writing and Practical Writing

The subjects set for compositions are different from those set for practical writing. Here are some typical syllabus descriptions of the two kinds of subjects set and of the different ways in which candidates are expected to respond to them.

Composition writing
1. The nature of the subjects will be such as to invite descriptive, narrative and imaginative (or 'creative') writing. Some discursive topics will also be offered. The content and form of the answer will be largely determined by the writer's individual response to the wording of the subject.
2. Candidates will be expected to write with some freshness and imagination. Opportunities to express opinions clearly and to sustain an argument will be provided. The content and form of the writing will be for each candidate to decide, but relevance, coherence and sound paragraphing are expected.

Practical writing
1. The content, purpose and audience will be prescribed in the instructions. The form of the writing (for example: letters, reports, operational instructions) will also be stipulated.

4

2. The particular task to be carried out will be strictly defined. Candidates will be assessed on the accuracy and clarity with which they communicate what is required, using given material in a practical situation.

Comparison of some typical subjects set for the two kinds of writing brings out the distinction between them.

(i) *Examples of Subjects Set for Composition*

1. A family feud.
2. Windows.
3. Describe the scene at a busy market in the week before Christmas.
4. Many people believe that corporal punishment and/or imprisonment should be used to deter young football hooligans and vandals. What do you think?

(ii) *Examples of Subjects Set for Practical Writing*

1. Write a letter to the mother of a friend of yours explaining why you are unable to accept her invitation to spend a few days at your friend's home during the summer holidays. Give your reasons clearly, but in such a way as to avoid hurting her feelings.
2. A group of foreign students is coming on an exchange visit to your home town. Write an introductory talk that you would give to them on one of the following topics:
    (a) Places of interest to visit in and around the town.
    (b) How to get the best out of local transport facilities.
    (c) Tips on suitable (and unsuitable) places to eat.
3. Write clear instructions on how to carry out one of the following:
    (a) Repair a puncture in a bicycle tyre.
    (b) Prepare suitable living quarters for a small animal to be kept as a pet.
    (c) Change films in a camera.

(d) Imaginative Writing and Practical Writing

The terms 'imaginative' (or 'creative') writing and 'practical' (or 'factual') writing are often used to describe the differences between the kind of answer required in composition and the kind of answer required in 'directed' writing. The specimen questions printed in Section 1.1(c) showed that there is a clear distinction between the two kinds of writing. Further study of typical papers will confirm that the subjects set in the two different questions are designed to test candidates in sharply contrasting ways.

Imaginative or creative writing

(i) Much of the material used in the composition must be imagined (created) by the writer, although its source is often (and best) found in personal experience.

(ii) The wording of the question invites a free and personal response from the writer.

(iii) The question is intended to be a 'trigger' for the writer's imagination. The emphasis is on self-

Practical, factual or directed writing

(i) Much of the material to be used in the writing exercise is supplied in the wording of the question.

(ii) The wording of the question controls the writer's response. The instructions demand an answer that takes a given form and develops along preset lines.

(iii) The question limits the writer's answer to a given area of communication. Clear treatment of

expression and creativity: a subjective approach is required.

factual material is looked for. The candidate writes to the examiners' 'brief': an objective approach is required.

Because composition and factual writing make such different demands, they are treated separately in this book. The writing of compositions of various kinds is demonstrated in this chapter, and ways of tackling practical writing exercises are demonstrated in Chapter 2.

(e) What the Examiners are Looking for

Both composition and practical writing are primarily tests of a candidate's ability to write well-organised, clear and accurate English. In each case the examiners are looking for a piece of writing that is:

- carefully planned as an answer to the chosen question;
- soundly constructed and clearly paragraphed;
- written in well-made and varied sentences;
- correct in its grammar, punctuation and spelling.

1.2 Different Kinds of Composition

(a) Classifications

The examiners make it clear that compositions of several different kinds are set. Here is just one typical statement to that effect: 'Dramatic, impressionistic, narrative and discursive subjects will be included.' Study of all the syllabuses and of representative question papers provides the following classifications of composition subjects: (1) narrative; (2) descriptive; (3) discursive; (4) dramatic; (5) impressionistic.

Candidates must learn to identify the category to which their chosen subject belongs, for each kind of subject has its own special features and must be treated accordingly. For example, an impressionistic subject requires a more subjective approach than a discursive subject.

Both the *form* of a composition and the *style* in which it is written must be suited to the kind of subject that has been selected.

The notes that now follow list the distinguishing features of each kind of subject. The work-out sections of this chapter demonstrate how those features affect the planning and writing of compositions of each kind.

(b) Narrative Writing

Narrative compositions tell (narrate) a story or give an account of a sequence of events. Their subjects are about *action*. For example: 'Write a story entitled *In the Nick of Time*'; 'Give an account of an exciting journey that you once made by land or sea or air'.

A story composition must have plot, characters and atmosphere. A plot is not needed for an account of events, but the narrator must introduce 'human interest' and set it against a realistic background. In both a story and an account of events the narration must move forward. Narrative compositions must not be static.

(c) Descriptive Writing

Obviously, descriptive compositions describe! They describe a scene or a place or an object or a person. For example: 'Describe either the sights or the sounds at a busy bus station on a winter's day'; 'Describe the appearance, personality and home surroundings of someone well known to you, either of your own age or much older'.

The key to success is the writer's ability to find an imaginative approach to the subject and to shape the composition so that every detail contributes to the overall effect that has been planned. Lacking that creative angle of attack, a descriptive composition is a mere list of details haphazardly strung together. Very boring.

(d) Discursive (Argumentative or Controversial) Writing

A discursive composition is one in which the writer presents facts, ideas and opinions about a given topic and *arrives at a conclusion by reasoning*. Typical discursive subjects are: 'What gives "pop" music its following?'; 'Do you think that smoking should be banned by law?'; 'What are the good and bad points about television?'; 'Consider the arguments for and against fox hunting'.

The alternative names for discursive compositions — 'argumentative compositions' and 'controversial compositions' — indicate the kind of subjects set and the kind of treatment required.

A genuine interest in and some information about the chosen topic are essential. So, too, are a respect for facts, a balanced attitude to the opinions of others and a clear presentation of the writer's point of view.

Discursive (argumentative or controversial) subjects are: *discursive*, because they require writers to reason their way to a conclusion; *argumentative*, because they require writers to set out the arguments on both sides and to weigh them fairly; *controversial*, because they require writers to keep cool and think clearly about topics that stir up strong feelings.

(e) Dramatic (Conversational) Writing

Dramatic compositions must be written in *direct speech*. Hence the alternative name 'conversational compositions'. Typical dramatic (conversational) subjects are: 'A lecturer and a student have had a disagreement. Write a dialogue between them in which the circumstances of their quarrel are made plain and in the course of which they come to a friendly resolution of their problem'; 'Write a short play by continuing the dialogue set out below in a manner which develops the dramatic situation'. (The first few lines of the dialogue are provided to introduce the characters and to establish the initial dramatic situation.)

Success in such compositions depends on the ability to write direct speech for two or more characters (dialogue) that sounds convincing and that develops the initial situation in an interesting way.

(f) Impressionistic Writing

Impressionistic compositions are highly subjective and imaginative compositions. Several pictures are provided as a starting point. The instructions then read like this: 'Write a composition suggested by one of these pictures. Your composition may be directly about the subject of the picture, or may be based on some suggestion that you take from the picture; but there must be some clear connection between the picture and your writing. You may choose to write in the form of a story or of a description.'

Another kind of impressionistic composition is based on a short poem (or an extract from a poem). Candidates are instructed to describe the ideas or thoughts or feelings that the poem suggests to them (in other words, the *impressions* it makes on their minds). Or they may be told to write (in prose, of course) a description of a place or a person well known to them in circumstances similar to those described in the poem. Or they may be asked to write a story based on the poem.

Whatever the particular form asked for, a successful impressionistic composition requires close observation of the details of the picture (or careful reading of the poem), an imaginative response and a clear link between the given stimulus (picture or poem) and the candidate's writing.

1.3 Examination Techniques

(a) Planning Your Time

Some of your assessed coursework in Expression will be written in your own time. In theory, you can take as long as you like over each piece of writing, for you are not under pressure to finish at a particular time or after writing uninterruptedly for a stipulated period. In practice, however, you need to set yourself a time limit for each piece of writing you do. Other work has to be done and you cannot spend more than a certain amount of your examination preparation in producing expressive pieces for assessment. Also, you will find that a self-imposed time limit is an aid to good work. Writing that can be finished 'any time' has a habit of not getting done or of being rushed through at the last minute. A sensible 'deadline' helps you to concentrate and to write better. A 'tomorrow-or-next-week-will-do' attitude encourages sloppy thinking, poor planning and careless writing.

Some of your assessed coursework (at least one piece — and more than one for some examining boards) will be written under supervision with a time limit for completion. And, of course, if you have been entered for an examination paper in Expression a time schedule is imposed and you must pace your writing within it. Find out how long the paper is and how many questions you must answer. Then practise answering papers and fitting your answers into the time available.

Sections (c) and (d) below give further advice on planning and timing.

(b) Choosing Your Subjects

In preparing for the examination, you will learn your own strengths as a writer and what kinds of writing you handle best. That experience will help you to reject subjects that are not suited to you. You have to demonstrate that you can write on different kinds of topics and in different forms, so your folder of expressive work must include various kinds of writing. Even so, there will always be the opportunity of selecting subjects that *interest* you. Your best work in composition is done when you can make a *personal* response and write in an individual and fresh way.

(c) Planning Your Writing

Skimped and careless planning is the commonest cause of poor work in composition. Every piece should be thoroughly planned *before* you start to write it. Three different (but linked) operations are involved: gathering material; selecting material; shaping the composition. Each of these operations is explained and demonstrated in the work-out sections of this chapter.

(d) Length and Timing

Each piece of writing that you submit for assessment will be between 400 and 500 words in length. Different examining boards word their requirements in different ways but they do not vary much in what they are looking for, as these typical regulations show.

1. *Five* units of work must be submitted to demonstrate a range of kinds of writing. *Each unit* should be *400–500* words in length, but a unit may consist of a number of related pieces of writing.
2. The coursework folder must contain *six* pieces of work of an approximate *total* length of *2500* words. A variety of writing is required.

Find out what length your own examining board stipulates, then practise accordingly. Quality is always more important than quantity, but you must not write shorter pieces than are asked for. Nor must you go much (if at all) beyond the maximum length laid down. If you plan carefully and practise frequently, you will learn to fit your pieces to the required length, while giving them a firm shape – a beginning, a middle and an end (see Section 1.6).

You will be advised how much time to spend on each of the coursework assignments that you write. Experiment too by setting yourself different time limits when you are practising. Aim to complete some pieces in an hour, some in an hour and a half, others in two hours.

The piece (or pieces) that you have to write under supervision will probably be written in about an hour. For the much shorter ('guided') composition pieces that you may have to write in an examination paper, you will be allowed about half an hour.

(e) Reading through and Correcting

In *all* your written work, the examiners expect:

- correct grammar;
- accurate spelling;
- clear punctuation;
- appropriate and effective vocabulary.

Always spend a few minutes reading through what you have written and correcting any careless slips you may have made. Valuable marks can be saved in this way. (Section 1.5(f) provides a demonstration.)

1.4 Summing up

1. 'Expression' tests your ability to write at some length on a variety of subjects and in different forms.
2. The term 'expressive writing' applies to pieces written in the form of *compo-*

sitions. It also applies to *practical* (factual and directed) pieces of writing.

3. Subjects for composition may be: narrative; descriptive; discursive; dramatic; impressionistic.
4. When you are writing a composition:

- Choose a subject on which you can write *interestingly*.
- *Plan* a piece of writing that suits the *nature* and *form* (narrative, descriptive, and so on) of the subject you have chosen.
- Write in an *appropriate* style.
- Take care with *grammar*, *spelling* and *punctuation*.
- Stick to the *length limits* laid down.

1.5 Work out Narrative Writing

(a) Getting to Grips with Narrative Subjects

The subjects set for narrative writing are of two distinct kinds:

1. Subjects that require you to write a *story*.
2. Subjects that require you to write an *account of events*.

In each kind of narrative the *action* provides the chief interest, but a story has some special features that are not required in a straightforward narration of events. The following table sets out the characteristic qualities of each.

A story	*An account of events*
(i) Must have a plot. It need not be complicated, but there must be a 'story line'. In a story things change. Perhaps a discovery is made or a problem is solved. Perhaps people's attitudes alter or their relationships with one another develop. In some important way a new situation is brought about and the story-teller must plan the events so that they lead to this development.	(i) Does not need a plot, but must progressively relate a sequence of events. The reader's attention is held by a series of incidents. The writer must provide links to connect successive events and to keep the narrative flowing in an interesting way. The action must move steadily forward from the beginning to the end. A successful narrative depends on a clear plan.
(ii) Needs characters to provide an interesting interplay of personalities and to create tension. There is no need to 'crowd the canvas' with people. Two characters will often be enough. The important thing is to involve people with events. A story is about people doing things.	(ii) 'Characterisation' (in the story sense) is not required, but some 'human interest' makes for a lively narration. Perhaps the personality of the narrator 'comes through' or there are some interesting glimpses of the people taking part in the happenings. The emphasis, however, is on action rather than on character.
(iii) Description of people and places is essential. The characters are placed against an interesting and convincing background. Much of	(iii) Description plays an important part in the narration. The emphasis is on action, but action does not take place in a vacuum.

the interest in a story is generated by the interplay of people, events and setting. A close connection between people and places creates an 'atmosphere'.

(iv) Dialogue (conversation between characters) is essential. People in stories talk to one another (as they do in real life). As they talk, they come alive for the reader and the plot is carried forward. The changing situations of a story — see (i) — are often brought about by or revealed through dialogue.

(v) A story is a piece of fiction. Plot, characters and setting are invented by the writer. Personal experience must be drawn on to create convincing people and places — 'write about what you know' — but a story is essentially made up: imagined.

Details are needed to help the reader to follow the events. Interest is aroused by lively description of a realistic setting.

(iv) Dialogue is not essential, but it can sometimes be introduced to good effect. Speech in a straightforward narrative composition is always directly related to the action. Its purpose is to advance the narrative flow.

(v) An account of events must be rooted in the writer's own experience. Firsthand knowledge of the happenings related — or of very similar happenings — is needed. Details may be invented to add life and colour, but this kind of narrative composition is essentially an imaginative treatment of actual events. It is not a piece of fiction, as a story is.

Sometimes the term 'anecdote' is used to distinguish between a story and a straightforward narrative. For example:

Write *either* a story *or* an anecdote based on one of the following: (i) a telephone ringing in an empty house; (ii) the non-arrival of an important letter; (iii) an ambulance speeding through a city on an icy morning.

An anecdote is the narration of an interesting or striking incident or a series of such incidents.

To sum up. If you decide to write a narrative, you must choose between:

A plotted piece of writing
A story. All the events lead up to and help to bring about the situation with which the story ends. This final situation develops out of circumstances and events earlier in the story.

An unplotted piece of writing
An account of events: a description of incidents: a relation of an experience: an anecdote. All these are examples of 'reportage'. They are narrations of interesting events happening in succession, one after another.

As this work-out section will show, 'unplotted' does *not* mean 'unplanned'. A clear plan is the basis of successful writing of whatever kind.

(b) Thinking about the Subjects on Offer

Here are some typical examples of subjects set for narrative composition.

(i) *Story Writing*

1. 'The Humber, the Menai Straits, the Tay, Sydney Harbour, the Golden Gate — what tales bridges could tell!' Write a story in which a bridge plays an important part.
2. 'It was the weirdest-looking object I'd ever seen.' Write a story in which those words are used at an important moment.
3. 'Even the smartest crook can make a silly mistake.' Write a story, using those words as its opening.
4. 'I never did discover its hiding place.' Write a story that ends with those words.
5. Write a story entitled 'A Broken Promise'.
6. Write a story suggested by the following quotation:

Hark, they are going: the footsteps shrink,
And the sea renews her cry.
The big stars stare and the small stars wink;
The Plough goes glittering by.
It was a trick of the turning tide
That brought those voices near.
Dead men pummelled the panes outside:
We caught the breath of the year.

Vernon Watkins

Note that each of those subjects contains a requirement that the writer must observe. Number 1 imposes some control over the contents of the story. Numbers 2, 3 and 4 influence the plot by insisting on the inclusion of given words at a particular point in the story. Number 5 influences both contents and plot by specifying the title of the story. Number 6 is less direct in its controls, but it lays down the condition that the source of the story must be the impressions the writer receives from the poetry. (This kind of assignment, combining narrative and impressionistic subjects, is often set.)

Candidates who can write a good story sometimes miss their opportunity by failing to recognise possible story subjects. When the particular form that a composition must take is not specified, candidates are free to choose whatever form suits them best. For example:

Write a composition based on one of the following topics:
(a) A family gathering.
(b) Lost property.
(c) Nightfall.
(d) A journalistic scoop.
(e) An unwanted present.

Instructions worded like those permit any of the given topics to be treated as story material. They are, of course, equally available for and suited to straightforward narrative or descriptive treatment.

(ii) *Straightforward Narrative Writing*

The instructions for the writing of an account of events, a description of incidents, a relation of an experience or an anecdote are worded in various ways. Here are some typical examples.

1. You were one of a crowd waiting for a celebrity to appear. Describe what happened.
2. Describe an experience in the course of which events occurred in a way that contrasted sharply with what you expected.
3. You saw a person knocked off a bicycle by a passing car that did not stop. Tell the story of what happened next.
4. 'I shan't do that again', you said. Give an account of the events that led up to that remark.

Only in the fourth example are candidates specifically instructed to give an account of events, but the wording of the others is a clear indication that straight-forward narrative writing (*not* story telling) is wanted. 'Describe what happened' (1) and 'Describe an experience' (2) instruct the writer to narrate a sequence of happenings. The writing is to take the form of a piece of 'reportage': an account of events that occurred one after another.

Do not be misled by the wording of the third example: 'Tell the story of what happened next'. That is not an invitation to write a story with a plot. It is an instruction to write an anecdote. The key words are: *what happened next*. An anecdote is not a story. It simply unfolds events in a straightforward chronological sequence. It does not bring about those plotted changes of circumstance and situation that are the essence of a story.

All these unplotted forms of narrative compositions — accounts of events, descriptions of incidents, relations of experiences, anecdotes — share the same essential characteristic: they run in a straight line from beginning to end. The writer must keep the narrative flowing. Any break in the continuity is a tiresome interruption at which the reader loses interest.

(c) Making a Choice

Most of the varieties of narrative subjects that you are likely to encounter are represented in Section 1.5(b), so it will be useful to consider them all while demonstrating how a good choice of subject can be made.

The work out is written in the first person singular because choosing a subject is essentially a personal decision. By showing you how *I* go about it, I can illus-trate all the points that you will have to consider when you are looking for a subject that suits *you*. In later sections, I shall gather and select material, then plan and write, thus providing a practical demonstration of methods that you can confidently use, whatever your choice of subject.

While steering you through the choice-making process, I do not assume that my choice of subject would be right for you. You may be able to write interestingly on a subject that is not for me. You may have ample material for a composition on that subject and the ability to make a good plan for it, whereas I am stuck for ideas and cannot see how to arrange what little material I have. The work out can-not tell you *what* to choose, but it can show you *how* to choose.

If I choose a story composition, I shall have to invent a plot. That is not easy, so I look first at the straightforward narrative subjects on offer, but none of them interests me so much that I feel confident of interesting my reader. I cannot see how I can tap my own experience to find the firsthand material that I need to write a lively composition on any of them.

Turning to the story subjects, I remember to look at those that *may* be written as stories ('A family gathering', 'Lost property', 'Nightfall', 'A journalistic scoop' and 'An unwanted present') as well as those that *must* be (numbers 1–6).

At first, I am tempted to have a go at 'A family gathering'. I think that my experiences at my Uncle Henry's house one Christmas provide me with useful material for characters and setting, although I cannot see plot possibilities. Of course, I might treat that topic by straightforward narration, using my imagination to provide some lively and colourful details.

'A family gathering' is a possible subject, but I do not warm to any of the others in that particular list. I cannot at once see plot material in them for stories and I am not very interested in the few ideas that they suggest to me for purely narrative treatment.

Turning to the subjects that are specified for story treatment, I reject the one in which a bridge is to play an important part. I think I *could* write such a story, but it would not come out of my personal experience. My story would be second-hand 'formula' writing; a stale imitation of stories that I have read. So, because I cannot see a way of putting something of myself into this particular story, I decide not to attempt it. Stories ought to be their writers' own creations. Only then can they be fresh and original and, therefore, interesting.

Subjects 2, 3 and 4 put me off by requiring me to include given words at particular points in the story. Many writers have the ability to carry out such instructions without losing their spontaneity. Indeed, the necessity of constructing a story line that brings the given words into the story at the right place seems to stimulate their imagination. But not mine. I know that my story would seem contrived and artificial. The plot would creak.

Again, I am not happy with number 5. I *can* sometimes write a story with a given title, even though that restricts my freedom to invent the contents and the plot; but I cannot recall interesting personal experience on which to base 'A Broken Promise'. (Now, if the given title were 'A Promise Fulfilled', I should have lively material ready for use and a good, simple plot needing just a little working up — but that isn't the title!)

I turn to number 6 and, as I read the lines of poetry, I find that I am getting strong impressions. The words are ringing bells in my memory, suggesting exciting possibilities for characters and setting; and I *think* I can see — rather dimly as yet — a possible plot.

At this point I realise that I have spent a lot of time considering possible subjects. My choice must be made. Which shall it be: 'A family gathering' or number 6? I can see good material for characters and setting in the former if I treat it as a story, but I have not had any ideas for a plot. If I treat it as a straightforward narrative, it may lack action. It begins to seem rather a static subject. Nothing much happened. On the whole, I think I see more scope in number 6.

(d) Gathering Material

Write a story suggested by the following quotation:

> Hark, they are going: the footsteps shrink,
> And the sea renews her cry.
> The big stars stare and the small stars wink;
> The Plough goes glittering by.
> It was a trick of the turning tide
> That brought those voices near.
> Dead men pummelled the panes outside:
> We caught the breath of the year.

I open my mind to the words. They stir up recollections and imaginings which I jot down as they occur. All that matters at this stage is to capture ideas: selecting and planning come later.

night — hushed — glittering stars — the sound of the sea — that lonely cottage in Cornwall where we spent a family holiday — a nightmare

The quotation has triggered off a personal recollection and I can link the poet's words with my own experience. This is promising. I explore the possibilities further, reading the words again.

Within the general impressions, certain words seem to be making a particular impact:

Hark, they are going/footsteps shrink/sea renews her cry/a trick of the turning tide/voices near/Dead men pummelled the panes

I add to the raw material already jotted down, letting memory and imagination work together. Some of my notes are based on fact, some are inventions suggested by the words of the quotation. The distinction between fact and fiction is of no importance when material for a story is being gathered.

an autumn holiday — starry nights — the sound of the sea — a lamp-lit living-room — my parents downstairs reading — my bedroom very quiet — the sound of footsteps dwindling — along a path? — the 'cry' of the sea again — a rapping at the window — something outside trying to get in — returning to claim something? — what? — 'It's only the sound of the sea' — 'the tide has turned' — the owner of the cottage kept the village shop — talking to him — his stories of days gone by

I can now see exciting possibilities in the material I have gathered. It should give me scope for lively writing and an original treatment, for it springs partly from the quotation and partly from an experience of my own which the poet's words have brought back to me. I must work on the raw material and shape it.

(e) Selecting Material and Arriving at a Plan

There is still a lot to do before I can start writing. The material I have gathered so far could be used in a straightforward narration of events, but I must now think out a plot so that I can turn an anecdote into a story. The connections between the words of the quotation and my raw material are well established, so I am at liberty to invent any details I need to construct a plot; and I am free to adjust the circumstances depicted in the poem to suit my story. I jot down some more notes, building up the material I have already gathered.

I had a nightmare — it frightened me very much — my parents weren't very pleased when I rushed downstairs into the living-room — 'Go back to bed. You've been dreaming.' — that big oak chest in the living-room — black with age — the initials 'I.R.T.' carved on the front — the man we rented the cottage from was called Tressilian — Reuben Tressilian — he kept the village shop and post office — his name over shop door — his family had lived in the cottage for many years — his great-grandfather was lost at sea in a great storm — we went to the shop for groceries the morning after I had my nightmare — he told us about his family that morning

I am beginning to see the bare bones of my story line and I feel confident enough to work on a more detailed plan. I set it out in two columns. The steps in which I shall tell the story are very carefully noted in the left column. In the right,

I make notes to help me to work out the details of character, setting and events as I go along. As I work on my plan, I reject some of the material I have already gathered and I alter and add to the rest.

(*Note:* As you study the plan that now follows, bear in mind that I have written it out at greater length than you — or I — would usually do. My purpose is to demonstrate the importance of thinking a subject through and becoming clear about how you are going to treat it *before* you begin to write. If you practise along the lines set out here, you will master the technique of sound planning and learn how to construct a short outline plan on which a good composition can be based.)

(i) *The Plan*

1. Introduce characters and setting — brief description of family, cottage and surroundings.

father, mother, son aged about ten — is story to be told in first or third person? — easier to bring about change in situation if son tells story as it happened — lonely cottage about 2 miles from nearest village — cottage near sea — sound of sea, especially at night

2. Sketch in holiday occupations and pleasures. Build up atmosphere before storm and nightmare.

warm autumn days — walks and picnics — cosy living-room — books and TV — son usually to bed at ten — parents stay up reading for a time — cottage interior described — important to bring old chest to reader's attention because it plays important part in story — initials 'I.R.T.' carved on chest — N.B. chest *not* in living-room — place it on landing outside son's bedroom door

3. The night of the storm. Son's fear. Parents explain it away. They're right, of course — he's been dreaming.

son wakes up — roaring of wind and waves (perhaps earlier?) — sudden hush — tapping at window — footsteps on path — fear — son rushes downstairs — 'someone at my window, trying to get in'/'you've been dreaming: it's only the wind rattling the panes — grating of pebbles on seashore'

4. Next morning — to village to shop.

this is a quiet stage of story — storm has died down — his nightmare is over and explained away — bright, calm morning — night fears seem unreal

5. Introduce Reuben Tressilian. He keeps the village shop. Conversation. He tells them about his family.

R.T. owns cottage — rents it to holidaymakers — Tressilians have lived in cottage for years — all fisherfolk — (some of these details to come in earlier? — when cottage is first described?)

6. Climax of story begins here. First mention of Tressilian's great-grandfather.

initials on chest ('I.R.T.') were great-grandfather's — he kept his valuables in it — story told about him — he was lost at sea in great storm — comes

7. Turning point of story here. Discovery made and situation changes. Son knows date of storm in which 'I.R.T.' was drowned.

back to find chest on anniversary of his death

care with details here — must be convincing — closely linked together to keep story moving — enough detail to keep reader in picture but don't clutter up the action — best if all told through dialogue? — son and Mr T. talking, but parents silent

8. End of story. Parents were wrong about 'nightmare' and son was right. Final situation follows from and is caused by 7.

don't over-explain — story ends crisply — parents realise what has happened, so does son — suggest this, rather than explaining — they look away — busy themselves in shop — mystery, but no loose ends

Now I can start writing. If I find, as I write the story, that I need to change any details or make minor adjustments to the sequence of events, I am free to do so. The plan is my guide and I shall stick to its main features, but I am not bound to follow it to the letter. I shall almost certainly think of improvements as the act of writing stimulates my imagination; but I shall not make fundamental changes in the structure of my story while I am writing it. I cannot afford to make false starts or leave loose ends in the plot, so it would be dangerous to depart far from this carefully constructed plan.

(f) Writing the Composition

When I was ten, my father and mother and I went ~~for our holidays~~ to a lonely cottage on the Cornish coast for a week's holiday.

It was a lonely place, perched above the sea and not another house near it. There was a village about two miles away where the owner of the cottage lived. His name was Reuben Tressilian. He kept the village post office and shop. ^and ~~He~~ rented the cottage to holidaymakers.

We had a lovely holiday. The days were warm, and although it went cold at night, we were cosy in the cottage. It was comfortably furnished with interesting old pieces and pictures. ^There was an open hearth in the living-room ~~The living-room had a big fireplace~~ which made it very cheerful. We had brought books with us and there was a TV set. We spent our days walking, exploring the cliffs and picnicking. In the evenings we sat reading or watching television until they pushed me off to bed at about ten o'clock. I didn't mind. There was a big black oak chest on the landing outside my bedroom door and I often made up stories about it. Some initials were carved on the front and as I lay in bed I used to wonder who 'I.R.T.' was. I guessed that he was the big, bearded man wearing a fisherman's jersey in the old, faded photograph that hung on the wall above the chest.

One night — I shall never forget it — there was a ^furious ~~big~~ storm. As we sat in the living-room, the wind roared in the chimney and we could hear the waves crashing against the cliffs. I thought it was exciting, but I don't think my parents liked it much.

At ten o'clock my mother looked at the clock on the ~~mantlepeace~~ mantelpiece. 'Off to bed now, Billy,' she said. 'We're going to the village early tomorrow. I need some ~~food~~ supplies for the rest of the week.'

'I shan't be able to sleep,' I said. 'Not with all this noise going on.'

'Nonsense! You'll sleep like a log. You've been out in the fresh air all day and you're yawning now.'

'Good night, Billy,' my father said, rather firmly. 'Sleep well.'

As I went past the chest on the landing, I stopped to look at the old photograph. It was ~~moving~~ swaying slightly on its cord in the draught.

'Good night, I.R.T.,' I said. 'Sleep well.'

In spite of the howling wind, I went to sleep at once. I didn't give old 'I.R.T.' another thought before I was off.

And then — I don't know how much later — I woke. I was cold and ~~I was~~ scared /stiff. ~~frightened~~. The noise of the storm had stopped. There was a sort of hush, as if the night was holding its breath, and the moon was bright on the window.

Then I heard a crunching sound, like heavy footsteps on the gravel path at the back of the cottage; and — seconds later — 'tap, tap, tap' on the glass. It was as loud as the beating of my heart and there was a shadow on the pane.

Downstairs I ran and into the living-room.

'Quick!' I said. 'Come up to my room. There's something tapping at the window — trying to get in.'

'You've had a nightmare, Billy,' my mother said. 'I'll get you some hot milk and you can drink it by the fire. Then back to bed you go.'

'It's the wind,' my father said. 'And waves beating on the shore. Listen!'

He was right. The storm ~~had started~~ was raging again. The wind was shaking the tiles and the sea roared below the cliffs.

He came up with me and tucked the clothes round me. 'No more dreams, Billy. Sleep well.'

And, strangely enough, I did. No more dreams and no more shadows at the window.

After breakfast we set off for Mr Tressilian's shop. The day was calm and bright and we enjoyed our walk.

'You're having a good time?' Mr Tressilian asked as he reached things off the shelves and loaded up ~~the basket.~~ our baskets.

'Oh, yes,' my mother answered. 'And it's such a lovely cottage. You've got some beautiful furniture there, Mr Tressilian.'

'All family stuff,' he said. 'Tressilians have lived in the cottage for years. They were all fisherfolk, till I gave it up and settled down to shopkeeping.'

'Who was "I.R.T."?' I asked.

He looked a bit surprised, but he answered me.

'He was my great-grandfather — Isaac Reuben Tressilian. That's his photograph that hangs on the wall above the big chest on the landing. He was lost at sea in a great storm, many a year ago.'

'It was his chest, was it?'

'Oh, yes. He had it made the year he was married — the year he built the cottage. He kept his valuables in it. It was always kept locked when I was a boy, though his valuables — such as they were — had long vanished. My father used to tell us a story about that chest. He said that Isaac Reuben always returned on the anniversary of the storm. Looking for his chest, he was. So my father said. He didn't believe it, of course. Nor do I. It was just a story he liked telling us and we liked hearing.'

'He was drowned on the fifteenth of September, wasn't he?' I asked.

'Yes,' Mr Tressilian said. 'He was — on the fifteenth of September 1865. How did you know?'

'It was the fifteenth of September yesterday,' I said. 'And I think your great-grandfather came looking for his chest last night.'

I turned to my parents as I said it, but they pretended not to hear. My father was reading a newspaper that he'd taken off the counter and my mother was unusually interested in the label on a bag of sugar.

(g) Reading through and Correcting

As you can see, I made some improvements in the couple of minutes that I allowed myself for reading through and correcting. I put right some careless slips of the pen and I was able to tighten up the writing here and there. One or two clumsy expressions jumped out at me as I read through what I had written, and it was easy to find better ways of wording them.

On the whole, however, the writing went smoothly because I had put a lot of thought into gathering and selecting my material and constructing my plan. The *form* of my composition was clear to me before I began to write it, so it was not difficult to find a *style* of expression that was suitable.

(h) A Different Choice of Subject

You may be reluctant to choose a story subject and you are right to be cautious. Never attempt a story unless you can see, quite early on, how you can construct a plot for it. The plot may be very simple, but it must be convincing (no loose ends) and it must bring about an interesting development in the story. In the work out you have just studied I was able to see plot possibilities when the words of the poetry connected with an event that I recalled from my own experience. I had to work on the details, of course, but the outline of my plot began to come through at an early stage.

Like many writers, however, I do not often find it easy to construct a plot, so I usually look for a straightforward narrative subject rather than a story. I hope to find one that interests me and to which I can bring some firsthand experience.

You cannot expect always to find an ideal subject, but things are never as bad as they seem in those first minutes as you read through the set topics and think despairingly, 'I can't write about *any* of these!' You can always find a subject on which you can write competently if you go about choosing and planning in the ways that I am demonstrating in this chapter.

Suppose the subject I chose in Section 1.5(c) had not been on offer. My second-string subject, you remember, was 'A family gathering', which the instructions permitted me to treat either as a story or as a straightforward (unplotted) narrative. Story treatment was ruled out for me because I could not see plot possibilities in the subject. As I considered it for straightforward narrative, I became less hope-

19

ful of success. I knew I could draw on personal experience and write interestingly about people and setting, but I knew also that my potential material lacked the essential ingredient of good narrative – *action*.

When a subject dries up on you like that, you have to look again at subjects that were not immediately attractive as you read through the assignments for the first time. By thinking hard along methodical lines, you will find a topic that you can tackle successfully.

Ask yourself these two questions:

- What are the chief features of a good composition of this kind on this subject?
- What opportunities does this subject offer me to write a composition that contains those features?

The whole purpose of these work-out sections is to help you to find the answers to those questions.

In my own case, looking again at all the composition subjects offered in Section 1.5(b), I should have to choose this: 'You were one of a crowd waiting for a celebrity to appear. Describe what happened.'

For various reasons, that is not my ideal subject for a straightforward narrative composition, but it does bring an item of personal experience to mind and I think I can work that up into a competent piece of writing, fragment though it is.

Faced with subjects that do not look very attractive at first sight, comfort yourself with the old proverb: 'Necessity is the mother of invention.' Necessity is there, without doubt: the necessity to write a composition! Don't panic. Think coolly. Your powers of invention and recall are greater than you realise. Necessity will bring them to your aid and a sound technique will enable you to make use of them.

In the next sections of this chapter I shall describe the qualities of a good narrative and then go on to demonstrate how, bearing them in mind, I feel reasonably confident of writing a successful composition on a subject that I chose because I had to.

(i) Action: the Essence of Narrative

Any composition that the examiners' instructions identify as an account of events, a description of incidents or the relation of an anecdote must be centred on action. Nothing must distract the reader's attention from the action, for it is in the action that the interest lies.

Any other features of such a composition – descriptions of people and places, passages of dialogue, for example – are secondary to the action. Their sole purpose is to make the narrative more vivid and to hold the reader's attention as the action unfolds. Anything that impedes the narrative flow is a tiresome interruption.

(j) Pacing the Narrative

Varying the pace of the narrative is a sure way of gaining and holding your reader's interest. Action described at a uniform pace is not very exciting. Your reader will be as bored by a narrative that races breathlessly from start to finish as by one that proceeds throughout at a steady jogtrot.

Try to begin with a striking incident to capture attention. You can then afford a *brief* description of the circumstances in which the action is taking place and of the people involved. Then be sure to get the action moving again at once. It is often effective to let it run slowly at first, then — at a clearly indicated turning point — to quicken the pace so that the narration carries your reader forward to its climax. Pay special attention to the end. Are you going to finish with the action at its highest point? Or does your treatment of your subject demand a brief rounding-off? Either of these endings can be effective but, if you prolong your composition beyond the highest point of the action, do be *brief*. An anticlimax at the end is a painful let-down.

(k) Narrative Links and the Narrative Thread

To write a successful narrative, you must:

- keep your reader's attention on the action;
- make your reader want to know what happens next.

You cannot achieve those two aims unless your narrative is easy to read.

The provision of narrative links makes for easy reading. These links connect the successive stages of the action and carry the reader along. Without such links, the narrative thread is snapped. Do try to vary their wording. A monotonous succession of 'then . . . and then . . . next' is boringly obvious. The links should be unobtrusive.

The more carefully you plan before you begin to write, the easier you will find it to provide the essential connections. Once the successive stages of the narrative are clearly set out in your plan, the sequence of events is established and you will be able to carry your reader through the action with only a sparing use of the more explicit verbal links. Incident will follow incident in a natural progression, and you will then not often need to provide obvious 'signals' that the action is moving on.

(l) Narrative Details and Descriptive Details

Some details play an essential part in carrying the action along. These are the narrative details that enable the reader to follow the course of events. For example, if your chosen subject hinges on a street accident and what followed, your reader *may* need to know the colour or make or size of a vehicle involved, or the age and appearance of the driver, or exactly where the accident happened.

You have to judge the relevance of each detail when you are considering whether to include it. Ask yourself: 'Does this detail help my reader to understand what is happening?' Obviously, you must provide the details that play an important part in the action, but be strict in your selection. A narrative cluttered with details is hard to follow. The reader's attention is distracted from the action.

The same considerations apply to descriptive details. Some are needed to make the narrative convincing and lively, but they must be sparingly used or the action will be held up. What matters most in a narrative is what happens. A few carefully chosen details will capture attention and hold interest, but your reader's main concern is with the events themselves.

(m) Human Interest

You are not creating 'characters' when you are writing a straightforward narrative, but people usually play the leading parts in the action. Just sketch them in with a few identifying details. It is especially important to do this when the events involve antagonism. Conflict may be present at the outset or it may be generated as the action unfolds. Skilfully revealed by a narrative in which the pace changes, conflict is a source of tension and rising excitement.

(n) Dialogue in Narrative

Though always less important than in a story, dialogue can be an effective means of identifying people and indicating that a new stage of the action is beginning. Keep it short. Too much talk interrupts the action. In a straightforward narrative, speech is useful to push the action along while, at the same time, informing the reader about who is doing what.

(o) Narrative Style

As we saw in Section 1.4, the style of your writing must be appropriate to your subject. A quick-moving style is appropriate to a straightforward narrative. Short sentences, active verbs and a sparing use of adjectives are generally effective when striking and interesting events are being described.

Variations of style, however, are as desirable as variations of pace. A deliberate slowing of the action (to increase tension and lead into a climax) will be marked by a more leisurely style. Descriptive touches are more telling when the language used contrasts with that employed in the purely narrative passages. Quick-fire sentences are an indispensable medium for rapid action, but a narrative that rattles along in staccato bursts from start to finish is no pleasure to read. The writer needs to get his breath from time to time — and so does the reader.

(p) Work out Another Plan

With all those considerations in mind, I tackle the subject that I have been forced to select. I have no more time left for making a choice and none of the other subjects seems more promising. At least, I can see a way into this one and I must work methodically to make the best use I can of the possibilities that it seems to offer me.

> You were one of a crowd waiting for a celebrity to appear. Describe what happened.

(i) *Gathering Material*

I jot down the material that comes to mind, just as it occurs.

> crowd in square in front of town hall — curiosity led me to join it — gradually discovered what it was all about — local hero expected to appear on balcony — had been given civic dinner and freedom of borough — long wait — crowd patient and good-humoured — gradually turned bad-tempered — I wasn't

very keen anyway, so I left — read about events in local paper afterwards —
eventual appearance — enthusiastic reception

That is not a lot to write about and it is sadly lacking in action. I shall have to
build it up.

Fortunately, the instructions give me some useful pointers: '*You* were one of a
crowd . . . Describe what happened.' I must narrate in the first person singular and
I must stay with the crowd longer than I actually did! I can draw on my memories
of the night and the crowd up to my departure, and I can reconstruct the later
events by using the newspaper report as the basis of my invented material. Although my starting point is an actual event, I can make up any extra material that
I need.

Also, I begin to see possibilities for changes of pace to create tension and rising
excitement.

crowd is good-humoured — crowd gets bored — crowd gets angry — celebrity
appears — crowd won over at once

And I can see how the action can be presented from various angles.

observer/narrator (me) — the crowd — the celebrity — the civic dignitaries
(especially the mayor) — the police

From some or all of those angles, contrasts and conflicts can be introduced into
the narrative to keep it moving and make it lively.

(ii)   *Selecting Material and Arriving at a Plan*

First, I shape my composition by mapping out the successive stages through
which the narrative will be unfolded. As I work on the outline, I can reject
material that does not fit in, adding whatever new material I need.

(1) I see a crowd. (2) I join in. (3) Eager anticipation — 'X' is to appear.
(4) Long wait. (5) Crowd gets bored. (6) Crowd gets restless. (7) Rumours
circulate. (8) Crowd gets angry. (9) Ugly mood develops. (10) Police inspector enters town hall. (11) 'X' appears on balcony accompanied by mayor?
NO: mayor appears alone. (12) Crowd furious. (13) Mayor brings 'X' onto
balcony. (14) 'X' talks to crowd, makes flattering speech. (15) Crowd's anger
evaporates: happiness all round.

That gives me a satisfactory start. Now I can work out a detailed plan. As I fill
in the gaps, I shall get a much firmer grasp of my subject. Some of the proposed
incidents will be compressed or omitted; others will be expanded. New ideas will
occur. I shall be establishing firmer links, varying the pace, introducing stronger
human interest, looking for conflicts and contrasts, placing snatches of speech at
strategic points in the narrative. Overall, what I aim to do is to increase the excitement of the narrative without destroying its credibility.

A good plan will firm up the possibilities that I have begun to see: possibilities
that were not apparent when I first began to gather my material. I am now confident that, if I can get my plan right, I can write a fluent composition on this
subject.

The Plan

1. Jump straight into the action. I am part of the crowd when the narrative begins: part of it but detached from it — there's a narrative angle here.

2. *Brief* description of situation. Action has been launched and reader now needs to know what it's all about.

perhaps like this? — 'We want Mel! We want Mel!' There must have been ten thousand people packed into Bursley Town Square that night . . .

names essential — reader must be helped to believe in narrative — Mel Jones, captain of Bursley football team — Bursley Town Square packed with people waiting for him to appear on balcony after civic dinner and award of freedom of borough — cold dark night — square and town hall floodlit

3. Pick up action again. Crowd has been waiting a long time. Mood is changing.

introduce little old man standing next to me in crowd — he's a useful way of carrying action forward and he's another 'angle' — he provides me with useful details about events — he's not a fan

4. Action quickens. Crowd getting very restless. Jokes rather savagely about mayor and councillors.

5. Rumours begin to fly through crowd. Action hotter.

'things'll get rough soon' (l.o.m. is talking to me) — 'it's gone ten now and he was due on balcony at nine'

'He's not coming out'/'mayor's driven away'/'it's all over'/'dinner's going on till midnight'/'toasts and speeches'

6. Crowd angry now. People surge forward. Police on town hall steps look apprehensive.

7. Police inspector enters town hall in a hurry.

'We'd best be going, lad.' — but impossible to shove through pushing mob

8. Mayor appears on balcony. Tries to make himself heard.

9. Mayor turns away. Goes back in. Climax of narrative begins here.

groans — jeers — crowd in ugly mood

fury of crowd — l.o.m. and I in danger of being crushed — trying to get away — perhaps better to go with crowd? confusion reigns — cheers and jeers — scuffles break out

10. Mayor returns. Mel Jones is with him. Some people can see him but most cannot.

11. Mel Jones begins to speak. Crowd gradually calms down. Listens. Cheers. Loves it. Purrs with self-congratulation. Good humour all round.

just hint at his soothing words: a phrase or two will be enough — 'fellow townsfolk . . . great honour . . . yours as much as mine' — acid comment from l.o.m.: 'half of them can't hear a word he's saying'

12. We make our escape. Action dies down. Keep this very short. I look back. Balcony is empty but they are still there — happy and singing in the cold dark night.

'Good night, lad. Those idiots'll wait all night for another dose of syrup.'

Obviously, your plan for a composition on that subject would be different from the one that I have just worked out; and I do not claim more for mine than that it provides ample material arranged in an effective order. You might give your narrative a different 'slant', emphasise other aspects of the action, or – of course – write about a completely different series of events occurring in wholly different circumstances. In expressive composition the examiners invite and reward an entirely personal response from candidates.

Even so, we all need the help that comes from a methodical approach to writing. By applying the techniques demonstrated in these work-out sections, you can make a good choice of subject, explore thoroughly the possibilities that it offers you, and then write a composition that does justice to the imaginative thinking that you have put into it.

1.6 Work out Descriptive Writing

(a) Facing the Problem

A descriptive composition seems easy compared with the other kinds. A story demands a plot; an account of events must be securely strung on a narrative thread; a dramatic composition tests the technical skill of writing realistic dialogue; an impressionistic composition exacts an imaginative response to a visual or verbal stimulus. In comparison, a descriptive composition appears to offer the writer much more freedom.

In fact, this apparent freedom can be a trap, for a descriptive composition makes its own special demands. You will probably not have difficulty in finding plenty of material for the descriptive subjects offered to you, but it is not easy to sort that material out and arrange it in an effective order of presentation.

(b) What You Must Do

A good piece of writing, of whatever kind, has a beginning, a middle and an end. That sounds obvious, but it is a fact that is often overlooked when a descriptive subject has been chosen. Unless the material is presented in a clear progression *from* the beginning, *through* the middle, *to* the end, a descriptive composition is just a ragbag of details. Descriptive items haphazardly thrown together cannot hold the reader's interest, however vivid and telling they are in themselves.

A descriptive composition must have *unity*. In other words, it must be a complete and self-contained piece of writing, all the *parts* of which contribute to the *whole*. To impose unity on your material, you have to do a lot of imaginative thinking and careful planning before you begin to write.

(c) Some Typical Descriptive Subjects

1. Write a description of a scene that you know well, bringing out its special character.
2. Write a descriptive composition entitled *either* (a) 'A lonely place' *or* (b) 'A night scene'.
3. My best friend.
4. Overheard remarks.
5. Breakfast.
6. A room of my own.
7. Describe the scene *either* at a railway station *or* at a public swimming-pool.

8. The river.
9. The street market.
10. Closing time at the supermarket.

(d) Making a Choice

A good choice depends on two factors: your interest in and personal experience of the subject; your ability to 'see into' the material that you gather and to find an 'angle of attack'.

Your material will not ring true unless you have some personal experience of what you are describing. For example, do not choose subject 10 in the above list if you have never been in a supermarket at closing time. Again, you will certainly have abundant personal experience from which to draw your material for subject 5, but what a very dull catalogue of details your composition will be unless you can find an 'angle' on it. A subject such as that demands a fresh and lively approach.

The wording of the first subject on that list sums up two very important points about descriptive writing. It instructs you to describe something that you know well (a scene in that case) and to bring out its special character.

- Whatever its particular subject, a descriptive composition must be about something (or somebody) you know well *and* bring out the special character or significance that it has for you.

(e) Working out a Descriptive Subject

I have chosen subject 5, 'Breakfast', for the purposes of this work out. As a candidate in the examination I should probably choose subject 2(a), 'A lonely place', because there is one particular moorland scene that I know especially well and I feel confident that I could describe it in a way that would bring out the very special character that it has for me. But the subject 'Breakfast' gives me a better chance of demonstrating two important techniques:

1. How to gather fresh and interesting material for a descriptive subject that could easily seem stale and secondhand.
2. How to find a personal angle of attack from which to plan a descriptive composition that is lively and original.

(i) *Gathering Material*

Think in particular terms, not in general terms. Not breakfasts in general, but breakfasts (or a breakfast) that *you* have taken part in. Open your mind to the subject and gather personal, not abstract, material.

> bacon and eggs — toast and marmalade — tea or coffee — a bowl of cornflakes and a rush — snatched piece of bread and butter — the bus leaves in 5 minutes — what a lovely day it's going to be! — what shall we do? — oh, lord, it's snowing! — where's Jean? — not out of bed yet — she'll be late again — breakfast/*break* fast — first meal of the day — new life — lovely — smells — toast's burning — no hurry — pass the butter — milk's boiled over — can't stop — what a start to the day! — why is everyone so grumpy? — yawn — switch that noise off — oh, this sun!

(ii) *Looking for an Angle of Attack*

Because I have been thinking about the subject in personal and particular terms — in other words, finding my material in my own experience — I am becoming aware of a pattern. My ideas have been jotted down just as they occurred, but I can see a way of shaping them:

> rush/leisure
> good humour/bad temper
> enjoying food/bolting food
> fine weather/bad weather
> zest/apathy

A strong contrast underlies the apparently haphazard collection of ideas. That contrast provides me with an angle of attack.

(iii) *Finding a Theme*

Following up this way of looking at my subject matter, I see that a theme is emerging: 'Breakfast as it *can* be, contrasted with breakfast as it usually *is*'. This emerging theme will now direct all my thinking and planning because, with it in mind, I can see how to describe breakfast in a purposeful way. For me, the subject now has a particular character and significance that I am aiming to express through my description. With that theme I can give my writing unity. Every descriptive detail that I include will bear on the theme.

Again, I can now make a plan that has a clear-cut shape. I can find a good beginning, link each paragraph to the others, arrive at an effective ending, because I have found a central idea to shape my writing. I know what I want to say.

Finding 'the idea behind the description' is the hardest job when you are writing a descriptive piece: the hardest and most important, for a composition without a theme is a mere catalogue of descriptive details, lacking unity, plan and purpose.

(f) Some More Descriptive Subjects

Sometimes the examiners' instructions draw your attention to the importance of providing a theme and implicitly warn you against producing a mere catalogue of details. Note the wording of this writing assignment:

> Treasured possessions.
> (You may wish to describe some of the things you value most and show why you would hate to lose them.)

By including the words *and show why you would hate to lose them*, the examiners are saying, in effect, 'A mere catalogue is *not* what we want. We want to read descriptions of the things you treasure that show us *why* you treasure them.'

If you were tackling that question, you would have to take that theme as your guide as you gathered and selected your material and arrived at your plan. Here are some of the considerations that I would bear in mind.

1. Personal and particular thinking — *my* treasured possessions. I'll make a list.
2. How many? I can't find time or space for more than three or four. In any

27

case, although I don't want to lose any, there aren't more than a few that I'd *hate* to lose. If I include too many, I can't bring out the significance of those that really matter.

3. Which shall I include? The *most* treasured, of course; but it's not easy to say which they are. Think hard about this, by going on to 4.

4. *Why* would I hate to lose each one? Let's have another look at the list I've made and start sorting them out by asking that question: my copper ring, because it was given to me by a very special person/my radio, because I get so much pleasure from it/my tool kit, because it's so useful/my post office savings book, because it's worth money. . .

5. I'll choose four possessions, each of which I'd hate to lose for a different reason. That will give my composition variety and, therefore, added interest.

6. Order of presentation? I must think ahead. How to arrive at an interesting *sequence* is a problem. I musn't make it a simple list of one thing following another. I know: start with the most *valuable* one (in money terms, that is); go on to the most *useful* one; go on to the one that gives me most *pleasure*; end with the one that isn't worth very much in money terms but *means most to me* because of the person who gave it to me.

7. That's the outline settled. Now I can work out a detailed plan. I've got to know *before* I begin to write exactly how I'm going to tackle the descriptions. Take the radio, for example. What sort of description can I give of that? What details are relevant? The theme gives me my way in. I'd hate to lose it because of the pleasure it gives me. How does it do that? Because of its splendid tone? Because of its world-wide wavelength coverage? Because it's small and portable? Whichever of its features are the ones that make it most treasured are the ones to describe in detail.

Directed thinking of that kind is the basis of a successful plan.

Getting the order right was a problem when dealing with that subject, but many descriptive subjects are so worded that the order of writing is plain. For example:

Describe the changing activities of your street from dawn to dusk of a summer's day.

If I choose that subject, I know where to begin (at dawn) and I know where to end (at dusk); but I must put more thought into it than that. The structure will be loose unless I can link the beginning and the end to round it off. If I can find a way of doing that, I shall be able to impose a unity on my composition, making each detail and each part contribute something important to the whole. Descriptive writing that is full of unrelated bits and pieces is very boring.

I try out several ideas and, in the end, decide on this as a unifying link.

dawn – day beginning – light   both are quiet times – the day begins
dusk – day ending – dark   and ends in silence

I think again. It's not as good as I thought it was! My street isn't very quiet at dusk! So I try for a unifying idea by working along different lines: the street is long; shops and houses on both sides; trees, street lamps, pavements, doorsteps; people walking, talking, laughing, shouting; cars moving, cars parked. I must take up a viewpoint – present the scene from an angle. Where? From a particular window? – whose? Downstairs window or upstairs? Or see the scene from a flight of steps? – church steps? – a memorial? – a monument? – a statue? (possibilities here: bustle of street contrasting with quietness).

Whichever angle I select, I can unify my composition by seeing and hearing everything from it. It is *my* street, after all, so I should be able to communicate its changing activities and personality as time passes over it on a summer's day.

Again, inside the dawn to dusk limits, I must select particular descriptive moments. I can't describe everything that happens at every successive minute of the day. Even if I could, it would be a rather boring and long-winded progression of 'then . . . and then . . . and then'!

Something like this might work: (1) dawn; (2) nine o'clock; (3) lunch time; (4) mid-afternoon; (5) dusk. I see the possibility of a three-part structure there. Beginning: (1). Middle: (2), (3) and (4). End: (5).

I suggest that you now work on some of the descriptive subjects in Section 1.6(c), gathering, selecting and arranging your material in the ways I have demonstrated. Find your angle of attack and establish your theme for each subject. Then make a detailed plan for one and write about it.

1.7 Work out Discursive Writing

(a) What the Examiners are Looking for

The special features of discursive (argumentative or controversial) compositions were described in Section 1.2(d). The subjects set are concerned with facts, ideas, opinions, and the examiners are looking for:

- a genuine interest in the subject and an adequate fund of information about it;
- the ability to give due weight to a contrary opinion, while coolly and reasonably rejecting it;
- the ability to set out an argument step by step and to arrive at a sensible conclusion.

To satisfy those requirements, discursive writing must be carefully planned and clearly expressed.

(b) Some Typical Discursive Subjects

1. Do you agree with the view that at a time of high unemployment women should give up their jobs so that unemployed men can get work?
2. 'We are squandering the natural resources of the planet and future generations will have to pay for our selfishness.' Put the case for three or four practical measures that you think we could and should take to safeguard the future of our children.
3. Do you agree that watching television is a waste of time?
4. Argue the case *for* or *against* the reintroduction in Britain of *either* capital punishment *or* corporal punishment.
5. 'Since alcohol causes as much suffering as any of the illegal drugs, the sale and consumption of alcoholic drinks should be banned.' What are your views on that statement?
6. 'No subject should be compulsory at school or college, for we never learn well what we learn unwillingly.' Suppose that you sympathise with that

point of view but, even so, believe that *one* particular subject should be compulsory. Make out your case.

7. Present your case for *either* believing *or* not believing in *one* of the following: (i) extraterrestrial life; (ii) the Loch Ness monster, or any other monster; (iii) ghosts; (iv) fortune-telling.

8. Do you agree with those who argue that everyone at the age of 18 should be conscripted into the armed forces for a period of military service?

9. 'We live in a world of which one half is affluent and the other half is poverty-stricken.' What are your views and what remedies would you advocate?

10. 'To derive pleasure from the death of living creatures is an abominable thing. I'd abolish hunting and all other kinds of blood sports.' What are your opinions on this contentious subject?

(c) Making a Choice

First, ask yourself whether you have enough knowledge of a particular subject to be able to write a composition of the required length. You do not have to be an expert to write well on any of the subjects offered, but you are expected to have the general information that a thoughtful person interested in the subject would have picked up from reading and talking about it and/or from discussions on television or radio. As you have seen, ideas for story, narrative and descriptive compositions are often generated as you gather and plan your material, but you will not obtain the material you need for a discursive composition by that method. Again, if you are short of information, this probably means that you are not very interested in the subject; and interest in your chosen subject is a prerequisite for successful writing.

This is not to say that a discursive composition must be crammed with facts. The examiners are less concerned with the quantity of your information than with the use you make of it in setting out your argument. Even so, to be able to deploy an argument and arrive at a sensible conclusion, you must have some knowledge of the subject.

(d) Read the Question Carefully

Consider very carefully the particular 'line' that the examiners are asking you to pursue. Are you being asked to put a case *for*? Are you being asked to consider both sides? Are you being asked to propose improvements? Marks are often thrown away because the candidate does not obey the instructions. For example, subject 7 on the list in Section 1.7(b) instructs you to present your case for *either* believing in *or* not believing in . . .'. There, you are not invited to consider both sides but to argue for or against belief. Because balanced views are wanted, it is always sensible to show an awareness of the opposing case, but a full exposition of it in this composition would be a waste of time. You would be marked on the part of the composition that obeyed the instructions. The other part would not be read.

Look at subject 6: 'Suppose that you sympathise with that point of view . . .'. In other words, do not debate that point of view. Take it for granted and deal with the meat of the question, which comes later.

(e) Planning and Style

A well-developed argument is required. It must be reasoned, balanced, thoughtful and interesting. It must, therefore, be based on a careful plan in which your ideas are arranged in a logical sequence. When you are planning, think in terms of a three-part structure: (1) introduction; (2) body of argument; (3) conclusion.

The introduction is best confined to one paragraph. Four or five paragraphs will suffice for the body of the argument. The conclusion is the destination towards which you have led your reader throughout the composition. It knits up the strands of your case and expresses your final opinion. Make it pithy. One paragraph should be enough if your argument in the body of the composition has been thoughtfully directed.

A clear, easily read style is essential. Your reader's attention should be concentrated on *what* you are writing, not distracted by *how* you are writing it. Firm, varied sentences and a crisp, accurate choice of words will sustain interest in and win agreement with the argument you are putting forward.

Never get carried away by the strength of your feelings. You are expected to have opinions and to express them, but in a reasoned manner. The point is well illustrated by subject 10 on the list in Section 1.7(b): ' "To derive pleasure from the death of living creatures is an abominable thing. I'd abolish hunting and all other forms of blood sports." What are your opinions on this contentious subject?' The quotation used as a 'subject trigger' expresses strong feelings, but the examiners are asking you to give your *opinions* on the controversial topic fired off by the quotation. What they want is a reasoned discussion of the question raised by the vehement words of the quotation. They expect you to have a decided point of view, but your conclusion must be reached by thoughtful argument. Your use of language should reflect your cool and reasoning approach to the subject. A discussion conducted in emotional terms — 'abominable', for example — would not be appropriate.

(f) Work out a Plan

As a rule, you know what your conclusion is before you begin to plan. The subject interests you. You have some information about it and you know what you think about it. Your problem is how to use your information in a developing and reasoned argument that justifies your opinions on the subject. In a sense, you are planning backwards from your conclusion and it is often helpful to do your preliminary thinking in this order:

1. This is what I think about this subject.
2. What are the facts and what are the arguments that lead me to this conclusion?
3. How can I best set out those facts and those arguments to show that I have good reasons for coming to my conclusion?

I shall now work out a plan for subject 5 on the list.

> 'Since alcohol causes as much suffering as the illegal drugs, the sale and consumption of alcoholic drinks should be banned.' What are your views on that statement?

I know that I do not agree that the sale and consumption of alcoholic drinks should be banned. What are my reasons? What facts am I relying on? (1) Alcoholic drinks need not be harmful. (2) There is some medical evidence to suggest that *moderate* drinking is beneficial. (3) Moderate social drinking is a source of pleasure. (4) Banning harmless pleasure can never be right. (5) In any case, a legal ban leads to law-breaking (e.g. the crime that accompanied prohibition in America; the evasions and severe punishments in some countries today).

Having jotted down my own positive reasons for the opinion I hold, I look at the arguments that underlie the proposition with which I am disagreeing. I must take opposing views into consideration if my argument is to stand up. (1) Yes, alcohol *can* cause suffering. (2) Whether it causes *as much* suffering as the illegal drugs, I do not know; and nor does the author of the statement. The proposition is very sweeping. (3) I suppose that cocaine and heroin — the so-called 'hard drugs' — are meant by 'the illegal drugs'. Their sale to and use by the general public should certainly be banned (even though they have their proper and beneficial *medical* uses). (4) The proposition makes no distinction between 'the illegal drugs', the general use of which *must* be harmful, and alcohol, the use of which *may* be harmful — but only when it is *misused*.

I have now sorted out my ideas. I know *where* my argument is going. I know, roughly, *how* it will get there. As I work out my plan, I have two remaining problems to sort out: (1) Where do I begin? (2) In what order shall I develop my argument?

(i) *Plan (with Notes)*

1 Introduction

Must be 'punchy' to gain reader's attention. Must make it plain that I am beginning a thoughtful discussion of the subject. *One* paragraph along these lines: the statement quoted is an assertion, not a reasoned opinion — it ignores the distinction between alcoholic drinks, which may be harmful, and hard drugs, which must be — on this dubious basis, it calls for an indiscriminate ban.

2 Body of Argument

Here I must do three things: (1) demonstrate weakness of proposition; (2) deploy my positive arguments for permitting sale and consumption of alcoholic drinks; (3) lead reader step by step towards agreement with my conclusion. Thinking about those three tasks suggests the following sequence of paragraphs.

PARAGRAPH 1

Cannot be denied that immoderate drinking causes mental and physical suffering — many alcoholics — families distressed — hospitals burdened — but this is misuse, abuse, of alcohol.

PARAGRAPH 2

Benefits of alcohol that statement ignores — social pleasure — medical evidence in favour of moderate use.

PARAGRAPH 3

Dangers of prohibition — the American experience — modern examples — law evasion and law enforcement — crime inevitably accompanies prohibition.

Some habits are so vicious, some substances so dangerous as to warrant banning — for reasons given, not alcoholic drinks — most people use them as source of harmless pleasure — cannot justifiably take away the pleasure of a majority because a minority misuses it.

CONCLUSION

One pithy paragraph, knitting together strands of argument. Banning pleasure always dangerous and rarely justified. Considering the inevitable harmful consequences of a legal ban, the case against alcoholic drinks is too weak to support their prohibition.

(ii) *A Note on Appropriate Language*

As you already know, emotional terms and excited writing must be avoided. You will not convince your reader by shouting. The cool, thoughtful tone of good discursive writing calls for a degree of formality in its style, but do not confuse formality with pomposity. Long-winded sentences and 'big', would-be important words will not impress your reader. An easy, plain style is best, but do not use slang or colloquialisms (see Chapters 6 and 7).

1.8   Work out Dramatic Writing

Remember that a dramatic (or conversational) composition must be written in direct speech, but — as you will see from the work out — you can use 'stage directions' to help to develop the action and to suggest the emotions and attitudes of the characters. A dramatic situation is tense and exciting because the characters are in some sort of confusion or conflict. The action rises to a climax and then ends with a quick clearing up of the confusion or resolution of the conflict.

(a) A Typical Question

> *David McKenzie, a young man of eighteen, is sitting at the table of a living-room making a model from a kit; his sister, Jacky, a bright-eyed nervous teenager, is curled up in an armchair watching television. Their father, who has just returned from work, is recovering his spirits by trying to read the evening newspaper.*
> *There is an insistent ringing of the doorbell. Mrs McKenzie is heard going to answer it, and there are muffled sounds of a serious conversation outside. The door of the living-room opens violently. She appears, disturbed and shaking.*
> *Mr McKenzie* [*casually looking up*] : What is it, dear?
> *Mrs McKenzie* [*breathlessly*] : There's a policeman at the door.
> *David:* Oh, no!
> *Jacky quickly unrolls herself from the chair and switches off the television; she looks anxiously at her father and bursts into tears.*

Write a short play by continuing the dialogue in a manner which develops the dramatic situation. (You are advised to continue the method of setting out the dialogue, but *do not copy out the extract*. If you wish, you may introduce one or two more characters or add a further scene.)

(b) Work out: Stage 1

Analyse the given dramatic situation out of which you must develop a short play.

    (i) Peaceful domestic scene suddenly interrupted by arrival of policeman.
   (ii) Four characters briefly introduced:
      David McKenzie (brother) – sitting working at model – quiet – eighteen.
      Jacky McKenzie (sister) – bright-eyed, nervous – watching TV – curled up – teenager.
      Mr McKenzie (father) – tired after work – trying to read newspaper.
      Mrs McKenzie (mother) – disturbed – shaking – opens door violently.
  (iii) Another character – policeman – as yet an unknown quantity.

(c) Work out: Stage 2

Identify possible dramatic 'growth points'.

    (i) Jacky's reaction – looks anxiously at father – bursts into tears – frightened of father's reaction – thinks she knows why policeman has called – nervous person, so assumes that policeman's visit means trouble for her.
   (ii) David McKenzie's exclamation ('Oh, no!') – is that caused by annoyance at interruption or does he think something is catching up with him? – quiet character, so has possibilities for surprising dramatic development.
  (iii) Father – no reaction given, so can be used in any way that develops drama – father-figure, so give him authority and some control over events – remember, he's tired and wants to read his paper in peace.
  (iv) Mother – upset – bewildered – worried – not so much an actor in the drama as a reactor to events?
   (v) Policeman – why has he called? – obviously the mainspring of the action – provide a harmless reason for his visit but do not reveal it at once – in meantime, let other characters react in confused, nervous or angry way.

(d) Work out: Stage 3

Outline development of dramatic situation.

    Suppose the policeman has called to interest the McKenzies in a police/public co-operation in a 'neighbourhood watch' scheme.

    Suppose David thinks he wants information about his motor bike. The licence is due for renewal.

    Suppose Jacky thinks he saw her and her friends leaving a disco late the previous evening. They were happy and excited and making a lot of noise. Perhaps there has been a complaint? What will her father say?

    Leave Mr and Mrs McKenzie in bewilderment. He's fed up because he's tired and wants to relax. She's anxious about her children. Give Mr McKenzie an active role. Give Mrs McKenzie a passive role.

Thinking it out has provided: (1) a development of the given dramatic situation; (2) action that rises to a climax; (3) an ending that untwists the strands of the action and resolves the tension.

(e) Work out: Stage 4

Write the dramatic composition in accordance with the instructions supplied.

Mr McKenzie [*wearily*]: What on earth does he want? You'd better bring him in. Oh, do be quiet, Jacky! What's the matter?

Jacky [*between sobs*]: We didn't mean . . . it was only fun . . .

David [*searching through his wallet*]: I filled it in the other day. Don't say I didn't post the blessed thing.

> *By this time, Mrs McKenzie has brought the policeman into the living-room. He is a young man, with a pleasant smile.*

Policeman: I'm sorry to disturb you, but I'd like to have a talk.

> *Jacky and her mother speak at the same time and nobody hears what they are saying. The policeman looks enquiringly at Mr McKenzie, whose patience is wearing thin.*

Mr McKenzie: I wish somebody would tell me what this is all about. Jacky, keep quiet until you have something sensible to say. Don't upset yourself, Alice. There's nothing wrong — as far as I know.

David McKenzie [*waving an envelope*]: It's here! All filled in and signed — *and* the money's inside. If I catch the last post, they'll get it tomorrow.

> *David makes for the door, smiling happily, but the policeman speaks to him before he can reach it.*

Policeman [*firmly*]: If you could just give me a moment . . . I'm particularly anxious to talk to young people, like you and your sister.

Jacky [*tearfully*]: I'm sorry, but — honestly — I don't know how to . . .

Mr McKenzie: Where d'you think you're going, David? Sit down. [*He turns to the policeman.*] Perhaps if you sat down too, we'd get somewhere. I think my two children have gone off their chumps.

Mrs McKenzie: Oh, yes, do sit down. I'll go and get us all a cup of tea. I'm sure you'd like one?

> *She turns towards the kitchen door, pleased to have something practical to do.*

Policeman: Well, that's very kind of you, but perhaps you'd just listen to me first. You are all concerned in this.

Jacky: No! You've got it wrong. It wasn't *their* fault. They weren't there. They were here, at home, when . . .

Mr McKenzie: Jacky, if I have to tell you to shut up once more, I'll go as barmy as you. [*He turns to the policeman.*] Now, young man, I think I can guarantee you a few minutes of silence. What's it all about?

Policeman: We're trying to start a neighbourhood watch scheme. Each station in our division is contacting the households in its area. There's to be a public meeting in the Town Hall at 7.30 next Tuesday and I'm here to invite you all to it.

David McKenzie [*putting the envelope back in his wallet*]: So that's it! Oh, what a pity! I can't go on Tuesday — it's my training night.

Jacky [*very enthusiastically*]: Oh, what a good idea! I'll be there and I'll bring some of my friends.

Mrs McKenzie: Tuesday, you say? I'm afraid I can't. I always spend the evening with Gran on a Tuesday. She's getting on, you know, and she looks forward to Tuesdays.

Mr McKenzie [*very firmly*] : I think we shall be well represented at the meeting, officer. Jacky's very keen — you can see that. And I'm sure David will put off his training for once. He takes a lot of interest in legal matters, don't you, David?

> *David is about to answer, but he looks again at his father's expression and changes his mind.*

Policeman: I'll leave these leaflets for you to read before the meeting. [*He hands one to David and one to Jacky*.] Thank you for your interest and I'll look forward to seeing you next Tuesday evening. I don't think I'd better have that cup of tea, thank you, Mrs McKenzie. I've got several more houses to visit.

> *Mrs McKenzie shows the policeman out. David returns to his modelling. Jacky reaches for the television switch.*

Mr McKenzie [*picking up his newspaper*] : Now, David, you'd better go and post that letter. And don't tell me it doesn't matter. If a policeman's visit reminded you of it, it matters all right. And, Jacky, you can forget about television for half an hour. Celebrate your lucky escape — whatever it was — by helping your mother in the kitchen. *I'm* going to read my paper.

1.9   Work out Impressionistic Writing

(a) The Examiners' Instructions

As you saw in Section 1.5, a composition on an impressionistic subject may be written in the form of a story. It may also be written as an unplotted narrative or a description, or in *any form that the particular instructions permit*.

Whether the provided stimulus is verbal (a few lines of poetry) or visual (a picture or a series of pictures), the examiners usually invite candidates to respond by writing *one* of several different forms of composition which they stipulate. Which form of composition you choose is entirely up to you, provided that it is one of the forms permitted by the question.

Instructions for impressionistic writing are worded in many different ways. You may be told to write a story based on a picture or a poem. You may be told to write a descriptive piece suggested by several pictures (or just one). You may be told to give an account of the thoughts and feelings that a picture or a poem suggests to you. (An instruction such as that calls for a very carefully planned piece of writing.)

To familiarise yourself with the range of instructions, study the list of typical assignments given in the next section. Before doing so, however, remind yourself of the stipulation that applies to *all* impressionistic compositions of whatever form: your writing must be directly and clearly connected with the given poetry or picture. That is its starting point.

(b) Some Typical Impressionistic Assignments

1. Using the picture as a starting point, write a story or compose a descriptive piece.
2. Write a story or a description or an account of your thoughts and feelings suggested by *one* of the pictures on the accompanying sheet. Your composition should be directly about the subject of the picture or take some central

suggestion(s) from it: *there must be some clear connection between the picture and what you write.*

3. Using the following lines of poetry as a starting point, write a story or describe your personal response.
4. Write a composition based on the accompanying picture postcard.
5. Write a composition suggested by the following quotation.
6. Write on an idea suggested by the picture below.
7. Write on an idea, *or* on places, *or* on persons, suggested by the following lines.
8. Look at the photograph printed below and then do *one* of the following:
    (i) Write a story in which the driver of the car in the picture plays an important part.
    (ii) Write a story entitled 'The car that broke down'.
    (iii) Write about the thoughts and feelings that the picture suggests to you.
    (iv) Describe what you imagine may have happened just *after* the photograph was taken.

(c) Work out Your Methods

Revise Section 1.5, where a sound method of writing an impressionistic composition is demonstrated in full detail.

In that work out the stimulus was poetry and the form chosen for the composition was a story. Here are some notes on how to use a pictorial stimulus to write compositions of various kinds.

(i) *Picture Subjects*

The picture material may be a photograph of a dramatic scene, or a 'still' from a television play or a film. It may be a news picture from a paper or a magazine, or it may be a landscape or townscape. It may be a photographic reproduction of a work of art. It may be a strip cartoon. It may be comic or serious; strictly realistic or imaginatively suggestive. The range of possibilities is large, but whatever the subject or the nature of the picture, your writing must spring out of a close and imaginative response to it.

(ii) *A Story Based on a Picture*

Imagine that you are one of the people in the picture, or imagine that you took the photograph or that you painted the picture. This way, you involve yourself in the possibilities of action, get to know the people, find an angle from which to tell your story.

Having identified with one of the people in the picture or with the photographer or artist, let your thoughts play on possible relationships (enmity, love, rivalry, support, and so on) between your 'angle character' and other people in the picture. The seeds of your plot lie here.

Study facial expressions, gestures, clothes, ages, postures, and so on, as shown in the picture. Sharp observation of such details will provide descriptive material and plot development for your story.

Only when you have 'interpreted' the picture in this way, by an imaginative exploration of *what* is happening and *why* it is happening, can you use it as the springboard for a story.

(iii) *Descriptive Writing Based on a Picture*

Study the picture closely, with a sharp eye for its details. You will find yourself responding imaginatively to some particular item. A frowning face, an open window, a shadow on a doorstep, a child's smile, a car without a number plate, a smart hat worn at a rakish angle . . . such are the pictorial hints that will start you off.

Look for your 'angle of attack' (see Section 1.6(d)) in the interaction of a detail with the overall impression that the picture makes. That crucial angle of attack may be discovered either by narrowing down your focus from the picture as a whole to a particular detail, or by focusing first on a detail and then widening your view to take in the whole picture. Try both ways of searching for your viewpoint.

Once you have established your angle of attack, move in an ordered sequence from your starting point to your planned ending. Unless you consistently maintain your chosen angle, you will let in irrelevant details and weaken the structure of your composition. Unity (each detail and each part contributes to the impact of the *whole*) is vital. Remember: 'No false starts and no loose ends.'

(iv) *Impressionistic Writing Based on a Picture*

Instructions such as 'Write about the impressions you receive from this picture' or 'What thoughts (and/or feelings) does this picture suggest to you?' require a different kind of answer from those we have been considering earlier. They limit you by excluding narrative or descriptive forms of composition, but they offer you great freedom of imaginative response to the picture. Provided that your subject matter is triggered off by something in the picture (and is clearly seen by the reader to be so evoked) you can allow your imagination to journey beyond the picture's bounds.

(v) *Model Structure*

Many candidates find that the following model structure provides a sound basis for picture compositions of the kind we are discussing here.

1 INTRODUCTION

Brief but vivid description of the 'trigger detail' in the picture and of your immediate response to it. One paragraph.

2 BODY OF COMPOSITION

Three or four paragraphs describing the associated ideas, thoughts and/or feelings that the 'trigger' has set off in your mind. It is essential to link these paragraphs so that each leads your reader on to the next. You must establish a clear forward flow of ideas, thoughts, feelings.

3 CONCLUSION

A final paragraph, rounding off the imaginative journey on which you have taken your reader. It is structurally effective and imaginatively satisfying to return to the trigger detail from which the essay began.

2 Practical Writing

2.1 General Characteristics

In practical (or factual) writing assignments and questions you are given certain material which must be used in a practical, everyday situation indicated by the examiners' instructions. The exercise tests your ability to write briefly, clearly and accurately. Because the instructions strictly control both the content and the purpose of your writing, practical writing is sometimes called 'directed writing'.

Now revise Sections 1.1(c) and 1.1(d).

Remember that practical writing is an essential part of 'Expression'. The quality of your practical writing (whether it is part of your assessed coursework or written under examination conditions) plays a major part in determining the grade you are given in English.

(a) Purpose and Form

Practical writing tests your ability to:

- write correct English;
- make accurate use of given information;
- carry out instructions.

The answer required may be in the form of:

- a letter;
- a report;
- a short article;
- a set of instructions;
- an ordered explanation;
- an outline of a point of view;
- an outline of advice on some problem.

(b) Style

A plain, 'no frills' style is appropriate to the practical purpose and factual content of practical writing. The letters, reports, instructions, etc., that are called for are best expressed in simple terms, with no wasted words or purple patches. 'Transactional' writing (writing that gets things done) is successful when it is crisp, clear and very much to the point, so your use of language must be objective, un-emotional and controlled.

2.2 Work out Letters

The instructions may or may not draw your attention to the importance of correct layout and the need to observe the conventions of letter writing. Whether they do so or not, your letter must always be set out properly and you must always conform to the conventions. Failure to do so is penalised.

(a) Work out 1

> factual material pro-
> vided and practical
> situation indicated

> writing task set –
> the writer is given
> two objectives

There is a proposal to resite the market in your town by moving it from its present open-air site in the town centre to a covered hall being built by property developers. This proposal has caused bad feeling between its supporters and its opponents. Write a letter to the Editor of your local newspaper, stating your own views and attempting to reconcile the two sides.

> writer's address –
> see notes

12, Grove Road,
St Mary's Way,
Boroughtown.
BT7 12GR
31 March 1985

> recipient's name and
> address – formal
> letter

The Editor,
Boroughtown News,
6, West Walk,
Boroughtown.
BT4 6WW

> correct salutation
> for Editor

Sir,

It is not surprising that the proposal to resite our market has caused so much bad feeling. Its supporters see only the advantages offered by a modern, spacious, weatherproof market. Its opponents regret the ending of a long tradition. Our market has been held in the Square for over three hundred years. Its stall-holders give us excellent service throughout the year. The objectors also argue that the move will cause market prices to rise to pay for increased rents in the new hall.

My own view is that the advantages of the move outweigh the disadvantages, but I sympathise with the objectors and I believe that their case merits a reasoned answer. If the market committee of the borough council would publish details of the new stall rents, the objectors would know whether their fears are justified. They also deserve an assurance that the layout of the new hall will be as convenient and efficient as the arrangements that we are used to.

I believe that the present bad feeling would be greatly reduced if those two suggestions were followed up.

Yours faithfully,

> formal close *Yours
> faithfully* matches
> salutation *Sir* – no
> full stop after sig-
> nature

Brian Jones

1 The Layout of Addresses

Choose either of the following styles. Whichever you choose, be consistent. Do not start with one style and change to the other.

Style 1	*Style 2*
12, Grove Road,	12 Grove Road
St Mary's Way,	St Mary's Way
Boroughtown.	Boroughtown
BT7 12GR	BT7 12GR
Closed punctuation.	Open punctuation.
Indented lines (except postcode).	Blocked lines (i.e. not indented)
The comma after the house number is optional.	If well-written, this is a neat and uncluttered address layout.
No full stop after St – it is a contraction (= *Saint*), not an abbreviation.	

2 The Date

All letters must be dated. The date form shown is clear and neat:

day (numerical)	month (in full)	year (in full)
31	March	1985

There are many other date forms. The following are often used:

31st March 1985; March 31st, 1985; 31.iii.85

Economy and clarity argue for the form used in the work out.

3 The Recipient's Name and Address

Must be included in formal letters. Out of place in informal letters. May be written above body of letter, as in work out, or below.

4 Salutation

The recipient of the letter must be 'greeted'. This greeting is called the 'salutation': *Dear So-and-so*. Formal ('business') letters require formal salutations. These are: *Dear Sir/Dear Madam*; *Dear Sirs* (to a Company); *Sir* (to the Editor of a newspaper). The correct salutations for 'non-business' letters are: *Dear Mr Jones*; *Dear Mrs Jones*; *Dear Miss Jones*; *Dear Ms Jones*; *Dear Tom*; *Dear Jane*; *Dear Uncle Fred*; etc.

5 Punctuation of Salutation

When indented paragraphs are used in the letter, it is customary to end the salutation with a comma.

Dear Mr Jones,
                   Thank you for your letter . . .

Note the capital for the first word of the letter. When the paragraphs are not indented, omit the comma at the end of the salutation.

Dear Mr Jones
Thank you for your letter . . .

6 Formal Close

Before 'signing off', the letter writer uses a *formal close*. The formal close must 'match' the salutation. Like this:

Dear Sir		*Dear Mr Jones*	
Dear Madam	*Yours faithfully*	*Dear Mrs Jones*	*Yours sincerely*
Sir		*Dear Sally*	

If the salutation does not name the recipient, the formal close is *Yours faithfully*. If the salutation does name the recipient, the formal close is *Yours sincerely*. Note that *Yours* begins with a capital Y, but *faithfully* and *sincerely* begin with small letters. There is no punctuation after the signature.

(b) Work out 2

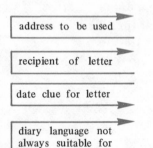

address to be used

recipient of letter

date clue for letter

diary language not always suitable for letter to aunt

You are on holiday with some family friends, the Robinsons, at 6, Quayside Cottages, Hartsea, Devon. On a morning walk along the cliffs, you witness the rescue of a person cut off by the tide. Write a letter to your Aunt Amy, describing the adventure. Make use of these notes from your diary.

Friday 13 August. Early walk along cliffs. Robinsons' dog Toby wittering away on cliff top. Barking like fury. Looked down. Figure on beach waving frantically. Faint calls. What to do? Return for help? Sound of helicopter. Hovered overhead. Then down cliff face. Winchman brought stranded walker up. Elderly woman. Bit shaken; not hurt. Took her to Robinsons. Surprise, surprise! Miss Agnes Smith — old family friend of theirs. Mrs R and Miss S quite overcome — shock/relief. Mr R's joke. Plans for party at Miss S's hotel tomorrow.

6 Quayside Cottages
Hartsea
Devon
14 August 1986

Dear Aunt Amy,

    I promised you a letter, but I didn't think I'd have quite such exciting news to send.

    Yesterday, I took the Robinsons' dog, Toby, for an early morning walk along the cliffs. Suddenly, he got very excited and started barking furiously. I looked over the cliff and saw a figure on the beach below, waving frantically at me. I could hear faint calls for help and I decided I must return to the cottage. I couldn't do anything on my own.

    Then I heard a helicopter in the distance. Quite soon, it was hovering overhead and then it descended the cliff face very slowly and carefully. The winchman was lowered and he lifted the stranded walker off the beach.

When they got her to the cliff top, I saw that she was an elderly woman. She was a bit shaken, but she assured them that she was not hurt, so they asked me to guide her back to the village.

Mrs Robinson came out to greet us and you can imagine how surprised she was to recognise the rescued woman as Miss Agnes Smith, an old family friend of theirs. It was quite a shock for them both and they were rather upset by it all, until Mr Robinson made them laugh by saying that this was an unusual way of paying calls!

We're having a celebration party at Miss Smith's hotel tonight and I must start getting ready now.

With lots of love,
Your affectionate niece,

Jane

(i) *Notes on Work out 2*

1 Layout and Conventions

The information required for the address was included in the instructions. (Style 2 was chosen for the layout, but style 1 would have been equally correct.) The date clue was also important. Notice the use made of it by Jane. The salutation *Dear Aunt Amy* was matched by the signing off, which accurately reflected the kinship and good feeling between writer and recipient.

2 Style

This is an informal letter (contrast it with Work out 1) in which colloquialisms (*didn't, I'd*, etc.) are appropriate. However, the slang expressions used in the diary notes were rightly rejected as being unsuitable in tone. Though not formal, this letter is from niece to aunt and slang would be ill-mannered. Jane very nicely achieved the easy, conversational style that the occasion required.

3 Contents

The letter writer was instructed to describe the adventure, but neither time nor length allowed space for descriptive detail, so a bare outline of events was required. A brief introductory sentence supplied a realistic beginning for the letter. Similarly, the last clause of the final sentence provided a neat and convincing ending.

(c) **Work out 3**

You notice this advertisement in your local paper:

Junior assistant required to work initially in Accounts Department of small but growing local firm, specialising in the preparation of research reports for electronics industry. Must be mathematically competent and willing to undertake part-time study for further qualifications in areas to be agreed. Apply in writing to Box 27, Bramshall Clarion, Mill Lane, Bramshall, BH12 6ML, giving details of qualifications and experience. Two referees required.

You left school 2 years ago with five O levels and since then have had work experience relevant to the post advertised. You have applied for admission to an electronics course at your local F.E. college and are waiting for the result of your application. Write a letter to the address given, applying for the advertised job.

---

16 Smith Street
Bramshall
BH8 16ST

30 June 1986
Box 27
The Bramshall Clarion
Mill Lane
Bramshall
BH12 6ML

Dear Sirs,

Junior Assistant in Accounts Department

     I believe that my qualifications and experience make me a suitable candidate for the above post.

     I am 18 years old and I left Bramshall Central Comprehensive School in July 1984 with five O levels: English Language (Grade 2); English Literature (Grade 2); Mathematics (Grade 1); General Science (Grade 2); French (Grade 3). I also gained life-saving and woodcraft badges in the Guides and I was secretary of the school discussion club.

     I then worked with Comma Electric for a year, gaining varied experience in components assembly and in the customer relations department.

     In the past year, I have had experience of part-time voluntary work in the Bramshall Youth Centre. I have now applied for admission to the first year electronics course at Bramshall F.E. college and, if you appoint me to the vacancy in your firm, I shall ask to be transferred to the evening course in order to pursue the further qualifications to which your advertisement refers.

     Yours faithfully,

Mary Young

Reference may be made to the following:
1. Mr J. K. Tompkins, M. A., Headmaster, Bramshall
   Central Comprehensive School, BH4 5CC.
2. Miss A. C. Bednall, Personnel Officer, Comma Electric,
   BH16 1TE.

Side annotations:

formal letter: recipient's name and address required

formal salutation

letter 'headline' provided: reader can 'tune in' to contents at once

start with personal details: list all qualifications and other achievements in non-academic fields

highlight aspects of experience that suit you for job

formal close *Yours faithfully*

clear and convenient way of listing referees

2.3 Work out Reports

When a practical writing assignment takes the form of a report, the examiners expect you to be:

- accurate in carrying out the instructions;
- logical in the arrangement of the contents;
- clear and brief in expression.

A report must be written in continuous prose (*not* in note form), but headings and/or numbered sections may be used as an aid to clear presentation. The test of a well-written report is the ease and clarity with which it can be read and understood.

Assignments of this type are often set:

> Your student council committee has asked you to report on the cafeteria service provided in your school or college. Write your report, suggesting practical ways in which the service could be improved.

(b) Layout: Headings

By its very nature, a report is an essentially practical piece of writing, intended to be *used*. It has been asked for by some person or some organisation. It is on a precise subject. It is needed for a particular purpose at a particular time. Therefore, it must be accurately and clearly identified. Always supply headings that provide the necessary details. The report called for in the question just quoted requires these headings:

> *To:* Student Council Committee, Fairplace F.E. College
> *From:* X. Y. Bloggs
> *Subject:* College cafeteria service
> *Date:* 15/9/86

(Note that all-numeral date forms are acceptable on reports, memoranda and brief notes. On letters, the date form recommended in Section 2.2(a) should be used.)

(c) Layout: Internal

Headings and/or numbered sections are usually required in the body of a report. They are essential when it contains numerous and varied items, and even the comparatively straightforward reports asked for in your examination are made much clearer by such divisions. Internal headings and/or numbered sections act as 'signposts' to the logical order in which a report is set out. Thus, they assist the reader to comprehend the contents quickly and clearly.

(d) Logical Order: Findings and Recommendations

When you have assembled the material for your report, sort it out into a logical order of presentation. In the question quoted in Section 2.3(a), you are instructed to do two things: (1) investigate the cafeteria service; (2) make practical suggestions for improvements. Logically, then, your report should consist of two main sections: (1) Findings; (2) Recommendations.

Since you will probably need to include more than one item under each of those internal headings, some such plan as this will be suitable:

1. *Findings*
   (i) or (a)   } arranged in a logical order when the
   (ii) or (b)   } material for the report has been
   etc.   } assembled — see below
2. *Recommendations*
   (i) or (a)   } arranged in a logical order after
   (ii) or (b)   } the findings have been sorted out
   etc.   } — see below

The precise nature and number of the sub-divisions under each main heading cannot be decided in advance. After you have jotted down the material for your report, you can then work out the classifications into which it can sensibly be divided. For example: favourable items; unfavourable items. Then you can decide upon the *order* of presentation: favourable items before unfavourable items — or vice versa?; proceed from most important item to least important item (*descending* order)?; proceed from least important item to most important item (*ascending* order)?

Provided that you are aware of the necessity of establishing a logical order, a scheme to suit the nature of the report will emerge as you sort out your material.

(e) Work out

practical situation indicated: instructions given →	Your student council committee has asked you to report on the cafeteria service provided in your school or college. Write your report, suggesting practical ways in which the service could be improved.

(i) *Stage 1 of Work out*

Jot down the material as it occurs to you. In an everyday situation you would gather this material by observing, asking questions and making notes. In examination conditions you must draw on your experience of the system to provide the material for the report.

> poor quality of snacks, sandwiches especially — lack of variety and imagination — hot and cold drinks expensive and not good — food, except for standard hot meal at lunch, poor value for money — hot lunch very good, varied, plenty of it, but too expensive for most students to eat every day — long queues — takes far too long to get to food bar — seats uncomfortable, and not enough — too much noise — lack of social atmosphere — cafeteria closes at five, no chance of hot drink or snack after lectures, evening students not catered for at all

(ii) *Stage 2 of Work out*

Suggestions for improvements have been asked for, so the logical order of presentation seems to be : (1) favourable items; (2) unfavourable items. Recommendations will then follow logically from the latter. Again, looking for ways of sorting the material out into sensible groups, you can see that the unfavourable items fall into three classes: (1) food; (2) surroundings and conditions; (3) opening hours. Of these, food is undoubtedly the most important, so take that first.

plan for report is emerging from close, analytical study of findings	

1. Findings

   (a) Favourable items

   (b) Unfavourable items

       (i) food

      (ii) surroundings and conditions

     (iii) opening hours

The details of this 'display code' — '(a), (b), (b)(i)', etc. — will not necessarily be followed in the report itself. Here they are useful in setting out the emerging plan for the report.

(iii) **Stage 3 of Work out**

The instructions asked for practical suggestions about ways of improving the cafeteria service. Now that the findings have been assembled and arranged in a logical order of presentation, the recommendations follow on logically. It is important to distinguish between what can and should be done immediately and what might be done in time and with extra funds. Those considerations suggest the logical order in which to present the recommendations.

recommendations follow logically from ordered presentation of findings and are themselves presented in a logical order	

2. Recommendations

   (a) Food   Detailed recommendations for immediate action can be made.

   (b) Surroundings and Conditions   Detailed recommendations for immediate and medium-term action can be made.

   (c) Opening Hours   Long-term problem because of serious financial implications. General recommendations can be made.

(iv) **Stage 4 of Work out: Writing the Report**

REPORT

To: Student Council Committee, Fairplace F.E. College
From: X.Y. Bloggs
Subject: College cafeteria service
Date: 15/9/86

1. Findings

   (a) Students consider that the hot lunch is a good meal, providing a variety of well-cooked dishes.

   (b) Most students, however, rely on the snacks because they cannot afford the hot lunch. The snacks — especially the sandwiches — are of poor quality. They lack variety and they are over-priced. The same criticisms apply to the hot and cold drinks.

   (c) Lunchtime queues are long and tiresome. The seating is uncomfortable and inadequate. There is too much noise in the cafeteria and a lack of social atmosphere.

   (d) Cafeteria service closes at 5.00 p.m. Consequently, students cannot obtain refreshments after lectures, and evening students are not catered for at all.

2. Recommendations

(a) *Food*   Immediate action can and should be taken to improve the quality and variety of the snacks and drinks. No additional funds are required to effect this improvement, just more care and imagination. A student/cafeteria staff liaison committee should be set up at once.

(b) *Surroundings and Conditions*   As a first step, more chairs should be provided. Then, queues, overcrowding and noise could all be reduced by more thoughtful timetabling. If half the morning lectures ended at 12 noon and the other half at 1.00 p.m. (with a consequent adjustment to afternoon lectures), the pressure on the cafeteria would be halved. Lunch service would have to be extended to 2 hours, but this should not cost more than present resources would allow.

(c) *Opening Hours*   I recognise that an extension beyond 5.00 p.m. would be costly, but I recommend that this problem be taken to the college authorities for urgent action as soon as financial conditions permit.

2.4   Work out Articles and Newspaper Reports

(a) Qualities to be Aimed at

Note, first, that the examiners' instructions often refer to a piece of writing intended for a newspaper or magazine as 'a report'. Such a report is very different from the kind of report worked out in Section 2.3. Its heading (or 'headline') is brief and eye-catching. It is not divided into sections and sub-sections (though it is clearly paragraphed and may have subheadings). It does not make recommendations.

An article is less concerned with events than is a newspaper or magazine report. For example, you would probably be asked to write a *report* of a village meeting called to discuss a local issue and to write an *article* about one of the speakers at that meeting. A report is more 'newsy' than an article. However, the distinction is not always sharply drawn. Instructions phrased like this are common: 'Write an article, suitable for your school or college magazine, reporting the major events (sporting *or* academic *or* artistic) of one term in the past year'.

An *article* and a newspaper or magazine *report* are very similar. The theoretical distinction between them does not affect the qualities looked for in your answer.

> ● An article or report written for a newspaper or magazine must be accurate, lively and readable.

(b) Two Kinds of Assignments

In one kind of assignment you are supplied with the information that you must use in the article. In such cases pay very careful attention to the instructions. Careless reading costs marks: a point illustrated by the following instructions.

1. Write an article for your school or college magazine, selecting your information from the notes below.
2. Write a report for your local paper, using all the information given below.
3. Write a report for publication in your college magazine, based on the notes supplied and any other information that you may wish to add.

The other kind of assignment stipulates the subject on which your article must be written, but leaves you to provide all the information. For example: 'Write an article for your local paper, reporting a measure proposed by the council and the strong feelings (for and against) that this has provoked'. Note that you are *not* asked for *your* opinions. Objective reporting is required. (Compare that assignment closely with the one set in Section 2.2(a).)

(c) Work out

Write an article for your local paper about Councillor Brown, your newly elected mayor, selecting your information from the facts supplied below.

Brown, Arthur Henry. b. Fairplace, 30 November 19–. Third son of William Henry Brown, foreman fitter Fairplace Engineering and a member of Fairplace Borough Council until his death in 19–. Educated at Fairplace Central School. Left at 16. Apprenticed to Fairplace Engineering. Later joined export sales division. Widely travelled. Numerous international conferences. Eventually managing director, his present post at Fairplace Engineering. Keen sportsman: Fairplace R.U.F.C. 1st XV; F. cricket club, captain 1st XI. Also F. dramatic soc. and civic soc. Member of Borough Council for past 10 years, Independent (Castle Ward), chairman library committee, member watch committee. In acceptance speech stressed desire to attract more industry to F. Hoped his year in office would be remembered for industrial expansion: 'more jobs and better jobs'. Married Mary Jones (Fairplace born) in 19–. Three children (two daughters, one son) now attending F. Sixth Form College

(i) *Stage 1*

The problem of order must be solved first. Think about the nature and purpose of the set task. You have to present facts about the new mayor in a way that will interest readers of your paper. A straightforward chronological arrangement of facts ((1) birth; (2) education; (3) early career; and so on) would work, but it might be rather dull reading. Can you think of a more interesting order? Here is one possibility.

NEW MAYOR'S AMBITIONS FOR FAIRPLACE

PARAGRAPH 1

A local family man

PARAGRAPH 2

Successful career — wide experience of industry and foreign travel lead to top job

PARAGRAPH 3

Yet, a Fairplace-centred life — local activities and local politics

PARAGRAPH 4

His ambitions for his term of office

PARAGRAPH 5

Conclusion: Councillor Brown, a mayor for our town and our times

The paragraph headings used in that outline will not appear in the article. They are useful signposts at this stage, when the objective is to group together and then to set out in a logical and interesting order the items of information supplied. You can probably improve on the suggested outline, but it does point out the possibilities for a livelier article than strict chronological order seemed to offer.

(ii) *Stage 2*

The reader's attention must be gripped by the beginning of the article and, an outline plan having been settled on, it is a good idea to try out one or two opening sentences. You do not have to distort the facts or to copy the broken English of the tabloids to be interesting. 'Fairplace's new mayor is a Fairplace man.'/'A truly local man is now Fairplace's first citizen,'/'Rooted in local life, our new mayor brings wide experience to his high office.' You may not use any of the trial openings exactly as worded (I am certainly not satisfied with any of those), but jotting them down tunes you in to the spirit of the article and helps you to get off on the right foot.

(iii) *Stage 3*

Think hard about your ending. Have it clearly in mind before you begin to write. Aim for a pithy and memorable summing up of the body of the article. No repetition, of course; but something that will stay in the reader's mind as epitomising the content and tone of the article. Look back at the outline. Paragraph 5 may suggest a good way of ending.

(iv) *Stage 4: Write the Article*

NEW MAYOR'S AMBITIONS FOR FAIRPLACE

Arthur Henry Brown was born on November 19— in the heart of the community whose first citizen he now is. The third son of William Henry Brown, foreman fitter at Fairplace Engineering and borough councillor until his death in 19—, he was educated at the Central School, leaving at the age of 16 for an apprenticeship with his father's employers. His marriage in 19— to a Fairplace girl, Mary Jones, strengthened these local ties, and their three children (two daughters and a son), students at Fairplace Sixth Form College, now follow in the family's footsteps.

Councillor Brown's apprenticeship was succeeded by an outstanding career in the export sales division, involving world-wide travel and attendance at many international conferences before he was appointed to his present post of managing director of Fairplace Engineering, the firm that he joined as a school-leaver.

Despite his many business commitments, he has always been involved in Fairplace activities. He played for the rugby club's 1st XV and was captain of the cricket club's 1st XI. His membership of the dramatic and civic societies was a reflection of his interest in the arts and in local history. Ten years ago, his election as a councillor (Independent, Castle Ward) led to service on the watch and library committees and the chairmanship of the latter.

His much-applauded acceptance speech, as mayor, epitomised his long and many-sided involvement with the life of our town. Above all, he said, he wanted his term of office to be remembered for the prosperity that would follow industrial expansion. 'More jobs and better jobs for Fairplace', in his own words.

Regardless of party ties, the people of Fairplace have welcomed their new mayor. An energetic and forward-looking man, deeply rooted in the community and devoted to its welfare, Councillor Brown is a mayor for our town and our time.

2.5 Work out Instructions, Descriptions, Explanations, etc.

(a) Typical Assignments

1. Give instructions (not in note form) on how to do *one* of the following: (i) recharge a flat car battery; (ii) build a kite; (iii) replace a faulty plug on an electrical appliance; (iv) prepare a nourishing soup.
2. Describe the layout of and the services offered at *one* of the following: (i) a public library; (ii) a filling station; (iii) a D.I.Y. store.
3. What advice would you give to a first-year student at your school or college to help him or her to settle in as quickly and happily as possible?
4. Write a leaflet for distribution to your fellow-students urging them to support a campaign for better library facilities.
5. You have been asked to speak briefly for or against *one* of the following: (i) that the voting age should be reduced to 16; (ii) that bicycles should be licensed in the way that motor vehicles are; (iii) that professionalism in sport should be abolished. Write your speech.
6. A visitor from overseas has asked you to suggest a place of interest in your locality suitable for an excursion. Write a brief description of an outstanding building or beauty spot that would be worth a visit.
7. A relative or friend about to travel abroad for the first time has asked for your advice. Write helpful tips on *one* of the following: (i) passing through customs; (ii) travelling light; (iii) language problems.
8. You want to encourage a friend to take up your own favourite hobby or pastime. Describe its attractions and rewards.
9. Advise a friend who is thinking of buying a camera on how to make a good choice.

(b) What You Must Do

Although the instructions may be worded in very different ways, practical writing is always a test of your ability to organise your material and to write clearly and to the point.

You must work out your plan before you begin to write. To work out a satisfactory plan, you must:

- arrange the individual items into sensible groups;
- decide on a logical order of presentation.

(c) Parts, Stages, Steps

When a straightforward subject has been set, thinking along these lines will help you to organise your material. Suppose you have chosen to describe the layout and equipment that you would expect to find in a well-planned kitchen. A number of unorganised items will spring to mind at once. They can be arranged into workman-like groups by thinking of the *parts* in relation to the whole. The essential parts of a kitchen are: cooker; sink(s); worktops; seating; lighting; utensils; etc. An organising idea has been found. If you are giving advice on how to perform some transaction, such as applying for a passport or a driving licence, divide the transaction into its *stages*. If you are giving instructions on how to build a kite or make a dress, divide the process into *steps*.

By following that method, you will train yourself to think analytically about your subject and — before plunging into the writing — you will be able to solve the two main problems posed by practical writing: 'Where do I begin?' and 'Where do I end?'

(d) More Complicated Subjects

The parts/stages/steps approach will not always work. For example, numbers 3, 4, 5, 6 and 9 in the list in Section 2.5(a) are so worded as to require a different solution of the organisational problem. Giving instructions on how to build a kite (question 1(ii)) is best done in a series of steps, whereas 'advice to help him or her to settle in as quickly and happily as possible' (question 3) must be organised differently. The plan has to take strict account of the task set, a point illustrated in the following work out.

(e) Work out

Advise a friend who is thinking of buying a camera on how to make a good choice.

(i) *Stage 1*

Jot down thoughts just as they come.

lens qualities, resolution, maximum aperture, etc. — exposure control, none/automatic/manual — film format, disc, 110, 35 mm — shutter speeds — size and weight — etc.

(ii) *Stage 2*

Look for a way of organising the items.

The essential parts of a camera can be grouped by function: (1) shutter; (2) lens; (3) exposure system; etc.

After a few moments, it is clear that the system of grouping tried out above is of no help in organising the material for this particular question. Organisation into parts grouped by their function would be a sound enough base for a plan if the task set were to describe a camera, but that is not what the instructions require. I have to advise on a good *choice* of camera. I must try to find another way of organising the material.

A good *choice* can't be made until you know what you want to do with the camera: what kind of photographs you want to take — sports (action) — portraits — landscapes — family snapshots — one kind of camera is a good choice for one kind of job, another kind is needed for a different job . . .

I think I have now found a way of organising my material into a suitable answer.

(iii) *Stage 3*

Keeping in mind the task set, group the items accordingly and decide on the order of presentation.

1. Good choice depends on what kind of work the camera will be used for.
2. Simple family snapshots need only a simple camera.
3. More ambitious photography needs a more sophisticated instrument. For example: action/shutter speeds; portraits and close-ups/viewfinder; etc.
4. Conclusion: decide what you want to do with your camera, then you can decide what features are essential.

(iv) *Stage 4*

An outline plan has been worked out, grouping the items and getting them into a logical order of presentation. The writing can now be done.

ADVICE ON CHOOSING A CAMERA

points 1 and 2 of plan taken together in opening paragraph

Your choice of camera depends on the kind of photographs you want to take. There are many very good, simple cameras that will take excellent family snapshots. They have fixed focusing and automatic exposure control. Consequently, they are practically foolproof to operate. They are light and portable and some of them are very cheap.

sufficient detail to support the point being made

However, those simple cameras are no good for more ambitious photography, such as sports shots, portraiture, close-up studies, landscapes, and so on. For such work, you will need a more complicated and more expensive instrument. Undoubtedly, a single lens reflex camera (an 'SLR') is the most versatile and accurate instrument yet designed. It offers you a range of shutter speeds and apertures that will cope with any problem. Its viewfinder is incomparable for brightness and precision, and its focusing system is unbeatable. A range of interchangeable lenses will equip you for any photographic task. The more expensive models give you a choice between automatic and manual exposure control.

personal, informal phrasing is in keeping with the task set: 'Advise a friend . . .'

In a nutshell, your choice lies between the cheap, light, easy-to-operate snapshot camera and the dearer, heavier, more complicated, but much more versatile SLR. When you have decided what kind of a photographer you want to be, I shall be able to give you more detailed advice.

NOTES

1. More detail is included in the plans in Sections 2.2–2.5 than you (or I) would need to include as a rule, but I want you to practise along the lines suggested in those sections until you have mastered the techniques of planning. Then you can speed up, and jot down a skeleton outline that will provide you with a sound plan for a clear and cogent exercise in practical writing, of whatever form you choose from the assignments on offer.
2. As you will see in Chapter 5, answers in the form of reports, letters and newspaper articles are often required in *directed writing*. The work outs in Chapter 5 assume that you have mastered the details of layout and procedure provided in this chapter.

3 Understanding and Response

3.1 Definition and Description

This part of the examination tests both your reading and your writing. The coursework on which you will be assessed *and/or* the examination paper you will take may be called 'Understanding and Response' or 'Comprehension' or, quite simply, 'Reading'. Whichever name it is given, it requires you to show that you can:

- *read* closely and accurately;
- *understand* fully what you read;
- *respond* intelligently and imaginatively to what you read;
- *express* clearly your understanding and your response.

Each of those requirements is explained in later sections of this chapter.

3.2 How You Are Tested

(a) Examination Paper and/or Coursework

Depending on the arrangements made between your examination centre (your school or college) and your examining board, you will be tested in one of the following ways:

1. You may be entered for an examination paper.
2. You may be required to submit a folder of coursework (five or six units) for assessment *instead of* taking an examination paper.
3. You may be required to submit some coursework (one or two units) *as well as* taking an examination paper.

Your centre will tell you at the beginning of your course what arrangements have been made.

The explanations, advice and demonstrations provided in this chapter apply *equally* to assessed coursework and to an examination paper. However, since the time factor may seem to be a more worrying feature of an examination paper than of assessed coursework, it is given special attention in work outs of specimen papers.

(b) What You Have To Do

You will be given some 'texts' to read very carefully. (The term 'text' is explained in the next paragraph.) Then you will have to write answers to questions designed to test your understanding of what you have read. You will also be given some tasks which test the response you have made to your reading. For example, you may be told to make comparisons between two texts, bringing out differences of purpose or attitude or style.

A 'text' is an extract (a passage) taken from a book or a newspaper or some other source. Two or more such passages are printed on the examination paper.

Similar passages will be supplied for you to use in assessed coursework. Or you may be told to use a particular book or newspaper or magazine as the source of your texts. Full details will be supplied. For example:

The following questions and tasks are based on a passage in *The Day of the Triffids*, by John Wyndham (Unicorn Books Edition). The passage begins: 'It took me longer than I had expected . . .' (page 55) and ends: '. . . as silent as the grave.' (page 58).

At least one unit of assessed coursework in understanding and response may be based on a complete book chosen by your centre for special study during your course.

3.3 An Organised Approach

In this part of the examination you are expected to show that you can read carefully; that you can think about and 'see into' what you read; that you can make an intelligent and imaginative response to your reading; that you can express your response in clear, fluent English.

Consequently, you will be asked the same *kinds* of questions and set the same *kinds* of tasks, whether they are based on extracts or on a complete book and whether you are taking an examination paper or submitting coursework.

Each kind of question or task has its own special point, designed to test your understanding and response in a particular way. So, before you start to write your answer, you must recognise what kind of question or task it is and precisely what it instructs you to do.

That is why an organised approach to this part of your work is so important, and that is why Section 3.7 of this chapter suggests *methods* of tackling all kinds of tests of understanding and response. Apply these methods when you are practising, so that you acquire the confidence and skills you need to do good work in the examination.

3.4 The Kinds of Passages Set

All kinds of writing are used to test your understanding and response. The passages (or complete books) on which questions and tasks are based may be narrative, or descriptive, or dramatic, or discursive, or impressionistic. They may be objective or subjective. They may be creative, or critical, or practical. They may be instructions or propaganda. They may be serious, or humorous, or satirical, or factual. It is not possible to list all the possibilities, for you may be asked to tackle any kind of writing.

Do not be alarmed by this. However wide the range of material, you will not be given a more difficult text than you can fairly be expected to understand. If you read the text and the instructions carefully, you will be able to tackle all the work you are set.

Here are some points to bear in mind:

- Do not panic if you know nothing about the subject on which the text is written – previous knowledge is not required (unless the text is a complete book that you have studied as part of your course).
- All the facts you need for factual answers are contained in the text.

- All the material you need for 'interpretative' (non-factual) answers is contained in the text.

3.5   What 'Understanding' Means

People often claim to 'understand' a piece of writing when, in fact, they have only a general and superficial impression of its content. The kind of understanding expected of you is much more detailed and deeper than that.

The examiners are looking for evidence that you have *comprehended* what you have read. In other words, they expect you to show them that you have really got to grips with it — that you have 'taken it in', as we say.

1. You have to understand its overall meaning *and* its details.
2. You have to take in both *what* is written (the content) and *why* it is written (the purpose).
3. You have to be aware of what is *stated* and what is *implied*.
4. You have to appreciate how the *style* of the writing (*how* it is written) reveals the writer's intentions and affects the meaning.

Your understanding is tested by questions that relate specifically to the content of the text. It is also tested by questions and tasks that explore the response you have made to what you have read. You cannot respond unless you have understood!

3.6   What 'Response' Means

The questions and tasks set on a passage will enable you to show that you have 'responded' to it. In other words, to show that you have read with interest and involvement — that you have thought about the passage and used your imagination. Depending on what kind of writing it is (see Section 3.4), you will be required to express your response in some or all of the following ways.

1. Comment on the writer's arguments, saying why you agree or disagree with them.
2. Detect bias or prejudice in the writer's selection of facts or arguments and/or in the way they are presented.
3. Bring out the writer's intention, saying how you discovered what it was from the way the passage is written.
4. Select material from the passage that you could use for a particular purpose.
5. Re-word part of the content of the passage.
6. Comment on the effectiveness of the writer's style, explaining why it works (or does not work) and expressing your own reactions to it.
7. Comment on the personality and motives of characters presented in a narrative or dramatic text.
8. Put yourself in the place of one of the characters and say how you would have reacted to the situation confronting her or him.

3.7   Working Methods

(a) Reading a Text

Close, careful reading is the basis of successful answers. You must understand *what* is written. You must note *how* it is written. You must try to discover *why* it was written. In other words, you must take in its *content*, be aware of its *style*, and recognise its writer's *intentions*.

Apply this method to each passage in turn.

1. Read it right through once at a steady pace, recognising what kind of writing it is — narrative, descriptive, discursive, and so on. Then sum up its main contents (its *gist*) in a *brief* note. Something along these lines is what is needed: 'Writer argues for conservation of earth's natural resources.' / 'Writer describes great drought of 1974 and details its effects on an isolated moorland community.' Do *not* look at the questions before you have completed this first reading and made your note of its main content. The questions direct your attention to particular details and aspects of the passage. Your first reading is an attempt to take it in as a whole.

2. With your summary of its contents in mind, read through the passage a second time, slowly. According to the kind of writing it is, trace the *development* of its narrative, description, argument, and so on. Discover its *structure* by noting the stages in which the writer sets the material out.

3. Note key words and phrases that throw light on the writer's intentions. Listen to 'the tone of voice'. Try to discover the *implications* of the language used. Respond to hints and suggestions. You are 'reading between the lines' now — 'seeing into' the passage — getting to grips with content, style and intention.

(b) Tackling the Questions

The two readings just described have enabled you to understand the passage *in depth* — to *comprehend* it.

1. Now read through all the questions and tasks *before* you start to answer the first. You will lose marks if you misunderstand the point at which each is aimed, and you will find that it is easier to understand what each is getting at if you have read them all. When you have read them, you may find it helpful to make a third (quick) reading of the passage to check on any doubtful matters.

2. Now start to write your answers. Deal with them in order, but if you are stuck for an answer, do not spend too long agonising over it. Leave it for the moment and go on to the next. You will often find that a question or task that seems baffling at first is much easier when you have answered later questions. It falls into perspective, and the answer 'emerges' as you work through the others.

3. Think hard about each question or task as you come to it, making sure that you have grasped its point — that you know *exactly* what you have to do (see Section 3.7(e)).

4. When you have completed your answers, go through them, correcting any careless slips in your writing. The examiners expect clear English and orderly presentation.

(c) Guided Reading

Different groups of examining boards have their own particular ways of wording their instructions. Some make it clear that you must read the passages in the purposeful and methodical way set out in Section 3.7(a). Others give more general instructions such as this: 'Read these two passages and then answer the questions'.

Do not let the wording of such 'open' instructions mislead you. Though you are simply told 'to read' the passages, the questions you will have to answer demand close, alert, sensitive reading of the kind already described. Unless you pay detailed attention to the content and the style of the writing and the intentions of the writer, you *cannot* meet the examiners' requirements.

Here is an example of detailed instructions such as some boards give. Notice the 'signposts' that are provided to guide your reading of the passage.

Read these two passages. Both give accounts of returning soldiers meeting some civilians who have little knowledge of what war is like. As you read, you should consider the following:

(i) The different experiences described by the two groups of people, and the facts used in presenting them.

(ii) Each soldier's behaviour, feelings and attitudes to the civilians.

(iii) How the age and personal history of each of the civilians affects his or her behaviour to the soldiers.

(iv) Ways in which the writer suggests the character of each of the people involved in this meeting.

(v) How changes in the style of the writing affect your feelings about these people and their meeting. (You may be struck by the choice of words, the use of figurative language or the use of short or long sentences, for example.)

You will be asked questions on all these points when you have completed your reading.

You have 15 minutes reading time. As you read, you may make notes, either on the printed sheets of passages or in your answer book.

Instructions such as those give you a lot of help. They guide your reading, directing your attention to the most important features of the passage. If you follow the 'signposts', they will lead you to a thorough understanding and *appreciation* of the writing.

- Your answers must be based on a thorough understanding and appreciation of the passages.
- When the instructions guide your reading, be sure to follow the 'signposts' they provide.
- When the instructions are of the simple 'Read these passages' type, apply the reading method set out in Section 3.7(a).

(d) Pacing Yourself

Whether you are taking an examination paper or writing coursework, you have to keep up with the clock. The time allowed is always generous, so there is no need to feel under pressure. Of course, if you ignore the advice given earlier and spend a disproportionate amount of time on one question, you will have to rush through the others – and probably make careless mistakes.

Be sensible. See how many questions you have to answer, and then divide your time equally between them. (If some questions carry fewer marks than others, you must spend less time on them.)

These examples show you how to pace yourself within the time limits imposed by two typical papers.

Paper 1

Total time allowed: 2 hours
Part I
Time allowed: 15 minutes
Two passages to study. The first contains approximately 600 words. The second contains approximately 500 words.
Part II
Time allowed: 1 hour and 45 minutes
Five questions to answer. They carry equal marks. Spend 20 minutes on each. That will allow you 5 minutes to read through your answers, correcting any careless slips.

Paper 2

Total time allowed: 1 hour and 30 minutes
Part I
Time allowed: 1 hour
Two passages to study. The first contains approximately 500 words. The second contains approximately 450 words. Four questions to be answered. Each carries 10 marks. Spend about 10 minutes studying the two passages. That leaves you 50 minutes to write and check your four answers. Spend about 12 minutes on thinking out and writing your answer to each question. That will allow you a couple of minutes or so for checking.
Part II
Time allowed: 30 minutes
One longer piece of writing to be done. It carries 20 marks, so it is the equivalent of two of the questions in Part I. Your writing must be based on the passages, but you have to include some material drawn from your own experience. Spend about 25 minutes planning your answer and writing it, leaving 5 minutes for revision and improvement.

(*Note:* This question in Part II is an example of the 'compositional' type of writing often asked for in an examination paper or coursework testing 'Understanding and Response'. See Section 1.1(b).)

Find out exactly what time limits your own examining board imposes. Then practise along the lines recommended above until you can comfortably complete the set tasks within the permitted time.

(e) Getting the Point

As you saw in Section 3.4, many different kinds of passages are used to test your understanding of what you read and your response to it. Consequently, many different kinds of questions are set. Depending on the kind of writing (narration, description, discussion, and so on) on which the questions are based, some questions test your grasp of the content and your understanding of the meaning of the passages. Others require you to comment on points of view expressed or arguments put forward. Others direct your attention to the way in which the passages are written (their style) and ask you to show that you have noticed and responded to the writers' use of language. The work outs later in the chapter show you how to tackle the various kinds of questions you will have to answer.

The particular 'target' at which a question is aimed may not always be obvious when you first read it. You must make sure that you have got the point, and to do that you must read the questions just as carefully as you read the passages.

- It is no use starting to answer a question until you are quite sure that you have got the point.
- Then – and only then – you know what kind of an answer is expected.
- In other words, you know what material in the passage is *relevant* to your answer; *and* you know how to *use* that material to produce a good answer.

Here is a list of typical questions arranged in groups according to their 'targets'. The questions come from several different papers.

1. Questions testing your grasp of the *content* and your understanding of the *meaning* of passages.

EXAMPLES

(i) The situation described in Passage 1 has been brought about because Kate is a lot younger than Jean. Although that fact is never stated openly, it plays a crucial part in the tense confrontation that the writer presents. In what ways is the fact revealed, and how does the age gap affect each of these two people?

(ii) Passage B gives an account of Councillor Brown's attempts to win popularity in the period preceding the elections. Describe in your own words the various ways in which he tried to get votes. What do the views of the five voters interviewed as they left the polling booth tell you about the effects of his campaign? Refer in detail to the opinions expressed by each voter.

(iii) Both passages maintain that road transport is more efficient than rail, but the evidence used in Passage A to support that point of view does not tally with the evidence used in Passage B. Show that the two writers rely on different and sometimes contradictory facts.

NOTE

Your answers must show that you have a thorough knowledge of the *content* of the passages. You are *not* asked to comment on them or to give your own views, so it would be *irrelevant* to do so and you would get no marks for doing it. As you read the passages, you may have felt that Jean deserved all she got. You may have despised or admired Councillor Brown's tactics. You may have agreed or disagreed with the two writers' views on transport. But *these* questions require you to confine your answers to *factual* matters as set out in the passages. Other kinds of questions ask for your opinions, as you will see later.

2. Questions testing your ability to *think* about points of view expressed and arguments put forward in the passages, giving your *reasons* for agreeing or disagreeing with them.

EXAMPLES

(i) In Passage A, James Johnson says, 'I now know that I made a good choice when I changed my job but, at the time, I wasn't at all sure that I was doing the right thing.' How far does his own description of his present circumstances bear out his claim that he did the right thing? Do you think that he has any reasons to be less sure than he says he is?

(ii) The detective in Passage 2 puts forward his case for arresting the suspect. Do you think that the evidence he has collected justifies his belief in the man's guilt?

(iii) The two passages set out opposing points of view as to the causes of vandalism. You may not be entirely convinced by either of the two arguments, but give your reasons for preferring one or the other.

60

All three questions assume that you have grasped the content of the passages and that you understand its meaning. What they are getting at is your ability to *reason*. Each requires you: (a) to follow an argument; (b) to judge its merits; (c) to say why you think that it is a sound or an unsound argument.

3. Questions about *style* direct your attention to the ways in which language is used in the passages. They require you to show how *a particular effect* is obtained by *a particular use of words*.

EXAMPLES
  (i) The first of the passages relates a sad anecdote, the second a humorous one. The two different effects are partly accounted for by the different circumstances in which people are placed, but the use of language in each passage also helps to create the mood. Show how the language of passage A contributes to the sadness and how the language of Passage B contributes to the comicality.
 (ii) The bare language used in the first part of Passage 1 contrasts with the colourful language used in the second part. Bearing in mind the different subject matter of the two parts, say why the writing is so different. Give some examples to help to explain the contrasting effects achieved in each part.
(iii) The writer of Passage I describes emotionally how she felt when she saw her home again after a long absence. She uses short, 'breathless' sentences and exclamations, and often conveys her mood in figurative expressions such as, 'The wind *laughed* in my ears' (1.10). Does her use of language help you to share in her feelings, or do you think she overdoes it? Would you have perhaps felt more in tune with her emotions if she had described her experience in a quieter and less obviously vivid manner? Describe your reactions to the way she writes. Give examples of what you like and of what you don't.
NOTE

At first, you may think that questions about style are difficult, but if you read them carefully you will see that they give you a lot of help. As those three examples show, they tell you exactly what to look for in the language used in the passages. They also tell you exactly what points your answer must cover.

4. Questions that require you to show that you have made an *imaginative response* to the passages. Such questions often direct your attention to what is *implied* rather than to what is stated.

EXAMPLES
  (i) From the way he treats them, what do you learn in Passage 1 about Peter's feelings and attitudes to (a) Mr Sampson and (b) the supervisor?
 (ii) What impressions are given of the atmosphere and conditions of the school described in Passage B?
(iii) 'This, Clarissa felt, was the right moment for the flamboyant gesture of defiance that she believed her public would expect of her.' What do those words tell you about Clarissa's motives for behaving as she does at this crisis in her career? From what you have learnt about her earlier in Passage II are you surprised that she behaves as she does?
NOTE

Questions such as these require you to show that your reading of the passages has gone deep. You have to show that you have recognised the writers' *inten-*

tions. You have to show that you are aware of their *implications* – deeper levels of meaning, which are often more important than direct statements. That is what is meant by 'an imaginative response'. As the examples show, the questions may be aimed at any of the following 'targets': people's characters, motives and behaviour; how they think and feel about themselves and about each other; how you might behave if you were in their place; atmosphere (of scenes and places) and its effects on people in the passages – *and* on you, the reader.

3.8 Work out 1 (with Comments and Answers)

Note: This first work out provides a detailed demonstration of how I would tackle questions if I were a GCSE candidate. Pay close attention to the details as you study the successive stages of working out the answers. It is essential to base your work on a methodical approach to the passages and to the questions set on them. The method demonstrated here will serve you well.

Read the following passage carefully and then answer the questions.

I stood at the window and smoked a small cheroot. Across the rooftops I could see the darkened hump that was Carlisle Castle. I peered at it through the gloom with a strange fascination. The sky behind the turrets looked mottled and angry, touched with red from the city street-lamps like the hammered bottom of a copper pot. It was a sky to steer away from, to button up against—a cloud-hung, wind-blown, rain-spattered sky. I shuddered. For the next few days, rain or wind, sleet or shine, my only shelter would be the tiny tent in the haversack on my back as I followed the trail of the Border Line across 110 miles of some of the wildest and most spectacular scenery in Britain. It would not be an easy walk.

Unlike Offa's Dyke or the Pennine Way, the Scottish Border was not a national footpath and because of the scarcity of highways had managed to remain largely intact, unspoiled by the incursion of the main summer tourist routes. It was a unique region, once the most disputed territory in the country, with wild hills, ancient castles and famous abbeys which had seen more turbulence and bloodshed than the rest of these islands put together. I would be following in the footsteps of those outlaws of ancient times who spread terror and devastation along the Border counties and I would be treading where the Border Line itself was conceived in more than a thousand years of the bloodiest battles in our history.

I peered silently at the huddled outline of the castle. Beneath the neon-splashed sky it looked oddly out of place, and yet it caught the very essence of the Border. It was some fortress: a symbol of austerity, no doubt, for the prisoners of the Wars of the Roses who were confined there. It had withstood siege for nine months against Parliamentary forces during the Civil War and had entertained Bonnie Prince Charlie. It was also the scene of one of the earliest commando raids when, in 1596, the bold Buccleuch crossed the Esk with eighty men and pounded on the castle gates, demanding the release of Kinmont Willie.

Stirring stuff: but that is what the Border was all about. For the next few days I would be recapturing some of the colour and tradition that made it such a romantic and fascinating locality.

I turned and peered at my hotel bed. It looked snugly inviting. Might as well make the most of it, I thought. I stubbed out my cheroot, took off my clothes and switched off the light.

Robert Langley

Stage 1: Studying the passage closely, making notes on its content, its structure and the way it is written

(a) What it is about

Writer recalls his thoughts and feelings at hotel in Carlisle on the night before he set out to walk the Scottish Border.

(b) Its structure – how it is developed

1. Describes view from hotel window.
2. Looks ahead to experiences of next few days.
3. Brings out special qualities of Scottish Border walk.
4. Describes some characteristic features of the history of the Border.
5. Adds to earlier description of castle.
6. Lists events in castle's history that typify Border's history.
7. Looks forward to rewards of walking the Border.
8. Tells of his thoughts and feelings on going to bed that night.

(c) Noting key words and expressions to discover the writer's intentions. Looking for the implications of the writing – 'reading between the lines' to discover what the language suggests as well as what it states

These seem to me to be the key words and expressions:

> the darkened hump that was Carlisle Castle – strange fascination – mottled and angry – city street-lamps – I shuddered – my only shelter – wildest and most spectacular scenery – disputed territory – terror and devastation – bloodiest battles – the huddled outline of the castle – neon-splashed sky – oddly out of place – very essence of the Border – commando raids – pounded on the castle gates – colour and tradition – romantic and fascinating locality – hotel bed . . . snugly inviting – make the most of it

They tell me a lot about the passage and the writer's aims and methods:

1. He wants his readers to enter into the situation that faced him that night. So he opens with vivid descriptions of the scene from his window and the walk that lay ahead. We see what he saw and we put ourselves in his place as he describes the conditions he's got to encounter.
2. Because he wants us to understand why that night was such a memorable experience for him, he's got to write in a way that will persuade us to share in the thoughts and feelings he recalls.
3. He doesn't often express his thoughts and feelings directly, but they are implied throughout the passage. His writing works mainly by suggestion. He relies on us to respond imaginatively to the details he includes *and* to the language he uses.
4. These seem to me to be the chief ways in which he works on our imagination to get the response he wants:

(i) Without overdoing it, he uses words to stir up feelings. They *suggest* as much as they state. For example: 'the darkened hump' / 'mottled and angry' / 'I shuddered'.

(ii) He builds the whole passage on two *implied* contrasts: (a) between the humdrum present and the turbulent past; (b) between the comfort of his hotel room and the hardships to be expected on the walk. Every descriptive and historical detail he includes brings out one or the other of those two contrasts.

(iii) Though he doesn't put it in so many words, he's facing up to an implied question throughout the passage: 'Why am I doing this?'

(iv) Near the end of the passage (in the penultimate paragraph) he finds the answer to that question. By that time, *if his writing has worked*, we know that we'd give the same answer.

Stage 2: *Studying the questions closely to get the point of each before starting to answer*

1. What information about the history of Carlisle Castle and of the Scottish Border does Robert Langley provide here? Your answer should be in your own words as far as possible, but you may include some *brief* quotations from the passage if you find it helpful to do so.

   This is a straightforward 'content' question, requiring a factual answer. I note the warning against copying out chunks of the passage.

2. What impressions are you given of the conditions and atmosphere of the Scottish Border walk that he is about to undertake?

   The wording of this question gives me a lot to think about. These are the points it raises.

   (i) It is a *response* question. I am *not* asked to list the factual details he gives. I *am* asked to say what *impressions* I get *from* those details. The question asks: 'What do the details and the way they are presented *imply* about the conditions and atmosphere of the walk?'

   (ii) There is a distinction between 'conditions' and 'atmosphere'. *Conditions* refers to the material (physical) aspects of the walk. *Atmosphere* refers to the thoughts and feelings suggested to the walker by the scenery, the history and the physical conditions of the walk. I must keep that distinction clear when I'm answering this question.

   (iii) The question directs my attention to the conditions and atmosphere of the *walk*. It asks me: 'What impressions does the writer give you of what it will be like to walk through the Scottish Border?' That is what I must concentrate on. I must not be tempted to include irrelevant details about the Border itself. The question is about the Border *as it affects somebody walking through it*.

3. Near the end of the passage, Robert Langley looks forward to 'recapturing some of the colour and tradition that made it [the Scottish Border] such a romantic and fascinating locality'. How far does he persuade you to share his view of the Border?

   (i) This is an *appreciation* question. It requires me to give my opinion of the writer's skill. (The wording '*How far* . . .?' is a favourite way of asking for an opinion.)

(ii) Take it step by step:

(a) I know what response the writer wanted me to make.

(b) Did the content of the passage and the way it is written succeed in persuading me to make that response?

(c) If so, how?

(d) If not, why?

(e) It follows from (c) and (d) that I must provide examples and illustrations to support the points I make. It's no use just saying, 'He writes so well about it that he succeeds in persuading me to share his view of the Border.' My answer must show what I mean by saying that he writes well. If I have a different opinion, I must show what I mean by saying that he doesn't write well.

(iii) Because it's *my* opinion that is asked for, I shall write my answer in a personal way. The question is directed at *me*; and though the examiners expect a reasoned answer, they also expect me to give them my personal response and judgement.

NOTE

It took a lot of time and space to set out Stages 1 and 2 of the work out in full. Under examination conditions, neither you nor I would need to make such extensive notes. But, as I have tried to show, close, methodical and imaginative reading of the passage and of the questions is essential. If you practise along the lines laid down here, you will soon learn how to get to the heart of a passage and to grasp the point of the questions.

Stage 3: Answering the questions

Note: Read each question again. Then read my answer. Think about it carefully, noting its good points. Improve it wherever you can. I've done my best to give good answers, but I don't suppose they're perfect!

1. Carlisle Castle was used to house prisoners in the Wars of the Roses. In the Civil War it resisted a besieging Parliamentary army for nine months. It received ('entertained') Bonnie Prince Charlie as a guest. In 1596 when Kinmont Willie was imprisoned there, 'the bold Buccleuch' led a raiding force of eighty men across the Esk, hammered at its gates and demanded the prisoner's release.

   These episodes in the history of the fortress were typical of the spirit ('caught the very essence') of the Border. The hills, castles and abbeys of that much fought-over ('disputed') region were the scenes of more violence and bloodshed than anywhere else in Britain. Outlaws filled all the Border with fear and laid waste to it ('spread terror and devastation'), and it took more than a thousand years of the worst carnage ('the bloodiest battles') in mainland Britain to agree on and establish a settled boundary where the Border Line now runs.

2. He will encounter tough conditions. A long walk (110 miles) through hilly country will be fatiguing. The stormy sky threatens wild weather, so he may often be cold and wet. His journey will take him through a remote, unpeopled and seldom-visited area in which he must be self-sufficient for food, cooking and shelter. The weight of his equipment will add to the physical strains imposed by the route and the weather.

The atmosphere will be partly menacing, partly exhilarating. He will be aware of his loneliness, knowing how little help and comfort he can expect in this empty land. Sometimes, especially at night, he may well be frightened by the space and silence all about him. The Border will often seem hostile. Yet the beauty of the landscape and the appeal of its legend and history will lift his spirits and make him glad to be there.

3. When I read these words I knew what Robert Langley meant by the 'colour' of the Border. By suggesting its excitement and its menace, his writing had already made me aware of the qualities of this wild and lonely land.

Right at the beginning he uses physical colours (mostly black and red) to suggest storm and battle. The 'darkened hump' of Carlisle Castle under a 'mottled and angry' sky 'touched with red' prepared me for his account of its violent past. Later, the castle's 'huddled outline' looking 'oddly out of place' under 'the neon-splashed sky' vividly conjured up the spirit of the Border and all those long-ago adventures and raids that he tells of. His figurative language and images make the Border seem very 'colourful'.

He made me even more aware of its 'colour' when he described the long journey that he was going to make, all alone, through 'some of the wildest and most spectacular scenery in Britain'.

His examples of its 'tradition' read like a thrilling adventure story, even though some — such as the Wars of the Roses and the Civil War — are historical facts. Others, such as the one about 'the bold Buccleuch' who 'pounded on the castle gates', sound more like legends, half true and half invented. As he says, it's all 'stirring stuff', and he writes about it in a stirring way.

He certainly persuaded me to feel the fascination and romance of the Scottish Border. He made it seem full of adventures. Having read this passage, I want to 'follow in the footsteps of those outlaws' and see those 'wild hills, ancient castles and ruined abbeys' for myself. I might have second thoughts just before I started, but I hope I would accept the challenge he describes so powerfully.

Of course, I am seeing it through his eyes. It may be different now, but he convinces me that when he walked the Border Line there really was romance to be recaptured.

3.9 Work out 2 (with Comments — Answers at End of Book)

Using the methods demonstrated in Work out 1, study this passage and then answer the questions. The answers that I would give if I were a candidate are printed at the end of the book, but do not look at my answers until you have written your own. Then compare yours with mine, referring closely to the passage and the questions as you do so. Try to discover the reasons for any major differences between us. Don't be afraid to stand up for your ideas whenever you think they are better than mine. I have tried to give clear, accurate answers, but you may have seen points that I missed or misinterpreted. If you disagree with any of my answers, say so — and say why.

Every year many millions enjoy the National Trust's open spaces. This freedom of access is one of the chief purposes of the Trust. None the less, its very volume creates serious problems. A careful tally on a bank holiday weekend at Clumber Park in 1964 recorded 106 000 visitors. In the following year at Hatfield Forest there were 28 300 cars, and at Runnymede 80 000. Two hundred sacks of litter have been collected on Box Hill after a Whitsun weekend. With the dumping of refuse and derelict cars on Trust property, litter begins to assume a quality of nightmare. No less worrying is the persistent hooliganism at many properties, particularly those near industrial centres such as Allen Banks in Northumberland. Even well intentioned visitors tend to damage trees, break fences and start fires. Uncontrolled dogs worry sheep, and on certain open spaces there is interference with the commoners' grazing rights.

A grave problem is the long-term effect of an excessive number of visitors on plant and animal ecology. If more than a given number of people pass over a dale or mountain path, regeneration becomes impossible and erosion follows. The bald and widening tracks scarring Dovedale and certain favourite cross-country routes in the Lakes are sad indications of this. At Kinver Edge in Staffordshire and Kynance Cove in Cornwall, which are much visited, the sward over large areas has been completely destroyed and erosion has set in. Consequently it has proved necessary to close and fence parts of the land in order to restore the natural ground cover. Sand dunes pose a similar problem, for with constant access erosion is unavoidable.

The problems raised by the increase in the number of visitors can be tackled in two ways. The first is a proportionate increase in the number of wardens. The Trust accepts this as an expensive necessity. They now constitute a growing army, recruited to help, advise and control the public. Many wardens are countrymen, sometimes naturalists or retired foresters, and their knowledge contributes directly to the pleasure of visitors. Happily, people are often ready to serve as part-time wardens in a voluntary capacity. On the Longshaw estate in Derbyshire there is a rota of forty voluntary wardens, and at Brownsea Island, where the fire danger is acute, no less than fifty people in the summer give unpaid service as watchers and wardens.

The second course open to the Trust, and one to which its publicity must be progressively directed, is to achieve a wider dispersal. An airman or a buzzard surveying the wide range of Trust properties would see some that seem to stir like anthills and others that preserve an almost Saxon solitude. The Trust's aim must be to spread the load, alleviating the pressure where it grows intolerable and dispersing it to spaces that may still be called 'open'. There is little danger in this. Solitude will always remain for those who wish to find it.

Apart from closure, which is contrary to Trust policy and which can only be justified for limited periods in desperate cases, there is a third course which the Trust may in extremity be forced to adopt at certain properties if numbers continue to increase as they have done in the last decade. It is the control of access by rationing. The brake could be applied either by charging an admission fee, or by limiting the numbers admitted on a given day. The Trust hopes that such measures can be avoided. They would only be necessary at peak periods. It is well to recall that most wardens have a well earned rest for six months, that dense visitor-traffic is usually as temporary as the holiday season, and that many of the airman's most restless anthills enjoy a long winter quiet.

Robin Fedden, *The National Trust, Past and Present*

Before you turn to the questions set on the passage, study these notes. They show you what to look for when you are preparing to answer questions that test your understanding and response. Such questions are always based on the content and style of the passage, on the writer's intentions, and on your judgement of how far those intentions are carried out. Put very simply, the questions ask: *What* does this passage say? *How* is it said? *Why* was it said? Does it *work*?

Notes On The Passage

1. The passage is an example of writing of a very different kind from the passage set in Work out 1. There the writer's aim was to persuade his readers to share in a vividly remembered experience which meant a lot to him. It was a personal — a *subjective* — piece of writing. Here the writer's aim is to explain a particular situation and certain problems which he wants his readers to understand. The passage is an *exposition*. (An *exposition* is 'a setting out' — an explanation given at some length and in considerable detail.) It is an *objective* piece of writing. Its purpose is to provide its readers with certain facts so that they can think about the described situation and its problems in an informed and constructive manner.

2. A piece of writing having those aims must above all be *clear*. As you study the passage, consider these questions. Are the words accurately used and well chosen? Are the sentences well-made and easy to read? Is the paragraphing helpful? Does the writer provide examples to show what he means as he explains the situation?

3. The nature of the subject matter demands the use of some special terms — for example, 'commoners', 'ecology', 'regeneration'. This presents the writer with a problem. He needs those special terms because they are precise, but he will lose touch with his readers if he uses terms they don't understand. However, he is entitled to expect his readers to have an adequate vocabulary. He is dealing with a subject of general interest, and the basic terms used in discussing that subject are pretty widely known. They are frequently employed in radio and television programmes and newspaper articles about conservation issues and the recreational use of the countryside. As you read the passage, consider how far the writer succeeds in using the special terms he needs while staying in touch with you. If he fails at any point, whose fault is it? Does he make any demands that cannot be met by a reasonably well-informed and intelligent reader?

4. Before you start to answer the questions, look up in your dictionary any words you didn't understand as you read the passage. This is one of the most effective ways of enlarging your vocabulary — an essential part of your preparation for the examination. (See Chapter 6.)

5. If the writer is to succeed in carrying out his intentions (see Note 1), he must hold his readers' interest. A dry-as-dust exposition stuffed with facts might offer an accurate explanation of the situation and its problems, but bored readers would not pay attention. Some would stop reading. Even those who plodded on to the end wouldn't feel inclined to spend further time and energy in thinking about the subject.

6. So, although this is a factual and objective piece of writing, it must be made as attractive and lively as possible. With that in mind, consider these points.

   (i) The sentences are varied. This helps to keep the writing fresh and interesting. Compare, for example, the perfectly clear but long sentence beginning 'Apart from closure . . .' with the short, crisp sentence 'There is little danger in this.'

   (ii) Note the sudden shift of perspective to a bird's eye view in the sentence beginning 'An airman or a buzzard . . .'. This is a surprising and dramatic way of bringing the facts to life.

   (iii) The figurative expression 'stir like anthills' is another vivid way of getting the facts across. Another telling use of language occurs in the phrase 'an almost *Saxon* solitude', which demonstrates how a well-chosen adjective can arouse interest and suggest a great deal of meaning to a responsive reader.

Those are just a few examples of the skilful way in which the passage is written. Questions set to test your understanding and response assume that you have become aware of such features of style by reading the passage closely and imaginatively.

QUESTIONS ON THE PASSAGE

(You are reminded of the need to write clear, careful English, paying proper attention to grammar, punctuation and spelling.)

1. The difficulties of the situation set out in this passage all arise from the fact that 'many millions enjoy the National Trust's open spaces' to which they have 'freedom of access'. Nevertheless, the particular problem described in the second paragraph has a different cause from those described in the first paragraph. Show that this is so.

2. What do you learn from this passage about the problem of 'erosion'? How far do you agree that, on the evidence supplied here, it is the National Trust's worst problem?

3. How far does the writer's way of presenting information and explaining problems help you to become interested in and to understand the issues he deals with?

4. Imagine that you are one of the voluntary wardens mentioned here. The full-time warden has asked you to give a talk to a party of students before they set out to walk across the National Trust estate that you help to look after. Write your talk as you would give it. Use information supplied in this passage and draw on any relevant experience of your own.

3.10 Work out 3 (with Comments — Answers at End of Book)

The passage on which this work out is based represents a different kind of writing from those on which you have previously answered questions. Study the passage closely with the aid of the notes. Then tackle the questions, writing out full answers of your own before you look at the answers given on pages 162–164.

Fiammetta had all the characteristics demanded of a prima donna: a magnificent voice well trained, an extremely beautiful person, a temperament passionate, fearless and headstrong. In body she was small, so that one marvelled such a superb volume of voice could pour out of such a fragile vessel— she was not in reality fragile, however, but brimming with a restless vitality, healthy, tough. Italian by birth, with an abundance of dark hair and huge dark eyes (grey or violet? Freeman never knew) which by some unusual coloration of iris and pupil had at times a silvery and starry appearance. Fiammetta dressed with the most exquisite taste; in ordinary life extremely neat, elegant, sophisticated, on the stage she could wear the flaunting costumes of operatic heroines with all the savage verve they required.

She was to sing the title-role in a production of *Carmen* for which Freeman was designing fresh costumes and scenery. Freeman considered this opera 'old hat', but had been assured by those in charge that he was employed especially to give freshness and originality to a somewhat stale theme. He had accordingly let his imagination gallop: the glowing result pleased him, and when he heard Fiammetta sing at rehearsal, his pulses quickened with delight. It appeared, however, that Fiammetta wished to sing in yellow instead of the traditional scarlet. Freeman was summoned to a conference on stage and informed of this desired change in an imperious tone. A new design for the dress would of course be needed.

'It can of course be done if you postpone the opening night for a month or two,' said Freeman with a smile.

'You require two months to design one dress?' said Fiammetta haughtily. (Her Italian-English, uttered in one of the finest contraltos of the century, was delicious.)

'By no means. But if the colour of Carmen's dress is changed, all the other costumes and the scenery must also be changed, or she will not appear the main character.'

'That is nonsense. Never have I heard such nonsense.'

'I think you're being a little unreasonable, Freeman,' said the stage manager anxiously.

Freeman shrugged his shoulders.

'If the signorina wishes to be a mere blur against the background, let it be so by all means, but take my name off the programme.'

'Now, Freeman!'

'What is that, a blur? I do not understand this word,' said Fiammetta, looking round the group angrily.

Nobody ventured to enlighten her, and there was an uncomfortable pause.

'Something such a beautiful Carmen should never be,' said Freeman eventually, laughing.

Fiammetta gave him a glance in which, as Freeman clearly saw, disdain was mingled with calculation. He was not surprised therefore when she suggested that they should lunch together and talk over the matter, not surprised when he presently found himself alone with her in her suite at the hotel. He was not surprised, because her intention to use the power of her beauty to get her own way about the dress was throughout sufficiently obvious.

Sure enough, she began to flatter and soothe him, to gaze up into his eyes with that expression of admiring interest which is always so seductive, so apt to lead a man into those intimate confidences which place him in the power of the recipient. Freeman had had sufficient experience, in various preceding *amourettes*, of this enticing look, to know exactly what it meant: he therefore watched Fiammetta with a smile—he had no objection in the world to being seduced, but nothing would induce him to yield about the yellow dress.

Fiammetta, it would seem, felt this, for she grew angry.

'You do not think me beautiful, Mr Freeman?' said she, her wonderful eyes sparkling with rage.

(They really sparkled, thought Freeman, surveying them admiringly; in her case the *cliché* was literally true.)

'On the contrary, signora,' he replied pleasantly: 'I think you the most beautiful woman I have ever seen.'

'Then why do you remain so cold? Come, kiss me! Do not be afraid.'

'I am not afraid,' said Freeman in an easy tone, laughing: 'but it is only fair to tell you that I am capable of taking many kisses and yet not making you a yellow dress.'

He rose and gave her a little bow, to take his leave.

'And yet you call yourself an honourable man?'

'No,' said Freeman, pausing. 'I have no such pretensions. I have come up out of the gutter and carry no sentimental luggage.'

'And I too, you fool!' cried Fiammetta, springing to her feet. 'I too am of the gutter. I am as relentless as you are yourself. I take what I want.'

'Ah! Now we understand each other.'

'Stay, then,' said Fiammetta, stretching out to him her small hot hand, on which the diamonds glittered.

'No. It is the dress you want, not the man,' said Freeman, turning away. He spoke soberly, but felt violence rising in him like fever.

She threw herself between him and the door.

'Are you so certain, Freeman?' she cried, panting.

'Don't try to lie to me!' shouted Freeman, plunging into rage.

For a moment they stood glaring at each other, furiously angry; then they both began to laugh.

'I shall not make you a yellow dress,' said Freeman stubbornly.

'*Basta!* What do I care?'

'But I will design a beautiful new scarlet dress; the old one is too dull, too spiritless for such a guttersnipe as you,' concluded Freeman, laughing and taking her in his arms.

Phyllis Bentley, Crescendo

Notes On The Passage

1. The kind of writing represented by this passage is fundamentally different from the kinds of writing studied in earlier work outs. The writer in Work out 1 was sharing a personal experience with his readers. The writer in Work out 2 was giving his readers information about a particular situation and its problems. *This* writer is telling a story. She is writing *fiction*, so she has different aims from theirs and she must use different writing techniques to achieve her aims.

2. Notice that she does not communicate with her readers *directly*. Her role is that of an invisible creator of imaginary people and imaginary events, so she does not intrude. She stays behind the scenes, letting her fictitious characters get on with living their own lives. If she were to 'appear' in the story, or if her readers became conscious of her as a manipulator of people and events, the illusion would be destroyed.

3. If her story-telling is to succeed, she must persuade us to believe in the people in it. We don't necessarily have to like or admire them, but they must be

credible. If we don't feel that we know and understand them, we can't get involved with them. So she wants us to respond to her characters just as if they were 'real' people. They reveal their thoughts and feelings and motives through their words and their actions, and that is how we come to know them. We get inside their minds. We recognise that they behave according to their natures. 'This', we feel, 'is how these people *would* behave in this situation.' It takes a lot of skill on the writer's part to bring about this kind of response.

4. Try to appreciate how she brings her characters to life. These are some of the points you should look for. Details of their appearance — eyes, hair, clothes, bearing. Ways of speaking and behaving that reveal moods and motives and atmosphere. Remember that she must work with hints and suggestions, relying on her reader to pick them up and draw the right conclusions. She can't break into her imaginary world and hold the story up while she says, 'Notice this' or 'Now I want to explain that . . .'. Here are a few examples of how she works: 'grey or violet? Freeman never knew' / 'in an imperious tone' / 'said Freeman with a smile' / 'said the stage manager anxiously' / 'Nobody ventured to enlighten her' / 'disdain was mingled with calculation' / 'he replied pleasantly' / 'plunging into rage'. Think about them. They tell you a lot about the people in the story and their developing relationship with each other. Then find some other similar examples of the writer's skill in creating living characters and involving her readers in this stormy episode.

5. The passage is *dramatic*. It presents a conflict between two determined, self-willed people. After a sharp quarrel, they arrive at an understanding and they resolve their dispute in a way that pleases them both. Notice how the writer structures and paces the narrative to bring out its drama. First, a confrontation. Then, rising tension. Then, a crisis in which they are deadlocked. Then, a sudden 'turn' in the action. Finally, a relaxation of tension as the combatants reach a solution. The characters of these two people and the nature of the situation in which they are placed at the beginning of the episode are full of exciting possibilities. But, to make the most of the potential excitement and conflict, the action must unfold in a carefully planned sequence of events. Yet it must seem to take a natural and spontaneous course. There must be no evident interference or string pulling by the author. Her characters must seem to be 'real' people, not puppets. What they say and do must strike the reader as being the inevitable expression of what they are. Skilful story telling depends very much on the author's ability to control the narrative — to quicken or slow the pace, to increase or decrease tension — while still presenting events as if they are the inevitable outcome of the personalities, moods and motives of the people involved. Whenever a passage of fiction is used to test your understanding and response, look closely at the way the author handles the narrative.

6. The background of the story is the world of opera. You may or may not know much about it, but there's nothing in the passage that careful and receptive reading will not make clear. The term *prima donna* (literally, 'first lady') is used in its strict sense, and the context makes it clear that Fiammetta is the principal female singer in an opera company. Similarly, it is obvious (to a careful reader, that is) that the *title-role* is the 'name part' and that she is to sing the part of Carmen in the opera of that name. Apart from these 'semi-technical' expressions, any problems of comprehension are matters requiring thoughtful and imaginative interpretation. A good reader will notice words and phrases that seem to carry particular weight. Don't start to answer the questions before you have done your best to sort out their implications. Here are some examples. The meaning of *old hat* (and what it tells

us about Freeman) in 'Freeman considered this opera "old hat" '. The impression conveyed both of Fiammetta and of Freeman by the adjective *glowing* in 'the glowing result pleased him'. The meaning of *traditional* in 'Fiammetta wished to sing in yellow instead of the traditional scarlet'. Why nobody '*ventured* to enlighten her'. The implications of the words *disdain* and *calculation* in Freeman's observation of Fiammetta's glance. Freeman's answer to Fiammetta's sarcastic exclamation 'And yet you call yourself an honourable man!' The significance of his use of the word 'guttersnipe' at the end. No doubt you have noticed other key words and expressions and got to work on them already. Don't forget to use your dictionary.

Questions On The Passage

(Choose your words carefully. Write clear, coherent and varied sentences. Where necessary, organise your answers in paragraphs, dealing with just one distinct topic in each. When you have finished all your answers, compare them closely with the answers printed on pages 162–164.)

1. What causes the quarrel between Fiammetta and Freeman and how does their dispute then develop? Answer in your own words as far as possible. Try to set out the origin and stages of the conflict so as to make them clear to somebody who has not read this passage and wants you to provide an outline of the events.
2. In what ways are Fiammetta and Freeman alike? Say, too, where they are different. Do you think that there is anything in Freeman's character that gives him an advantage over her in their tussle?
3. Did you enjoy this passage? Give reasons for your answer, saying what you found to admire in the writing.

3.11 Work out 4 (Complete Examination Paper with Notes — Answers at End of Book

So far, each work out in this chapter has been based on one passage. They have shown you:

- how to study a passage and the questions set on it;
- how to recognise the point of a question so that you can find in the passage the material that is *relevant* to your answer;
- how to *organise* that material and to *present* it in a clear and appropriate way.

You are now ready to practise answering tests containing more than one passage, so this work out is based on a complete examination paper. Questions are set on each passage separately, but one question (sometimes more than one) requires an answer based on both passages. You are asked to compare or contrast some particular feature or features of the two passages – the content; the writers' attitudes to their subjects; the atmosphere created; the ways in which they are written; and so on.

The methods practised already will help you to write good answers to the questions set in this work out. Then, having used them successfully in answering this specimen examination paper, you will know how to apply them to your own assessed coursework and/or examination papers in 'Understanding and Response'.

The *Notes* that follow the examination paper are an important part of this work out. They guide your reading of the passages and the questions. They point out exactly what you have to do. You will *not* be given detailed help like this in the examination, but, if you have absorbed the lessons taught in this chapter, you will not need it. You will know how to set about the work without being told.

To use this work out to best advantage, proceed as follows.

1. Read both parts of the examination paper.
2. Study the *Notes* in detail, referring closely to the examination paper as you do so.
3. Write full answers to the questions, paying strict attention to the examiners' instructions and trying to keep to the time limits given. If you find it hard to stay within the time limits, don't panic. With further practice – and always trying to keep up with the clock – you will speed up. By the time you take the examination, you will be able to complete your answers in the time allowed. (The importance of regular practice has often been stressed in this book, but it is worth repeating here that you cannot hope to do well unless you get into training.)
4. When your answers – carefully and clearly set out – have been completed, turn to the answers given on pages 164–166. Compare your answers closely with mine. Refer to the passages and the questions wherever there is anything in my answers which you do not understand or with which you disagree.

ENGLISH – UNDERSTANDING AND RESPONSE

Part I of this examination paper consists of two passages about which you will be asked to do some writing in Part II. 15 minutes is allowed for reading the passages and for making any notes you wish, after which you will be given Part II with the questions based on the passages.

Part I

Read the following passages. Both give accounts of teenagers meeting some old people. As you read, you should consider the following:

each person's behaviour, feelings and attitudes towards the old people;
the old people's feelings about them;
and the ways in which things are described.

You will be asked questions on these points in Part II.

You have fifteen minutes' reading time. You may make notes on details of the passages in your answer book.

After fifteen minutes you will be given **Part II** *This will give you the questions to answer on the passages.*

Passage One

The person keeping the diary is Adrian Mole, aged 13¾.

Sunday July 4th

FOURTH AFTER TRINITY. AMERICAN INDEPENDENCE DAY

I was just starting to eat my Sunday dinner when Bert Baxter rang and asked me to go round urgently. I bolted my spaghetti Bolognese down as quickly as I could and ran round to Bert's.

Sabre, the vicious Alsatian, was standing at the door looking worried. As a precaution I gave him a dog choc and hurried into the bungalow. Bert was sitting in the living room in his wheelchair, the television was switched off so I knew something serious had happened. He said, 'Queenie's had a bad turn'. I went into the tiny bedroom. Queenie was lying in the big saggy bed looking gruesome (she hadn't put her artificial cheeks or lips on). She said, 'You're a good lad to come round, Adrian.' I asked her what was wrong. She said, 'I've been having pains like red hot needles in my chest.'

Bert interrupted, 'You said the pains were like red-hot knives five minutes ago!'

'Needles, knives, who cares?' she said.

I asked Bert if he had called the doctor. He said he hadn't because Queenie was frightened of doctors. I rang my mother and asked her advice. She said she'd come round.

While we waited for her I made a cup of tea and fed Sabre and made Bert a beetroot sandwich.

My mother and father came and took over. My mother phoned for an ambulance. It was a good job she did because while it was coming Queenie went a bit strange and started talking about ration books and stuff.

Bert held her hand and called her a 'daft old bat.'

The ambulance men were just shutting the doors when Queenie shouted out, 'Fetch me pot of rouge, I'm not going until I've got me rouge.' I ran into the bedroom and looked on the dressing table. The top was covered in pots and hair nets and hairpins and china dishes and lace mats and photos of babies and weddings. I found the rouge in a little drawer and took it to Queenie. My mother went off in the ambulance and my father stayed behind to comfort Bert. Two hours later my mother rang from the hospital to say that Queenie had had a stroke and would be in hospital for ages.

Bert said, 'What am I going to do without my girl to help me!'

Girl! Queenie is seventy-eight.

Bert wouldn't come home with us. He is scared that the council will take his bungalow away from him.

Thursday July 29th

My father has been working flat out on the canal bank for the past three days. He hasn't been getting home until 10p.m. at night. He is getting dead neurotic about leaving it and going on holiday.

Went to see Queenie in hospital. She is in a ward full of old ladies with sunken white faces. It's a good job that Queenie was wearing her rouge, I wouldn't have recognised her without it.

Queenie can't speak properly so it was dead embarrassing trying to work out what she was saying. I left after twenty minutes, worn out with smiling. I tried not to look at the old ladies as I walked back down the ward, but it didn't stop them shouting out to me and waving. One of them asked me to fetch a nice piece of cod for her husband's tea. The tired-looking nurse said that a lot of the old ladies were living in the past. I can't say I really blame them; their present is dead horrible.

Sunday September 19th

FIFTEENTH AFTER TRINITY

Took a deep breath and went to see Bert and Queenie today. They were hostile to me because I've neglected them for a week.

Bert said, 'He's not bothered about us old 'uns no more, Queenie. He's more interested in gadding about.'

How unfair can you get? I can't remember the last time I gadded about. Queenie didn't say anything because she can't speak properly because of the stroke, but she certainly looked antagonistic.

Bert ordered me to come back tomorrow to clean up. Their home help comes on Tuesdays and Bert likes the place to be tidy for when she comes.

Sunday November 7th

Went to see Bert and Queenie with my mother.

Everyone we met on the way asked my mother when the baby was due, or made comments like, 'I expect you'll be glad when the baby's here, won't you?'

My mother was very ungracious in her replies.

Bert opened the door, he said, 'Ain't you dropped that sprog yet?'

My mother said, 'Shut your mouth, you clapped-out geriatric.'

Honestly, sometimes I long for the bygone days, when people spoke politely to each other. You would never guess that my mother and Bert are fond of each other.

Everyone was too old, or too ill, or too pregnant to do any cooking (I developed a sudden ache in both wrists). So we ate bread and cheese for our Sunday dinner. Then in the afternoon we took it in turns to teach Queenie to speak again.

I got her to say, 'A jar of beetroot please', dead clearly. I might be a speech therapist when I grow up. I have got a definite flair for it. We got a taxi back home because my mother's ankles got a bit swollen. The taxi driver moaned because the distance was only half a mile.

Passage Two

It was mid morning — a very cold, bright day. Holding a potted plant before her, a girl of fourteen jumped off the bus in front of the Old Ladies' Home, on the outskirts of town. She wore a red coat and her straight yellow hair hanging down loose from the pointed white cap all the little girls were wearing that year. She stopped for a moment beside one of the prickly dark shrubs with which the city had beautified the Home, and then proceeded slowly toward the building, which was of whitewashed brick and reflected the winter sunlight like a block of ice. As she walked vaguely up the steps she shifted the small pot from hand to hand; then she had to set it down and remove her mittens before she could open the heavy door.

'I'm a Campfire Girl . . . I have asked to pay a visit to some old lady,' she told the nurse at the desk. This was a woman in a white uniform who looked as if she were cold; she had close-cut hair which stood up on the very top of her head exactly like a sea wave. Marian, the little girl, did not tell her that this visit would give her a minimum of only three points in her score.

'Acquainted with any of our residents?' asked the nurse. She lifted one eyebrow and spoke like a man.

'With any old ladies? No — but — that is, any of them will do,' Marian stammered. With her free hand she pushed her hair behind her ears, as she did when it was time to study Science.

The nurse shrugged and rose. 'You have a nice multiflora cineraria there,' she remarked as she walked ahead down the hall of closed doors to pick out an old lady.

There was loose, bulging linoleum on the floor. Marian felt as if she were walking on the waves, but the nurse paid no attention to it. There was a smell in the hall like the interior of a clock. Everything was silent until, behind one of the doors, an old lady of some kind cleared her throat like a sheep bleating. This decided the nurse. Stopping in her tracks, she first extended her arm, bent her elbow, and leaned forward from the hips — all to examine the watch strapped to her wrist; then she gave a loud double-rap on the door.

'There are two in each room,' the nurse remarked over her shoulder.

'Two what?' asked Marian without thinking. The sound like a sheep's bleating almost made her turn around and run back.

One old woman was pulling the door open in short, gradual jerks, and when she saw the nurse a strange smile forced her face dangerously awry. Marian, suddenly propelled by the strong impatient arm of the nurse, saw next the side-face of another old woman, even older, who was lying flat in bed with a cap on and a counterpane drawn up to her chin.

'Visitor,' said the nurse, and after one more shove she was off down the hall.

Marian stood tongue-tied; both hands held the potted plant. The old woman, still with that terrible, square smile (which was a smile of welcome) stamped on her bony face, was waiting . . . . Perhaps she said something. The old woman in bed said nothing at all, and she did not look around.

Suddenly Marian saw a hand, quick as a bird claw, reach up to the air and pluck the white cap off her head. At the same time another claw to match drew her all the way into the room, and the next moment the door closed behind her.

'My, my, my,' said the old lady at her side.

Marian stood enclosed by a bed, a washstand and a chair, the tiny room had altogether too much furniture. Everything smelled wet — even the bare floor. She held on to the back of the chair which was wicker and felt soft and damp. Her heart beat more and more slowly, her hands got colder and colder, and she could not hear whether the old women were saying anything or not. She could not see them very clearly. How dark it was! The window blind was down, and the only door was shut. Marian looked at the ceiling . . . . It was like being caught in a robbers' cave, just before one was murdered.

*Part II of this examination paper consists of questions based on the passages given to you in Part I. You have **1 hour and 45 minutes** in which to answer them. Answer all the questions, which carry equal marks.*

You are reminded of the importance of clear English and orderly presentation in your answers.

Part II

*The questions which follow are based on the passages given to you in **Part I**. Using only the information you have gained from reading these passages, **answer questions 1–5**. The five questions carry equal marks.*

You may make any further notes to help you in your answer book. Cross out all your notes when you have answered all the questions.

Passage One

1. Describe in detail Queenie's 'turn' and what happens to her afterwards.
2. What do you learn about Adrian Mole's behaviour, feelings and attitude towards Bert and Queenie from the way he treats them?

Passage Two

3. What impressions are given of the atmosphere and conditions of the Old Ladies' Home?

4. Imagine that Marian keeps a diary. Write her diary entry for the day she visits the Home. Include the important things that she notices and what she feels about them. Bear in mind that a diary entry need not be too long (see Adrian Mole's).

Both Passages

5. Imagine that you are an elderly person reading these two passages. Give your impression of the two young people involved.

NOTES ON THE PASSAGES

1. Both are fiction.
2. Both are about a teenager visiting old people, but Adrian Mole and Marian have very different attitudes to them, and they visit them in very different circumstances and with very different motives.
3. Passage One is written in the form of a diary. The events are narrated in the first person. Adrian Mole himself tells the story in which he plays the central part.
4. Passage Two is written in the form of a novel. The events are narrated in the third person. Marian's story is told by the author.
5. Written from different 'angles', the two passages are also written in different styles. The language of Passage One is everyday (though Adrian Mole from time to time — and with evident pleasure — draws on a quite impressive vocabulary). It is colloquial — full of spoken expressions. The language of Passage Two is more formal — more 'bookish'. Compared with Passage One, it is essentially written language.
6. Passage One is easier to read than Passage Two. Up to a point — but *only* up to a point — it 'gives itself up' more readily. It is easy to get involved with it quickly, but at the same time it is a subtle piece of writing. Many of the most interesting impressions we get from it — of Adrian Mole's character and of his relationship with Queenie and Bert — are made by implication. This passage asks for (and deserves to get) close and responsive reading. The experience it offers lies deeper than it appears to at first, and a reader taking this passage at face value would miss a lot.
7. In contrast, the writing in Passage Two more obviously 'signals' its author's intentions and methods. We recognise at once that we are expected to pick up and respond to significant details and figurative language conveying character, situation and atmosphere. The swift 'pictorial' introduction of Marian and the suggestive description of the outside of the Home (it 'reflected the winter sunlight like a block of ice') tells us that this is 'literary' writing in a way that Passage One is not. We are 'tuned in' right away to the 'wavelength' of the language, and we know that we have got to keep alert. For example, the nurse's comment on Marian's potted plant tells us a lot about her attitude to the girl, just as Adrian Mole's remark about the home help's visit tells us a lot about Bert and about Adrian, but the implications are conveyed in strikingly different language. The writing in Passage Two makes deliberate use of literary skills. It uses the writer's arts. But the writing in Passage One gives the *appearance* of being 'artless'. (It is *not* artless, of course. It is full of art — very skilful writing indeed.)

Those comments on the two passages do not pass value judgements on their merits, nor do they argue that one passage is 'better' than the other. They make objective statements about the different ways in which the two pieces of fiction are presented.

Readers who have noticed those comparable and contrasting features of the two passages (without necessarily going into such detail) are well prepared to answer questions testing their understanding and response.

Notes On The Questions

1. This question requires you to show that you have a clear understanding of the events recorded by the diarist. You have to pick out the main points and present them in order, setting them out one after another as they occurred. You are expected to give a fluent account of the successive events and developments in your own words as far as possible. Here is a list of some of the information provided in the passage.

> Queenie was taken ill on Sunday 4 July. She stayed in bed, not bothered — for once — about her appearance.
> She had sharp pains in her chest and was able to describe them.
> The doctor had not been sent for, because she was afraid of doctors.
> Adrian's mother sent for an ambulance to take her to hospital.
> Before it arrived, Queenie started to talk ramblingly about the past.

Carry on from there, noting each important stage in the story of Queenie's illness.

You are not expected to include in your answer every piece of information that the passage gives, but you must include sufficient detail to show that you have grasped the main developments from Sunday 4 July to Sunday 7 November. Those two dates mark the beginning and the end of these entries in Adrian Mole's diary, and Queenie's illness is mentioned throughout.

Be careful! The question refers to Queenie's 'turn' and what happens to her afterwards. Nothing else in the passage is relevant to your answer. There is a lot of interesting material about other people as well — about Adrian's mother and father, for example, and about Adrian himself and Bert — but it has nothing to do with *this* question, so don't be tempted to include any of it in your answer.

2. This question asks you to show that you have noted the details of Adrian's behaviour to Bert and Queenie. It also requires you to show that you have *inferred* from his behaviour what his feelings and attitude to them are. He does not often say in so many words what his feelings and attitude are. They are *implied* by his behaviour. Some simple and obvious points will spring to mind at once, but several quite complicated and subtle ideas are suggested too. You have to read between the lines to become aware of them. Look closely at the language Adrian uses and try to interpret its tone. Here are some of the points you may want to make.

> He cares for them.
> He hurries to help them.
> He sees the funny side of Bert.
> He is sensitive to their feelings.
> He makes an effort to see them when he doesn't really want to.
> He recognises that Bert is demanding and unreasonable.
> He is patient with them, especially Queenie.

Find some more points for yourself. There are plenty. Remember, though, you are not expected to get everything into your answer. Make a selection from the material you find. Try to give a lively account of this complex relationship, keeping a balance between its serious and comical aspects. It is both touching and amusing, and a good answer will reflect this.

Don't forget to refer closely to the diary when you are answering. You must give the evidence for the points you make.

3. Your answer to this question must show that you have noted the descriptive details *and* that you have responded to the mood and atmosphere they conjure up. When you are describing the atmosphere and conditions, be sure to refer to the particular details used to create particular impressions. For example, it is not enough to say that the Home seemed a cold, unwelcoming place. You must say what features cause it to give that impression.

You may want to use some of these points, among others that your own reading will discover.

It seemed unwelcoming, even hostile, because of 'the prickly dark shrubs' beside one of which Marian paused on her way up to 'the heavy door'.
The coldness of the whitewashed brick which 'reflected the winter sunlight like a block of ice' is repellent.
The nurse looks cold and grim. She's dressed in white and has 'close-cut hair'.
It smells musty and shut up, 'like the interior of a clock'.
It's a sinister place in which human beings make animal-like noises.

4. This sets a more difficult task. It requires you to do these things.

(i) Imagine that you are Marian and try to write as you think she would.
(ii) Change the form and style of the writing from the third person narrative of the passage to the first person narrative suitable for a diary.
(iii) Select relevant material from the passage.
(iv) Record Marian's feelings as well as what she saw and did and what happened to her.

You must give your answer a suitable heading. No date is provided in the passage, so you must invent one. Bear in mind that this episode took place in winter.

Consider, too, how to end your answer. The passage breaks off with the action unfinished. You *can* end in the same way, but is it a realistic way of ending a diary entry?

An answer to this question might start something like this.

Saturday 3 February
Terrible 'Campfire Visit' to old ladies' 'Home' (Prison? – Madhouse?). Scared out of my wits for three miserable points – if I ever get them! Cold, creepy place . . .

You will not be able to include everything that is recorded in the passage, but try to mention everything that you guess would be uppermost in Marian's memory when she wrote about this experience in her diary.

Note the examiners' guidance about the expected length of your answer.

5. This is the hardest job of all. You have to put yourself in the place of an imaginary elderly person (*not* Queenie, *not* Bert, *not* one of the old people in the Home) who has formed impressions of Adrian and Marian by reading these two passages. You have formed your own impressions of them, of course, but now you have to look at them through another pair of eyes and from a different perspective.

However, it is not too hard a job for an imaginative reader who has studied the passages closely and responded to them sensitively. Ask yourself these questions.

What characteristics of these two young people would be of greatest interest to an elderly person?

What would an elderly person's feelings be about Adrian Mole and about Marian?

Which of the two would an elderly person prefer to have as a visitor?

In what ways would an elderly person's attitude to Adrian Mole be different from his/her attitude to Marian?

If you think about this task along those lines, you will find plenty of relevant material for your answer. Then you must work out a suitable order of presentation and decide on the best way of writing, remembering that you have to write 'in character' — as if you were the elderly person.

I think I'd start something like this.

People of my age often say they want 'respect' from the young. I don't. 'Respectful' behaviour is cold and distant . . .

That is just an idea, and you are not meant to copy it. Think out your own way of answering.

4 Summarising

4.1 An Essential Skill

As you saw in Chapter 3, good answers to questions testing understanding depend on your ability to:

- select and extract relevant information from a given source;
- restate that information accurately and coherently.

Similarly, in *directed writing* (see Chapter 5) you are required to select relevant information from various sources and to make use of it for specified purposes. For example, you may be told to take what is needed for a given purpose from maps, or diagrams, or tables of figures, or articles, and then to use it in, say, a report, or a letter, or a 'feature' suitable for a newspaper or a magazine. Successful performance of such tasks is based on your ability to *summarise*.

Summarising is the process of extracting the essential points from a given source and then rewording them briefly without falsifying them. They must also be set out in a clear and logical sequence.

Because it is a process that we all have to use frequently in our working lives, the examiners rightly expect candidates to be competent summarisers. The examination questions based on summarising are rehearsals of a skill on which efficient communication quite often depends.

For example, you may need to make a summary of papers, correspondence, articles, books or parts of books in order to *abstract* information needed for working purposes. So there is nothing 'artificial' about an examination question that requires you to demonstrate your ability to do this. The examiners are simply asking you to show that you are capable of going to the heart of the given material and rewording its essential information for use in different circumstances.

As an example of the very practical point and purpose of summary, consider this typical question and its accompanying instructions.

What does the first passage tell you about the weather conditions during the 1947 attempt to scale the mountain? Trace the successive changes in those conditions, making clear precisely how each new development affected the climbers' chances of success. Then, drawing your material from the second passage, show what use the later expedition made of the lessons learnt from the earlier attempt.

4.2 The Importance of Practice

You will not find it easy to answer questions like that (or similar kinds of questions already worked out in Chapter 3) until you have become proficient in the art of writing summaries. As you will see, too, when you study examples of *directed writing* in Chapter 5, your performance of the kind of writing tasks set in that part of the examination depends on the accuracy with which you extract the points you need from the source material on which those tasks are based.

That is why this chapter provides you with full instructions about summarising. It teaches a method which you can then apply whenever you have to select relevant information from passages and make use of it according to the examiners' instructions. Practise along the lines laid down here, so that examination tests of understanding and directed writing will not give you unforeseen problems of comprehension or rewording.

4.3 Definition and Description

A summary is

- a short, pithy restatement of the *chief points* made by a writer (or speaker); a *concise summing up* of the contents of a passage of writing, or of information derived from maps, diagrams or tables.

A summary must be

- written in *continuous* prose (*not* in note form). As far as possible, it must be written in the summariser's *own words* (*not* in the words of the original passage).

A good summary is

- *accurate*. It includes *all* the chief points of the original passage and, although they must be expressed in the summariser's own words, they must *not* be altered. However much the summariser may dispute or dislike the facts set out or disagree with the ideas or opinions expressed in the passage, they must not be tampered with. The 'slant' and the 'feel' of the original passage must not be changed.

A good summary is

- *brief*. The summariser must *condense* the original passage by *selecting* the essential points and expressing them in *economical* language. Minor points must be omitted. All decorative writing, figures of speech, verbal flourishes, illustrations and examples must be omitted. In a summary there is room only for the essential meaning — the bare bones — of the original passage.

A good summary is

- *clear*. It must be *clearly planned* so that its successive items follow each other in a logical sequence. It must also be *clearly expressed* in plain, easily understood English.

4.4 The Skills Required

Summarising employs all the skills required for general competence in the use of language, for it is a test of reading comprehension and writing aptitude. To make a good summary you must be able to:

- understand what you read;
- and then express your understanding in words of your own.

The first step in summarising is to arrive at a thorough comprehension of the passage. Then, and only then, you are ready to plan and to write your summary. Those two operations demand:

- the *judgement* to distinguish between *essential points* (which must be included) and *minor points* (which must be omitted);
- the *organising ability* to work out a *coherent* and *logical* plan;
- the *writing skill* to frame *clear* sentences, *correct* in grammar, punctuation and spelling;
- the *word power* to *condense* the passage while restating its essential contents, and to select *appropriate* expressions to reflect the 'slant' and the 'feel' of the passage.

Each of those points is discussed and demonstrated in later sections of this chapter.

4.5 Different Kinds of Summary

(a) Whole-passage Summary ('Précis')

(*Note:* The word *précis* (French) is still in common use as a synonym for *summary*.)

> ### Typical Instructions: Whole-passage Summary (Précis)
>
> Summarise (make a précis of) this passage in clear and correct English. Some words and phrases in the original writing cannot be accurately or economically replaced, but you must not copy out long expressions or whole sentences. Use *your own words* as far as possible. Your summary *must not exceed 150 words*. State at the end the exact number of words you have used.

The word limit may be expressed in other ways. For example, '. . . in about 150 words'. In that case, you should aim at being not more than 5 words above or below the stipulated number.

Whole-passage summary requires you to include in your summary *all* the chief points expressed in the passage set.

(b) Selective Summary

Often, the examiners' instructions direct attention to one particular subject dealt with in the set passage or passages. In that case your answer must be based exclusively on the information that is supplied about that specified subject. No other information in the passage is relevant.

For example, the set passage might recount the history of a legal reform (the abolition of child labour, say), proceeding from the early days of the struggle to enlist public support to its passage into law and its effects on society. A question set on that passage might ask you what you learn from it about either the early stages of the reforming process, or the parliamentary battle, or the subsequent developments. Your answer must be confined strictly to the specified subject.

Another kind of question demands the selection and rewording of material occurring in various places throughout a passage or passages. For example, in an account of the career of a famous person there might be details of how, at various stages of his/her life, particular qualities of character and personality led to success or failure. The instructions might tell you to say what part one quality (rashness, say) or another (ruthlessness, perhaps) played in his/her career.

Instructions of that kind demand close attention and an alert mind. The examiners are testing your ability to follow their precise wording by extracting and rephrasing only the particular information required. Much that is important in the passage as a whole must be disregarded in your answer, because it is *irrelevant* to the task you have been set. You will lose marks if you include any point that does not bear directly on the particular topic you have been told to write about.

If you have practised summarising in the ways suggested here, you will be unlikely to make that mistake when tackling tests of understanding and directed writing.

Typical Instructions: Questions Based on Selective Summary

1. This passage gives an account of the various courses of action open to the leaders of the new party. Say, in your own words, what you learn about their reasons for rejecting the policies that were pressed upon them by an influential group of their supporters.

Use in your answer only that part of the passage that is concerned with the specified subject. Much that is important in the passage as a whole (for example: other courses of action open to the party leaders; the policies that they adopted) is irrelevant to the task you have been given.

2. Study these letters exchanged between Mr J. K. Smith and the Northtown planning authority. Bring out in your own words their points of disagreement about the roofing materials to be used on the house that Mr Smith seeks planning permission to build.

Other matters may be covered in the correspondence (design of roof and windows, colour of paintwork, access road to the house, and so on), but the subject matter of your answer must be restricted to the topic specified in the instructions.

4.6   Summarising Method: Step by Step

Practice in whole-passage summarising ('précis writing') is the best way of learning the art of summary. While you are learning how to make a good summary of a whole passage, you are at the same time mastering the kind of thinking and the language techniques needed for answers based on a selective summary.

Step 1 Get the *gist* of the passage. State it briefly and in your own words.

Step 2 Get to grips with the writer's *purpose* by 'tuning in' to the 'slant' and 'feel' of the passage.

Step 3 Make a *skeleton outline* of the writer's presentation of the *main theme* by noting each *key point* as it occurs in the passage.

Step 4 Use your list of key points as the framework of a *detailed plan* for your summary.

Step 5 Write a *draft* of your summary.

Step 6 *Prune* and *polish* the draft.

Step 7 Write the *final version* of your summary.

That list of the necessary steps may look daunting, but each step is explained and demonstrated later in this chapter.

Summary writing is an essential skill and you must take pains to learn it. Method is vital: nobody can make a good summary 'off the cuff'. With practice, you will speed up and become so versed in these well-tried procedures that you will find it second nature to apply them efficiently in your examination.

4.7 Applying the Method

(a) Step 1: Get the Gist of the Passage

Follow the reading method set out in Section 3.7(a) to arrive at a thorough comprehension of the passage. Then write (*in your own words*, as far as possible) a brief statement of the main theme(s) expressed in the passage. (The *theme* is the basic, bedrock subject.) Your statement should sum up in as few words as possible ('encapsulate') what the passage is essentially about: the very heart of the matter. You will find it helpful to begin your statement of the theme with some such formula as 'The writer argues that . . .' *or* 'This passage gives an account of . . .'. Such an opening helps you to make an objective and accurate statement of the writer's main subject matter.

(b) Step 2: Get to Grips with the Writer's Purpose

The need to be objective and accurate was emphasised in Section 4.3: 'However much the summariser may dislike or dispute the facts set out . . . they must not be tampered with.' You may not like the factual contents of the passage. You may even know or think you know that they are wrong, but *it is not your job to alter or correct them in any way*. If the passage states that the moon is made of green cheese, you must not query it or comment on it in your summary. When you make a summary you must reproduce *faithfully* the gist of the original. Your concern is with what the writer says, *not* with what you think he/she ought to have said.

The subject matter is not always factual. It may be an expression of ideas, opinions, arguments for or against a point of view or a course of action. Again, you must reproduce the writer's 'slant' accurately, however much you may disagree with it. It may arouse strong feelings in you — either for or against — but *you must not allow those feelings to appear in your summary*.

Again, without actually stating a point of view, the writer may indicate his/her standpoint indirectly. The passage may be satirical (mildly or savagely; in whole or in part). It may be objective or subjective, part factual, part persuasive. It may be warmly enthusiastic or 'tongue in cheek' writing. There are many possibilities, but whatever the 'feel' of the passage, you *must reflect it accurately and without comment* in your summary.

So, keeping in mind your brief statement of its theme, read through the passage again, looking for the writer's point of view and purpose in writing. As you read, note key words, phrases, sentences that indicate the 'feel' of the piece. Ask yourself these questions: '*What* is the writer trying to do?' '*Why* is the writer trying to do this?' '*How* is the writer trying to do this?'

(c) Step 3: Skeleton Outline—Key Points of Main Theme

Keep in mind your statement of the main theme as you look for the key points. Include every one that bears on that statement. If in doubt about a point, include it; you will prune later. You can list the key points either by underlining them in the passage or by jotting them down on rough paper.

(d) Step 4: Make a Detailed Plan for Your Summary

Base the plan on your list of key points. When writing the plan:

- Use *your own words* as far as possible.
- Include sufficient *detail* to enable you to write your draft summary from your notes *without referring to the passage*.

There are two good reasons for that advice. First, if you use the writer's words in your notes, you will be in danger of incorporating them in your summary. Second, if you have to refer to the passage as you write your draft, you will be in danger of departing from the scheme of key points worked out in Step 3 and will probably mix minor points and other irrelevant matter in with the key points.

A good summary plan is:

- *coherent* — all the items that sensibly go together are grouped together — they 'stick together' (*cohere*) — they are *not* 'dotted about' in various parts of the summary;
- *logical* — each part follows on sensibly from the preceding part — the summary is presented in an ordered sequence, *from* its beginning, *through* its middle, *to* its end.

(e) Step 5: Write a Draft of Your Summary

Stick to your plan. Do not be tempted to alter it as you go along. Revisions come later (Step 6). Choose your words carefully and think out well-framed sentences. The language of summary is:

- clear and easily understood;
- condensed — no wasted words or long-winded expressions;
- correct — in grammar, punctuation and spelling.

(f) Step 6: Prune and Polish the Draft

1. Check the length of your answer. If you have included only the essential information and written clear, economical English, you should have used about one-third of the number of words in the original. A 'long summary' is a contradiction in terms. A summary is always a *brief* account of the chief points made in the passage on which you are working.

2. Prune by removing unnecessary words. Look especially for overworked, verbose expressions and tautologies (see Section 4.8 and Chapter 7).

EXAMPLES

check up on	= check
period of time	= period
in this day and age	= now *or* nowadays
advance forward	= advance
reverse backwards	= reverse

Apart from such misuse of language, some perfectly good expressions must be pruned because brevity is so important: figurative language, illustrative examples, rhetorical questions and repetitions, decorations — all of which have a part to play in writing *of a different kind*.

3. Condense wherever possible. Search your vocabulary for *compendious* words (see Section 4.8). Make every word tell.

EXAMPLE

Those who argued in favour of a nuclear generation plant raised powerful objections to their opponents' plan, which offered them some but not all of the resources for which they were contending.	The nuclear lobby objected strongly to their opponents' suggested compromise.

4. Check for errors of grammar, punctuation and spelling.
5. Look out for and remove *all*: colloquialisms; slang; quotations; direct speech.
6. *Finally* ask yourself these questions:

- Would this summary be readily understood by a reader *who had not seen the original passage*?
- Would it convey to that reader *the essential meaning* of the passage?

If the answer to both questions is 'Yes', you have written a good draft which you can fair copy and confidently hand in.

(g) Step 7: Write out the Final Version

1. Head your summary with a suitable title and underline it. Keep it *short*. Do *not* try to write a 'clever', 'punchy', newspaper-type headline. A plain, accurate, brief title is what is wanted. It does *not* count towards the number of words used.

2. Write the final version in your best and clearest handwriting. Be sure to incorporate all the corrections and improvements made as you pruned and polished the draft.

3. If you have been given a word limit, state at the end the *exact* number of words in your summary, *excluding* the title. Do *not* be tempted to falsify the number. If it looks wrong (and the examiners have a shrewd idea of how many words occupy how many lines of the answer sheet), it will be checked.

4.8 The Language of Summary

(a) Plain, Clear, Brief

1. *Plain*, because a summary is a restatement of the bare bones — the *essential* meaning — of a given passage. So, no 'frills' of any kind: no figures of speech; no illustrative examples; no rhetorical questions or repetitions; no 'decorative' writing.

2. *Clear*, because a reader *who has not seen the original passage* must be able to grasp its essential meaning quickly, easily and accurately *from the summary alone*.

3. *Brief*, because the word limit imposes a strict discipline and not a word must be wasted. (If no word limit has been stated, keep within one-third of the original length.)

That description sums up points made in earlier sections, but certain other features of the language of summary must now be singled out for special attention.

(b) Condensed

See Section 4.7(f). The use of *condensed* language (language that boils down a lot of meaning into very few words) is necessary. You must take every opportunity of contracting clauses into phrases and phrases into single words. *Compendious* words (*compendious* = 'space-saving') are needed to encapsulate the essential meaning of longer expressions.

You must also *remove* all *redundant* (superfluous) words. *Verbose* language (language that uses more words than are necessary) is always a fault: in summary, it is fatal.

EXAMPLES

1. The popular press is full of crime stories, violence in the streets, scandals, thefts and horrifying incidents of every kind.	The popular press is full of sensational items.
2. She made a list of things she needed such as butter, cheese, raisins, salt, sugar, flour and frozen foods.	She made a list of groceries she needed.

3. The auctioneer moved on to the old barn where harrows, ploughs, seed-drills, rakes and mowers were stored.

The auctioneer moved on to the old barn where agricultural implements were stored.

4. The ship was crowded with people who were leaving their native land for a new home.

The ship was crowded with emigrants.

5. Jean decided to train as a teacher of spinning, weaving, basket-making, china-painting and similar skills.

Jean decided to train as a handicrafts teacher.

6. He was handicapped in examinations by his inability to recall accurately facts and theories that he had learnt.

He was handicapped in examinations by his bad memory.

7. The book tells how Ben Gunn was put ashore and abandoned on an uninhabited island as a punishment.

The book tells how Ben Gunn was marooned.

8. Her small, unexpected good fortune was quickly and wastefully spent on tastelessly showy ornaments.

Her windfall was soon squandered on garish ornaments.

9. Brown says his new job involves a great deal of very hard work.

Brown says his new job is laborious.

10. We tried in vain to persuade the conflicting parties to agree to submit their respective cases to the decision of an independent umpire.

We failed to persuade the adversaries to go to arbitration.

11. The treasurer reported that there were serious financial difficulties in respect of the prospect of completing the new housing estate by the target date that had been set.

The treasurer reported that lack of funds was endangering the completion of the new housing estate on time.

12. In the majority of instances, householders informed the council through the investigating officers enquiring on the council's behalf that they were satisfied and had no complaints in the matter of the scheme regulating the system of differential rating.

Most householders told the council that they were satisfied with the differential rating scheme.

(c) Correct and Appropriate

Errors in *grammar, punctuation* and *spelling* will cost you marks in questions based on summary (as in all the other questions), but correct language alone is not enough: it must also be *appropriate*. The language of summary is *formal* (without being stiff or pompous). Therefore, you must *not* use:

colloquialisms ('free and easy' expressions suited to conversation and informal writing);

contractions ('didn't' = 'did not', and so on);
abbreviations;
slang.

(d) Reported Speech

The language of summary is *impersonal*. Therefore, you must *not* use direct speech. Any direct speech in the passage that contributes to the essential meaning must be turned into *reported* ('indirect') speech in the summary.

Direct speech is a *direct representation* in writing of the words *actually spoken*. Reported speech is a *report* in writing of what was said.

Direct speech	*Reported (indirect) speech*
Jones said, 'I shall be forced to resign.'	Jones said that he would be forced to resign.
(*Quotation marks round the words actually spoken*.)	(*No quotation marks, because no words are actually spoken*.)

(i) *The Rules*

1. A 'saying' verb followed by 'that' introduces reported speech. The use of an *expressive* 'saying' verb helps to convey the tone and 'flavour' of the speech being reported.

   EXAMPLE

   The customer *maintained* that the goods were faulty when delivered.

2. The tense of the 'saying' verb governs the tenses of the verbs that follow. When the 'saying' verb is in the past tense, the other verbs must also be in the past tense. When the 'saying' verb is in the present tense, the other verbs must be adjusted to fit the sense.

   EXAMPLES

   (i) The witness *declared* that he *had* often heard the accused threaten to set fire to the factory and that he *had* not been in any doubt that the threats *were* serious.

   (ii) Our agent in Brussels *reports* that the new regulations *will* favour our products and that he *foresees* a steadily growing market.

3. All pronouns and possessive adjectives must be in the third person: *I* becomes *he/she; we* becomes *they; my* becomes *his/her*; and so on.

   EXAMPLE

   (*Direct speech*)   The retiring president said, 'I am grateful for the support that I have always received from you, the officers of the association. Your help and friendship will remain a precious memory.'
   (*Reported speech*)   The retiring president expressed *his* gratitude for the support that *he* had received from the officers of the association, adding that *their* help and friendship would remain a precious memory.

4. All expressions indicating nearness in place and time in direct speech are 'distanced' in reported speech: *here* becomes *there; this* becomes *that; today* becomes *that day*; and so on.

> (*Direct speech*)   Councillor Brown said, 'My supporters have not sent me here to prolong these conditions. They expect decisive action before this year is out.'
>
> (*Reported speech*)   Councillor Brown said that his supporters had not sent him *there* to prolong *those* conditions. They expected decisive action before *that* year was out.

5. Colloquialisms, contractions and slang expressions used in direct speech must be removed in reported speech. If they contribute to the essential meaning, a formal equivalent must be substituted.

EXAMPLE

> (*Direct speech*)   At this point, the sergeant blew his top. 'Don't dodge the question!' he yelled at the suspect.
>
> (*Reported speech*)   The sergeant now angrily accused the suspect of being evasive.

6. As the examples have made clear, quotation marks must never be used in reported speech.

The following demonstration gathers together all the rules. Note that a rearrangement of the order of the original passage helps to condense the material. Note, too, the use of compendious words and the way in which the 'flavour' of the direct speech is reflected in the shortened version.

Direct speech

'May all the plagues of Hades fall upon you!' the furious Hassan shouted at the trembling courier. 'You arrive with a message from my brother, asking for instant help, and I find that you have been over a week on the way. This letter should have been in my possession last Tuesday at the latest. I've half a mind to string you up with my own hands!'

'Pardon your wretched slave, pardon!' howled the distraught courier. 'The river at the frontier was in high flood and I could by no means cross until the waters subsided. You know how swift and faithful I have been in your service for many a long year.'

Shortened version in reported speech

Hassan cursed the terrified messenger and threatened him with execution, saying that his brother's request for immediate help, which should have arrived no later than the previous Tuesday, had taken over a week to deliver. Begging for mercy and reminding Hassan of his past services, the messenger protested that he had been delayed by a flooded river.

4.9   Work out 1 (Step by Step)

Write a summary of the following passage in good continuous prose, using not more than 120 words. State at the end of your summary the number of words you have used. The passage contains 348 words.

When social historians look back, they will be astonished at our almost obsessive concern with sufficient supplies of energy. Our planet is, after all, one vast system of energy. The sun's rays that fall on the roads of North America contain more energy than all the fossil fuel used each year in the whole world. The winds that rage and whisper round the planet are a vast energy reserve caused by unequal solar heating of blazing tropics and arctic poles.

Nor should we forget the energy locked up in plants. Indeed, in some developing lands, ninety per cent of the energy is derived from wood. Experimentally, a U.S. Naval Undersea Centre has an ocean-farm project cultivating seaweed. The hope is that the solar energy captured by the plant on an ocean-farm of, say, 470 square miles could theoretically be converted into as much natural gas as is consumed in America at present. All in all, the fear of running out of energy must be said to have a social, not a rational base. Modern citizens simply do not see that their whole life is surrounded by a variety of energy reserves which not only exceed present sources but have a further advantage that they are not exhausted by use. A ton of oil burnt is a ton lost. A ton of seaweed will be growing again next year. Even more reliably, the sun will rise and release an annual 1.5 quadrillion megawatt hours of energy. There can be no running out of such resources.

But can they be harnessed? A tornado is a fine exhibit of energy unleashed but it is hardly a useful one. The fundamental question with all renewable sources of energy is how to develop the technologies for using and storing them at reasonable cost. Perhaps the first need is for citizens to open the eyes of their imagination and conceive of energy in new shapes, forms and sizes. If they do, they will find that the technologies *are* available, *will* become cheaper, and *could* even lead to a more civilised mode of existence.

Barbara Ward

(a) **Step 1**

Discover the theme. Make a brief statement of the gist of the passage.

> Writer argues that our worries about supplies of energy are unnecessary, since nature provides abundant renewable supplies if we learn how to tap them.

(*Notes:* (i) Objective statement, beginning with formula ('Writer argues that . . .'). (ii) Own words used.)

(b) **Step 2**

Read passage again, slowly and carefully. Jot down (or underline in passage) expressions that highlight writer's ideas/views/aims. Get to heart of subject matter.

> they will be astonished/our almost obsessive concern/Our planet . . . vast system of energy/fear of running out of energy . . . social . . . not rational/ simply do not see . . . whole life surrounded . . . energy reserves/exceed present sources . . . not exhausted by use/no running out of such resources/ can they be harnessed?/fundamental question . . . to develop the technologies/open the eyes of their imagination/conceive of energy in new shapes/ technologies *are* available/*will* become cheaper/*could* lead to a more civilised mode of existence

(*Notes:* (i) Writer believes people misunderstand true position. (ii) Uses facts to back this up. (iii) Wants to persuade people to look at position differently. (iv) All those points made clear by scrupulous examination of *what* writer says and *how* it is said.)

(c) Step 3

Keeping statement of theme in mind, make skeleton outline of key points.

1. . . . social historians . . . will be astonished at our almost obsessive concern with sufficient supplies of energy.
2. Our planet is . . . one vast system of energy.
3. All in all, fear of running out of energy must be said to have a social, not a rational base.
4. Modern citizens simply do not see . . . not exhausted by use.
5. There can be no running out of such resources.
6. But can they be harnessed?
7. The fundamental question . . . reasonable cost.
8. Perhaps the first need is for citizens to open the eyes of their imagination . . . energy in new shapes, forms and sizes.
9. If they do . . . more civilised mode of existence.

(*Notes:* (i) *Only* key points included. All supporting points and illustrative examples omitted (e.g. 'The sun's rays . . . the whole world'/'The winds . . . arctic poles'/'A ton of seaweed . . . next year'). (ii) This effects a considerable reduction of the original material; but there are nine major points, so condensed writing will be required. (iii) *Question*: How vital is 'social historians' point? Not sure, so include *at this stage*.)

(d) Step 4

Make plan for summary. Base plan on list of key points. Use own words in plan as far as possible and include sufficient detail to be able to write a draft of the summary without referring to the passage.

1. Future social historians will be very surprised by our constant worries about not having enough energy resources.
2. Since the planet is a huge reservoir of energy, it is not reasonable to be afraid of running out of energy. There must be a social reason for our fears.
3. People today do not see that there are many different sources of energy all around them. These sources are not only greater than those now used, but they cannot be used up because they constantly grow again or they are permanent forces.
4. There are technical problems of how to make use of these sources economically, but the chief problem is getting people to use their imagination and think about energy in new ways.
5. If they can manage to do that, they will see that we have the techniques to exploit the natural resources and that they will get cheaper and could make life more civilised.

(*Notes:* (i) The plan is based on the key points, but it 'telescopes' some of them: nine key points become a five-point plan. (ii) There is a lot of repetition of words in the plan (e.g. *energy/sources*) and this must be removed in the draft. The detail of the plan is important; polishing comes later. (iii) A good deal of rephrasing will be needed — compendious words must be found to boil down the meaning of some straggling expressions which waste words. (iv) Connecting phrases and linking words will be needed to turn the separate points of the plan into a piece of good, continuous prose.)

(e) Step 5

Write a draft of the summary, working from the plan. Refer to the passage *only* if stuck; but it should not be necessary to do so.

> Future social historians will be very surprised by our constant worries about not having enough energy resources. Since the planet is a huge reservoir of energy, it is not reasonable to be afraid of running out. There must be a social reason for our fears. People today do not see that there are many different sources of energy all around them and that these are not only greater than those now used, but they cannot be exhausted because they grow again or they are permanent forces. There are technical problems of how to use them economically, but the first necessity is for people to use their imagination and think about these new forms of energy. If they do that, they will realise that we have the essential technologies and that they will become cheaper and could make life more civilised.

(f) Step 6

Prune and polish the draft.

    (i) *Word count*   The word limit is 'not more than 120 words' and there are 139 words in the draft. Hard pruning is required: 19 surplus words make the draft 15% too long!

    (ii) *Look for unnecessary material*   First, check the 'social historians' point listed as 'doubtful' at Step 3. Further thought shows that it ties in with 'a *social* reason', so it makes an important point and must stay. All the other material seems essential, so words cannot be saved by pruning the subject matter.

    (iii) *Look for wasted words*   The language of the draft needs to be much tighter in construction and more condensed in expression. For example: '. . . it is not reasonable to be afraid of running out'/'. . . because they grow again or they are permanent forces'. The first is loose; the second is both loose and ambiguous. Disciplined rewriting will save words and put the meaning across much more crisply.

    (iv) *Look for badly chosen words*   One leaps out at once: *reservoir*. There is nothing wrong with the word itself, of course, but *in this context* it seems to suggest that the natural energy sources are all to do with water-power; and that is *not* what the writer says. Again, is there confusion in the use of *techniques/technologies*? Does 'very surprised' give the right 'feel'? Is it strong enough?

    (v) *Is the draft a connected and readable piece of prose?*   The last two sentences are not linked firmly enough to bring out their logical connection. Apart from that, the 'flow' of the draft seems satisfactory. The ideas and the argument move steadily forwards.

    (vi) *Check grammar, punctuation and spelling*

    (vii) *Final tests to be applied*   Would this summary be readily understood by a reader who had not seen the original passage? Yes. Would it convey to that reader the essential meaning of the passage? Yes.

(g) Step 7

Write final version.

    (i) *Head* the summary with a *suitable* (brief, plain, accurate) *title*.

(ii) *Write out* the final version in your best and *clearest* handwriting, remembering to incorporate all the improvements of Step 6.

(iii) *State* at the end the *exact* number of words used, *excluding* the title.

THE EARTH'S UNTAPPED AND RENEWABLE ENERGY RESOURCES

Our besetting anxiety about energy supplies will astonish future social historians. Since Earth is itself a huge energy system, our fear that our supplies may fail is not reasonable. Its cause is social. People today are blind to the fact that all around them are different kinds of energy, far greater than those now used. These natural sources of energy can never fail, for they are renewable and, therefore, inexhaustible. There is the problem of how to exploit them economically, but the first necessity is for people to think imaginatively about these new possibilities. Then, they will realise that we have the essential technologies, which will get cheaper and which could make human life more civilised.

(116 *words*)

4.10 Work out 2 (with Notes)

Summarise this passage in clear, concise English, *using your own words as far as possible*. You may retain words and brief expressions which cannot be accurately or economically replaced. Do *not* take whole sentences from the passage and simply replace key words. Write your summary in about 110 words and state at the end the exact number of words you have used. Spend about 45 minutes on this question.

A man can stand being told that he must submit to a severe surgical operation, or that he has some disease which will shortly kill him, or that he will be a cripple or blind for the rest of his life; dreadful as such tidings must be, we do not find that they unnerve the greater number of mankind; most men, indeed, go coolly enough even to be hanged, but the strongest quail before financial ruin, and the better men they are, the more complete, as a general rule, is their prostration. Suicide is a common consequence of money losses; it is rarely sought as a means of escape from bodily suffering. If we feel that we have a competence at our backs, so that we can die warm and quietly in our beds, with no need to worry about expense, we live our lives out to the dregs, no matter how excruciating our torments. Job probably felt the loss of his flocks and herds more than that of his wife and family, for he could enjoy his flocks and herds without his family, but not his family — not for long — if he had lost all his money. Loss of money indeed is not only the worst pain in itself, but it is the parent of all the others. Let a man have been brought up to a moderate competence, and have no specialty; then let his money be suddenly taken from him, and how long is his health likely to survive the change in all his little ways which loss of money will entail? How long again is the esteem and sympathy of friends likely to survive ruin? People may be very sorry for us, but their attitude towards us hitherto has been based upon the supposition that we were situated thus and thus in money matters; when this breaks down there must be a restatement of the social problem so far as we are concerned; we have been obtaining esteem under false pretences. Granted, then, that the three most serious losses which a man can suffer are those affecting money, health and reputation. Loss of money is far the worst, then comes ill-health, and then loss of reputation; loss of reputation is a bad third, for, if a man keeps health and money unimpaired, it will generally be found that his loss of reputation is due to breaches of parvenu conventions only, and not to violations of those older, better established canons whose authority is unquestionable. In this case a man may grow a new reputation as easily as a lobster grows a new claw, or, if he have health and money, may thrive in great peace of mind without any reputation at all. The only chance for a man who has lost his money is that he shall still be young enough to stand uprooting and transplanting without more than temporary derangement.

Samuel Butler, *The Way of All Flesh*

LOSS OF MONEY IS THE WORST OF MISFORTUNES

The prospect of a major operation, fatal illness or crippling disability is more courageously borne than financial disaster. Indeed, that worst of sufferings, loss of money, is followed by all other miseries. Health is lost because habitual comforts are removed. Friendships and social regard are destroyed because sympathy alone cannot sustain former relationships once they are seen to have been based on false financial assumptions. Loss of money is worse than loss of either health or social standing. With money, illness is endurable. Lost social standing is easily recovered or readily dispensed with if money and health are preserved, but financial ruin can be survived only by those young enough to start again elsewhere.

(113 *words*)

NOTES

1. The opinions expressed in the passage are contentious, deliberately challenging the usual points of view on these matters. The summariser must not be jolted out of an objective approach to the task. The writer's opinions must be restated accurately, without alteration or comment.
2. Because the writing is itself condensed, the word limit is hard to observe. In fact, the summary is just below the upper limit ('about 110 words' allows a plus or minus of 5 words). The material omitted consisted mainly of supporting points and illustrative examples (e.g. 'Suicide is . . .'/'Job probably felt the loss . . .'/'as easily as a lobster. . .').
3. Compendious words (e.g. 'crippling disability'/'habitual comforts'/'financial assumptions') were used to encapsulate longer but essential statements. Useful tips can be learnt by comparing the vocabulary of the summary closely with that of the original passage.
4. An attempt was made to convey the ironical tone of the writing (e.g. 'Lost social status . . . *easily recovered . . . readily dispensed with* . . .'), though the need to condense inevitably diluted the full flavour.
5. Some rearrangement of the order in which the key points are presented in the passage helped to establish coherence in the summary. For example, 'With money, illness is endurable' encapsulates the meaning of 43 words in the passage ('If we feel . . . torments.') *and* moves the point to a later stage in the summary than in the passage. Such shifts in the order are often necessary, for the coherence established in a longer piece of writing may be destroyed unless adjustments are made to preserve it in a small-scale version of the essential meaning.

5   Directed Writing

5.1   Definition and Description

A piece of *directed writing* is a composition of some length written 'to order'. The examiners provide you with 'source material' and with detailed instructions which stipulate:

- the *nature* of the material to be used in your answer;
- the *form* your writing must take;
- the *audience* for which it is intended.

Sometimes the length of the piece of writing is strictly and explicitly controlled by a stated word limit. More often, the length depends on the time allowed for the question, which may be as little as 30 minutes or as much as one hour. You will, of course, find out what time limits your own examining board sets, and practise accordingly.

A directed writing task may be one question in an examination paper testing understanding, or it may be part of your assessed coursework. Some examining boards set a separate paper with the title *Directed Writing*.

5.2   Some Typical Instructions for Directed Writing

1. Passage One gives an account of the meticulous planning of the raid on the bullion van. Passage Two details what happened and how the driver and the security guard rather luckily succeeded in foiling the attempted robbery.

   Having studied both passages, write a report of the incident such as the driver might have made to his employers, pointing out weaknesses in the security arrangements and procedures which so nearly allowed the raid to succeed, and making recommendations for improvements.

   Use only the material supplied in the two passages, and remember that this is an official report, not a journalistic 'write-up' of a sensational event.

   Spend about 15 minutes in studying the two passages and making notes. You will then have 30 minutes in which to plan and write the report, which must be clearly ordered and written in plain, direct English.

2. The following passage (written soon after the events occurred) describes some of the effects of the Blitz on London in 1940.

   Imagine that you have been asked to write a 'feature article' for your local paper commemorating the anniversary of these historic events.

Use only the information supplied in the passage, and do not try to include everything mentioned there. Select those details that you think will be of greatest interest to readers to whom 1940 is a long time ago. Your article should reflect your admiration of Londoners' behaviour as described in the passage.

Use your own words as far as possible. If you do include any expressions from the original passage for their vividness or historical flavour, be sure that they are such as your readers will readily understand.

Write in an appropriate style. Provide a headline for your article. Subheadings may also be used.

You are allowed one hour for this question, and your article should be between 400 and 450 words in length.

3.   ENGLISH – PAPER 2

Time allowed: 1 hour 30 minutes

Look carefully at Map A which shows the start and Map B which shows the route of the Northtown Charity Marathon Run. Then read the official hand-out following the maps. When you have studied all this material, you must answer both questions which carry equal marks.

Your answers must be based on the information given to you, but you must use and organise the material in your own way and not simply copy from the passage.

Questions

1. Write a letter from the chairperson of the Marathon Run Committee (Mr James Penny) to prospective entrants for this year's run, giving them all the information they need to appreciate the physical demands that the Run will make on competitors. Base the information on the maps and the hand-out.

Begin the letter 'Dear Enquirer' and end with 'Yours sincerely', followed by the appropriate signature. Provide it with a sensible date.

Before starting to write, study this additional information.

(i) In last year's Run, several entrants who were not physically fit had clearly underestimated the strain involved. Mr Penny wants to ensure that this year's entrants have a medical check before they run.

(ii) Learning from last year's experience, the organisers are providing an ample supply of sugar and salt drinks and greatly increased first aid facilities at regular intervals along the route.

Mr Penny wants to emphasise both these points without frightening prospective (and fit) entrants off.

2. Imagine that you have taken part in the Run and that, having completed the course, you have raised £50 from your sponsors. You are handing the money over to a local charity. Write a suitable letter to the treasurer of that charity, using this information.

Charity: Northtown Senior Citizens' Social Club.
Treasurer: Ms Julia Blake.
Appeal target: £10,000.
Objective: To buy a minibus to provide transport for Club outings, hospital visiting, etc.

You may want to draw on additional information extracted from the maps and the hand-out, but be sure that it is relevant to this letter.

Write in an appropriately warm tone, but do not forget that the recipient of this letter is a good many years older than you. Remember, too, that although you have made a big effort and are handing over £50, that is a small amount in relation to the sum needed. On the other hand, false modesty about your achievement and your donation would also strike the wrong note.

Begin and end your letter suitably. Date it and remember to include your address.

5.3   What You Have To Do

The length of the instructions quoted in the previous section is typical of directed writing questions. You have to study them closely, because it is essential to do exactly what you are told to do.

Their length and detail will not seem so frightening once you realise that, whatever the nature of the given source material (maps, diagrams, tables, written passages of various kinds) and whatever the form of writing required of you (reports, letters, articles, diary entries, instructions, and so on) all directed writing questions make the same three basic demands.

1. You must study the source material closely, reading it for full comprehension. (You have already learnt how to do this, in Chapters 3 and 4.)
2. You must then extract from the given material all the information required to perform the particular writing tasks you have been set. Go about this in the methodical way recommended in Chapter 4. The thinking and procedures needed are exactly the same as those needed when you are preparing to write a summary.
3. Finally, you must use the information you have extracted, ensuring that every item you use is relevant to the jobs you have been given. Again, the process is similar to summarising in that you must set the relevant information out in a logical order and reword it to suit the job you are doing. As the instructions quoted in Section 5.2 put it: 'Use your own words as far as possible.' / 'You must use and organise the material in your own way and not simply copy from the passage.'

5.4   Appropriate Style

In Section 5.1, it was pointed out that directed writing instructions specify the *form* in which you must write and the *audience* for whom you must write. Those two specifications (form and audience) determine what *style* of writing is appropriate.

The examiners provide you with all the guidance you need — if you pay attention, that is.

For example, the first set of instructions in Section 5.2 called for a report from the security van driver to his employers. Both the form of the required writing (a report) and the audience (his employers) make it appropriate to write in a formal and objective way. To make sure that candidates did not choose an inappropriate style, they were reminded later in the instructions that 'This is an official report, not a journalistic write-up of a sensational event'.

The second set of instructions stipulated a piece of writing in the form of 'a feature article for your local newspaper'. The audience was not described, because there was no need. The nature of the audience (the readers of a local newspaper) is implicit in the stipulated form. You are expected to draw on your own experience and have a pretty shrewd idea of what such readers would respond to. In any case, key words later in the instructions provided plenty of indications of what would be an appropriate style for this piece of writing: 'interest . . . admiration . . . vividness . . . historical flavour'.

The third set of instructions set two tasks. Both were to be written in letter form, but to very different audiences. The first was an 'open' letter aimed at a public audience. It was to be 'personalised' in its beginning and ending, but it was not truly personal. It was not written to one, individual person. Its content was official and its purpose was to inform and caution. Its style had to match its content, its purpose and its audience while, at the same time, striking a reassuring note. The second letter was to be written to an individual person, and its content was personal. The examiners gave careful advice about the style and reminders about the audience: 'an appropriately warm tone . . . do not forget that the recipient of this letter is a good many years older than you . . . a small amount in relation to the appeal target . . . false modesty would also strike the wrong note'.

Only by paying very close attention to the instructions in the ways just demonstrated can you be sure of getting the style right.

The basic requirement, of course, is to write clear sentences, cogently linked to form a continuous and connected piece of English. But even a correctly written answer that makes accurate use of relevant information cannot be given a high grade unless

- its style is appropriate to the form in which it is written and to the audience for whom it is intended.

5.5 Work out 1 (with Notes)

The passage below deals with certain aspects of vandalism. Using only the material contained in this passage write an article, in *two* paragraphs, for your local newspaper, setting out:

(*a*) the serious effects of vandalism;
and
(*b*) the possible causes of vandalism.

Your two paragraphs should correspond to (*a*) and (*b*) above. *Do not add ideas of your own* but select and arrange material from the passage. *Write in good, clear, accurate English and use an appropriate style.* Your article should be in your own words as far as possible; do not copy out whole sentences or expressions.

The editor has told you not to exceed 200 words:

A feature of the last twenty years has been the rapid increase in vandalism in Britain. Vandalism itself, however, is not a new phenomenon, since through the ages there have always been those who preferred to destroy rather than to create; even the word 'vandalism' owes its origin to a race of barbarians
5   who devastated parts of Europe as long ago as the fifth century.

The misspelt graffiti, uprooted newly planted trees, abused train carriages, smashed phone boxes, and bus-stop shelters recklessly destroyed spoil the environment and deprive the public of their amenities for which they have paid. Those who perpetrate such outrages seem to be without any self-
10   discipline and show scant respect for the rights of their fellow-citizens. More-over, they increase the taxes and the rates that they themselves have to pay.

Some argue that the vandals feel rejected by society with its predominant middle-class standards and have far too much time on their hands. It is con-ceivable that poor housing and squalid living conditions may lead to this
15   anti-social behaviour, but, if these are the principal causes, it needs to be explained why most of the socially deprived are not vandals. One thing is certain: in order to repair the damage done, local rates have to be increased and national levels of income tax have to take account of the increased ex-penditure needed to maintain services. Scarce material resources and human
20   skills are unnecessarily wasted in the attempts to reduce the danger to life and property caused by vandalism.

Those who practise vandalism are often of poor education and without parental control. They would defend their behaviour, perhaps, by arguing that society provides them with few youth clubs and recreational activities
25   and that they have nothing better to do with their time. The truth is that they are insecure and feel they must put on a show of bravado in order to impress their peers and members of the gang. Perhaps the growth of gangs and movements such as the punks, mods and greasers has played a major rôle in the increase in vandalism.
30   It is a pity that the development of new schools and improved health services has been jeopardised because of a lack of financial resources when these very resources are being squandered in repairing the damage and making good the destruction caused by vandalism. The situation poses a real challenge to those responsible for educating the young or maintaining law
35   and order. The evidence everywhere of vandalism demeans the standing of the country in the eyes of foreign visitors who are amazed to read the obscene remarks scrawled illiterately across walls or step through the broken glass of street lamps smashed 'just for a joke'. The pride, too, of local people in their environment is being eroded.
40   Some of the socially minded politicians give up their efforts to improve the quality of life in the face of such mindless destruction; imaginative designers and developers are reduced to designing amenities which are vandal-proof rather than beautiful and attractive. The older generation, with some justification, blames the younger one and age-groups become even more
45   sharply divided. Some local authorities have become reluctant to improve recreational and social facilities because of vandalism, which is aided and abetted, it is sometimes suggested, by the reduction in police surveillance and an apparently uninterested public which looks the other way when it sees vandals at work. Too many are content to blame the invention of the
50   aerosol can and the felt-tip pen, which make it easy to vandalise buildings and other people's property. Ostrich-like, many ignore what they see and hope that the trail of devastation will cease with the coming of a new genera-tion.

1. Start work by abstracting the material asked for, listing each key point under one or the other of the headings provided in the instructions: (a) the serious effects of vandalism; *and* (b) the possible causes of vandalism. Use of the given headings ensures that all the material selected is *relevant* to the set task. Restate each key point *in your own words* as you note it down. Have an eye to the style required by the assignment (an article for your local newspaper) as you reword the points.

2. In the passage the relevant key points may be divided from each other. For example, the physical damage detailed in lines 6 and 7 is a serious effect of vandalism. So are the reactions of politicians, designers, developers, older people and local authorities described in lines 40–46. Having found one key point bearing on one of the set topics, do not conclude that you have finished with that topic. Keep looking.

3. When you are sure that you have abstracted *all* the relevant material and listed each key point under its correct heading, read through the passage again. Have you included any non-essential material? (For example, nothing in the first paragraph is relevant to the task you have been given; nor is the second sentence of the second paragraph.)

4. You are now ready to plan the article you must write. You know its shape: two paragraphs. As you plan, think out a sensible way of linking the two. Your paragraphs must be connected. Each is part of the *same* article, although each deals with a distinct aspect of the shared subject matter.

5. You must also look for a way of making each paragraph *coherent*. (All the items must 'stick together'.) Perhaps you see that the separate items fall into groups? (For example, *paragraph (a)*: group 1, physical effects; group 2, financial burdens; group 3, less tangible effects – reactions of foreign visitors – erosion of local pride – widening of generation gap; and so on.) If you can hit on coherent groupings, you will be able to present the material in a logical sequence.

6. Now think hard about the style. An article for a local newspaper must be interesting and informative. If you have made an accurate selection of material from the passage, your article will be informative, but unless you present it in an interesting way, the information will not make an impact on your readers. Try to write *plain* but *lively* English. Your language must be *condensed* (or you will exceed the permitted number of words) and it must be easily understood. The *style* in which you write must not get in the way of *what* you write. It must be a smooth-running vehicle to carry information to your readers.

7. Finally, an article must have a *title*. Make it eye-catching (but *not* 'gimmicky'), brief, crisp, accurate. The title does *not count* towards the word limit.

LIFE IN VANDALISED BRITAIN

The visible effects of vandalism are sickeningly evident in our damaged surroundings. To repair the havoc, rates and taxes are increased and scarce funds diverted from pinched education and health services. Less tangible effects also diminish the quality of life. Foreign visitors think poorly of us. Local pride is worn down and local authorities hesitate to embark on amenities. Caring politicians lose heart. Innovative design and development must concentrate on security to the impoverishment of aesthetics.

Conflicting theories explore the causes of this pernicious disease. Superficially, some blame the vandals' much-used tools, the aerosol can and the felt-tip pen.

Public apathy and the removal of the bobby from the beat play their part. The alienation of vandals from a society whose values and advantages they cannot share undoubtedly contributes. Yet that does not explain why most who are poor, badly housed and ill-educated do not turn to vandalism in protest. Certainly, insecurity and its consequent bravado — intended to impress fellow-members of proliferating anti-social gangs — underlie conduct that corrodes our national life.

(175 words)

COMMENTS AND QUESTIONS

1. The *title* was chosen to attract a newspaper reader's attention without being sensational or inaccurate. Can you improve on it?

2. In draft, the article overran the word limit. It was *pruned* in the following places:

Draft	*Final version*
The visible effects of vandalism are apparent in our damaged surroundings, from illiterate scrawls on buildings to wrecked bus-stop shelters.	The visible effects of vandalism are sickeningly evident in our damaged surroundings.
Some simply blame the aerosol can and the felt-tip pen because they are often used by vandals, but this is surely to confuse means with reasons.	Superficially, some blame the vandals' much-used tools, the aerosol can and the felt-tip pen.
It is often said, with some justice, that vandals feel shut out from the prevailing standards and occupations of a dominantly middle-class society.	The alienation of vandals from a society whose values and advantages they cannot share undoubtedly contributes.
Certain it is that insecurity and its consequent bravado . . .	Certainly, insecurity and its consequent bravado . . .

3. The *order* in which the key points are presented in the passage was *extensively rearranged* in the article, partly because the imposed two-paragraph structure dictated this and partly because the passage itself is not remarkable for its coherence. Compare the two closely, trying to appreciate the reasons for the changes and weighing their effectiveness.

4. Consider the *style* in which the article is written. Remember that the given task was to write in a style *appropriate to a local newspaper*. Therefore, the relevant subject matter had to be presented in a lively, readable way without altering or distorting the information supplied in the passage. Note (and comment on) the use of emotive expressions — for example: 'sickeningly'/ 'pernicious disease'/'anti-social'/'corrodes our national life'. Remember that a style that is appropriate to *this* directed writing assignment would not be appropriate to another. (Nor, of course, to 'straight' summary.) If, for example, the required writing had to take the form of a report to a committee, then 'the removal of the bobby from the beat' would *not* be an appropriate rewording of 'the reduction in police surveillance'. When considering the effectiveness of the style, look closely at these points: (i) use of compendious

words; (ii) compression of sentences to save words and tighten up the writing; (iii) the linking of the two paragraphs; (iv) the vocabulary. Finally, ask yourself whether the article would be easily understood by the readers of your local newspaper. If you think that you can improve its readability, do so; but do *not* exceed the word limit and do *not* omit or tamper with any of the essential information.

5.6 Test Papers in Summary and Directed Writing

(*You will find suggested answers on pages 167 and 168, but do not look at them until you have completed your own answers. Then study them closely, making detailed comparisons with your own work.*)

1. Make a summary of the following passage in not more than 100 words. Write good continuous prose. Provide a suitable title and state at the end the exact number of words you have used, *excluding* the title. You should spend about 40 minutes on this question. **(20 marks)**

Prospective students hoping to start this autumn should already be involved in making inquiries about getting grants from the local education authorities. The best advice is to start the process in January; there is certainly no need to wait until you have received an unconditional offer of a place at college or university. The rules are quite complicated and the forms which have to be filled in by the student (and, probably, his or her parents or spouse) will help to determine the nature and amount of the grants which can be expected.

These will depend on (a) the nature of the course to be followed, (b) the student's personal history (he or she must have been treated as an ordinary UK resident for three years and must not have received any previous grant for higher education) and (c) the financial status of the people involved.

Government regulations require LEAs to pay **mandatory grants** ('awards') to young people who are about to take first degrees at universities, polytechnics or colleges, as well as Diplomas of Higher education, B.TEC (Business and Technical Education Council), Higher or Higher National Diplomas, initial teacher training courses leading to PGCE or Art Teachers' Certificates or Diplomas, and a range of other eligible courses about which information can be obtained from the local education authority or direct from the Department of Education and Science.

Discretionary Awards are for those who take a variety of other courses and are made by LEAs in accordance with policies which are reconsidered at the beginning of each financial year.

They vary and some are competitive in terms of exam results. Wherever finite and diminishing public funds are concerned, it's best to get in early. It is worth noting, however, that if an LEA decides to offer a discretionary grant to someone who doesn't fill all the requirements of the Education Act (about residence, etc.) but has been accepted for a degree-equivalent course the award must be the same amount as a mandatory one.

Mandatory awards are expected to cover course fees, examination fees and compulsory contributions to students' unions; these sums are usually paid directly to the educational institution. At present, the undergraduate actually receives reasonable travel costs over £50 (this system is under review) and a maintenance grant, the amount of which is determined by the 'residual income' of the student, his or her parents, or possibly spouse. Deductions are made on a sliding scale when the undergraduate's own residual income is over £345 per annum, or that of the parents exceeds £7100. A minimum grant of about £410 is always payable. Special allowances will be paid to mature students and those with dependents and a grant of up to £520 may be paid at the discretion of the local authorities to students with disabilities.

The only people who can draw social security benefits during term time are single parents and handicapped people.

Education Guardian (April 1984)

---

2. Summarise the passage below in clear continuous English, using your own words as far as possible. Your summary should be about 150 words in length and you must state at the end the exact number of words you have used. Remember to provide a suitable title. Spend not more than 1 hour on this question. **(30 marks)**

In politics, again, it is almost a commonplace that a party of order and stability and a party of progress or reform are both necessary elements of a healthy state of political life; until one or the other shall so have enlarged its mental grasp as to be a party equally of order and of progress, knowing and distinguishing what is fit to be preserved from what ought to be swept away. Each of these modes of thinking derives its utility from the deficiencies of the other; but it is in a great measure the opposition of the other that keeps each within the limits of reason and sanity. Unless opinions favourable to democracy and to aristocracy, to property and to equality, to co-operation and to competition, to luxury and to abstinence, to sociality and to individuality, to liberty and to discipline, and all the other standing antagonisms of practical life are expressed with equal freedom and enforced and defended with equal talent and energy, there is no chance of both elements obtaining their due; one scale is sure to go up, and the other down. Truth, in the great practical concerns of life, is so much a question of the reconciling and combining of opposites that very few have minds sufficiently capacious and impartial to make the adjustment with an approach to correctness and it has to be made by the rough process of a struggle between combatants fighting under hostile banners. On any of the great open questions just enumerated, if either of the two opinions has a better claim than the other, not merely to be tolerated, but to be encouraged and countenanced, it is the one which happens at the particular time and place to be in a minority. That is the opinion which, for the time being, represents the neglected interests, the side of human well-being which is in danger of obtaining less than its share. I am aware that there is not, in this country, any intolerance of differences of opinion on most of these topics. They are adduced to show, by admitted and multiplied examples, the universality of the fact that only through diversity of opinion is there, in the existing state of the human intellect, a chance of fair play to all sides of the truth. When there are persons to be found who form an exception to the apparent unanimity of the world on any subject, even if the world is in the right, it is always probable that dissentients have something worth hearing to say for themselves and that truth would lose something by their silence.

John Stuart Mill, *On Liberty*

3. *Read the following instructions carefully before beginning your work.*

Write an article for inclusion in a local newspaper deliberately setting out to persuade the readers that noise is a real threat to everyone in today's society. It should consist of *three* paragraphs, as follows:

    (a) deploring the potential dangers of noise in modern life;

    (b) suggesting how the dangers can be reduced or eliminated;

    (c) admitting that it is neither possible nor desirable to eliminate all noise in life.

Do not write more than 200 words.

Use only the information given in the passage and the table below; do not attempt to use all the details and examples given but select and arrange the material best able to make your article really persuasive. Use your own words as far as possible, although you may retain words and expressions which cannot be accurately or economically replaced.

As you write, bear in mind the kind of readers who take a local newspaper and your own attitude as a writer seeking to persuade others. You should use an appropriate style but you must write in clear and accurate English.

Remember that your work will be assessed on the number of facts you use and their accuracy, as well as on the way you direct your writing towards your readers.

Spend about 1 hour on this question.   **(30 marks)**

NOISE

The unit in which noise is measured is known as the *decibel* (db). The threshold of hearing, that is the point at which man has the capacity to hear, is at zero decibels; somewhere around 180 decibels is the lethal level. Rats exposed to levels approaching this turn cannibalistic and eventually die from heart failure; short exposure to 150 db can permanently damage the human ear and cause excruciating pain; slightly lower levels can cause temporary deafness and if there is a long-term exposure to noise above that found near a motorway where traffic is continually passing there is a grave risk of permanent hearing-loss and nervous exhaustion.

Table: Common noise levels

Jet aircraft at 200 feet near a large airport	150 db
Pneumatic drill	130 db
A 'hard-rock' band	115 db
Power mower; accelerating motor-cycle	110 db
Food mixer (2 to 4 feet away)	100 db
Underground train (inside)	100 db
Heavy city traffic	90 db
Passenger cars on nearby motorway	65–86 db
Normal conversation	60–70 db
Telephone conversation	60 db
Quiet residential street noises	50 db
Tick of watch (2 feet away)	30 db
Leaves rustling in the wind	10 db

It is best, of course, to minimise the potential danger from noise at its source; much of it is within our control in the kitchen, living-room, and the play or workroom. Dishwashers, food-mixers, tumble-driers, electric drills and washing-machines can raise the noise level to dangerous levels but if they are placed or operated in rooms separate from the living accommodation the noise level is reduced or even eliminated; if the machines are stood on sound-absorbing pads the nuisance and risk are diminished. The acoustic power of a full orchestra is rarely more than ten watts and yet music systems used in some living-rooms can produce sounds at more than a hundred watts of audio power. Young people, too, often feel it necessary to amplify the sound of their musical instruments and they also plug their transistor outputs into their ears with the volume turned up at full blast. Perhaps they want to follow Beethoven into deafness.

Most television sets are turned up to dangerous levels while the viewers' attention is distracted from the threat by the picture flashing in front of their eyes. Noisy dustbins, squeaky gates or machines strangers to the oil-can, loud lawn-mowers shattering the peace of suburban afternoons, honking car-horns, and children reliving the latest TV Western in the street, all contribute to the noise pollution of our own time. Curtains, carpets, large furniture and wall-fittings help to reduce noise levels within the home by their deadening effect; outdoors, trees and shrubs, high walls and fences act as noise-breaks; even lawns and flower-borders make the environment quieter just as carpets reduce sound levels indoors.

However, there are those who think that noise is preferable to washing clothes by hand, cutting grass with scythes and walking long distances. Noise, they argue, is a necessary part of man's advance. One man's noise is another's sweet melody. Some think that a crying baby, the explosive roar from a motor-bike's exhaust, the throbbing beat of a pop-group or the rattling of bells as cows slither down idyllic mountain slopes are all beautiful sounds. The living world is full of sounds; only the world of the dead is uniformly silent.

---

6 Using Words

6.1 Basic Skills

Chapters 6-10 concentrate on word choice (vocabulary), grammar, punctuation and spelling. Used together with Chapter 11, which provides varied practice in solving all sorts of common problems, they give you help with your written English.

The explanations, advice and work outs in each of the earlier chapters have referred to a particular area of the work tested by the GCSE examination in English: expression (both composition of various kinds and practical writing in various forms), understanding and response, summary and directed writing. However, you have been given frequent reminders that your performance in all these tests finally depends on your competence in the basic skills of written English. As a rule, examination papers include similar reminders. For example, the paper worked out in Section 3.1 contained this statement:

- You are reminded of the importance of orderly presentation and clear English in your answers.

In all your coursework you will certainly be encouraged to pay careful attention to the clarity and correctness of your written English.

A caution about the need for 'clear and correct English' may be a useful reminder, but it is worded too generally to be of much practical help. You may feel that it does not throw a great deal of light on what is expected of you — and unless you have learnt beforehand what is meant by 'clear and correct English' (and practised writing it), it won't!

The fact is that, in issuing their reminder, the examiners assume that you have learnt the ground rules of written English and know how to apply them. What they are saying, in effect, is this:

- No matter what kind of question they are answering, all GCSE candidates are expected to be competent in the basic skills of written English. Those who are not will lose marks.

The various examining boards phrase their requirements in their own way, but they all have common aims and apply the same standards. Careful study of their syllabuses and grading criteria makes it possible to draw up a list of the qualities of written English looked for in the work of all candidates.

1. Paragraphing

Every piece of writing you do must be carefully organised. Its subject must be introduced, developed and carried onwards to its conclusion. (In other words, it must have a thought-out beginning, middle and end.) The firm overall structure required cannot be achieved unless it is based on a linked and logical sequence of paragraphs, each of which deals with one (and only one) main topic.

2. Sentences

Your sentences must be grammatically correct. In their construction and their tone they should be appropriate to the particular ideas and feelings you are trying to express. Your awareness that you are attempting to achieve a particular effect in one sentence and a different effect in another will be reflected in the variety and range of sentence structures that you employ.

3. Choice of words

You must choose your words carefully and sensitively. You can do this only if you have a large vocabulary on which to draw, and some feeling for the way words work. Evidence that you have tried to suit the expression to the particular sense you want to convey and to the tone of voice you consider to be fitting will be a very strong point when your work is assessed. 'Correct', 'varied' and 'appropriate' are the terms used by the examining boards when describing the qualities they hope to find in candidates' use of words.

4. Punctuation

Correct grammar and appropriate word choice must be supported by well-judged punctuation consistently applied. Clear, accurate use of the basic punctuation marks is one of the most important ways you have of getting your meaning across and avoiding ambiguity and misunderstanding. Punctuation and sense go hand in hand.

5. Spelling

Although you are not expected to be faultless, you *are* expected to spell all commonly used words correctly. Ignorance and/or carelessness will cost you marks — and rightly so. As in grammar and punctuation, so in spelling, the examination demands a standard of literacy below which you must not fall.

The importance of structuring your answers — both overall and in paragraphs — has been demonstrated frequently and in detail, especially in Chapters 1 and 3. The basic skills of written English described in points 2–5 of the above list of the examiners' requirements are dealt with in this and subsequent chapters. Do not fail to study them closely. Then work through the exercises and tests in Chapter 11. The benefits will be apparent in all your written work in English — and in all your other subjects too.

6.2 Enlarging Your Vocabulary

Your vocabulary is the range of words that you can use. The larger that range, the better your work in all the English questions — and the better your performance in all your other subjects.

To enlarge your vocabulary you must be interested in words: their meaning, derivation, pronunciation and spelling. While preparing for your examination (and afterwards, I hope) pay attention to every new word you meet: words that you have not heard or seen before; *and* familiar words used in ways that are new to you.

Get the dictionary habit. First, you must learn the 'signalling' system of abbreviations, different typefaces, brackets, and so on, that your dictionary uses to convey a lot of information in a small space. Different dictionaries use different 'codes', so, to get full help from the entries, you must study the 'preliminary matter' in your own dictionary. As this example shows, 'knowing' a word involves more than simple definition, although that is the essential starting point.

> **summary**, a. & n. Compendious, brief, dispensing with needless details, done with dispatch, (a *s. account*; *s. methods, jurisdiction*, etc.); hence **summarily**, adv. (N.) brief account, abridgement, epitome. [n. f. L. *summarium*.]

To build up a vocabulary that will be adequate for your examination, you must make frequent and proper use of your dictionary.

6.3 Meaning and Context

Examination questions, especially in tests of understanding, often draw your attention to the fact that the meaning of a word depends very largely on the context in which it is used. A typical instruction reads like this: 'Explain the meaning of the following words and expressions *as they are used in the passage*.'

- Remember that a word can have several meanings and can act as different parts of speech, *according to the context in which it is used*.

For example, my dictionary tells me that the word *pat* can be used as a noun, as a verb, as an adjective or as an adverb. It can mean (among other things): a stroke or tap; a small mass formed by patting; to strike gently; opportune(ly); apposite(ly). In all the following sentences, *pat* is correctly used but it means something different in each.

1. Get me a pat of butter.
2. Don't pat yourself on the back.
3. The startling news came pat to their purpose.
4. Question him again if you like, but he has his story pat.

Context must always be considered before meaning can be established. Your dictionary gives you as many meanings as it has space for and indicates the common ways of using a word, but it cannot tell you which particular meaning and which particular usage you need. Your study of the context provides the solution.

6.4 Prefixes and Suffixes

- A **prefix** is a letter or a group of letters joined on at the *beginning* of a word to change its meaning and to make a new word (*un* + 'happy' = unhappy).
- A **suffix** is a letter or a group of letters joined on at the *end* of a word to change its meaning and to make a new word ('friend' + *ship* = friendship).

You must learn to recognise the meaning and the function of the prefixes and suffixes most frequently found in English. For example, you must know the difference between *ante*date and *anti*dote; between *ab*ject, *in*ject, *ob*ject, *pro*ject and *re*ject; between occu*pancy* and occu*pant*; between wood*ed* and wood*en*.

The language tests in Chapter 11 provide useful practice, but you must reinforce them with work along the lines suggested in Section 6.2.

6.5 Synonyms, Antonyms, Homophones

- **Synonyms** are words having the same (or very nearly the same) meaning. For example: *blend/mixture*; *change/alteration*; *start/begin*.

But when you need to substitute one word for another, as so often in directed writing and summary, you must remember that words are *not* lifeless counters, instantly interchangeable. You have to consider whether the proposed substitute carries the required *shade* of meaning. The following points must be borne in mind.

1. Words often convey feelings as well as ideas; and the feelings associated with a word are an important part of its meaning. For example, *evil* 'means' *bad* (and *bad* 'means' *evil*) but *evil* carries with it different (and much stronger) feelings than *bad*. The two words cannot simply be interchanged. You could not sensibly write (or say), 'Travelling overnight was an evil decision, for we were tired out when we arrived.' (See Section 6.8.)
2. Very rarely do two words mean exactly the same thing, although they may be close enough in meaning to be interchangeable. You have to be satisfied that the word you choose is precisely right for the particular meaning you want to express. For example, *end* and *finish* are very close in meaning and they may be interchangeable in some contexts, but they may convey quite different senses in other contexts. Compare: 'There was a dead heat at the finish of the Tadcaster Hurdle' with 'The loss of sponsorship funds means the end of the Tadcaster Hurdle'.
3. Words must be appropriate to their context. You have to consider not only the sentence in which a word is to be used, but also the paragraph in which that sentence occurs and — often — the passage as a whole. You have already seen that a particular use of language demands a fitting (appropriate) choice of words (see especially Sections 4.8, 5.4 and 5.5) and you must bear this in mind when selecting synonyms. For example, *respire* 'means' *breathe*, but the two words cannot be freely switched around. There are many contexts in which *breathe* is appropriate but in which *respire* would be inappropriate. Similar considerations apply to *buy/purchase*; *live/reside*; *house/residence*; and to many other synonyms.

- **Antonyms** are words of opposite meaning: *difficult/easy*; *happy/unhappy*; *strong/weak*.

The considerations that apply to the selection of synonyms apply equally to the selection of antonyms. In respect of length, a long journey is the opposite of a short journey. Opposite moral judgements are expressed in the two sentences: 'He is a good man'/'He is a bad man'. *But* is the meaning of 'Those sausages were bad' the opposite of 'Those sausages were good'?

- **Homophones** are words that sound the same or nearly the same, but are spelt differently and have different meanings: *complement/compliment*; *fair/fare*; *gait/gate*; *sail/sale*.

There are a great many of these 'confusables' — a name that epitomises the danger they present to a careless writer.

6.6 Compendious Words

The need to know (and to know how to use) these 'space-savers' was demonstrated in Chapter 4. Essential when summarising, they are invaluable in all uses of written (and spoken) language. They pack a tremendous punch. With a wide range of compendious words in your vocabulary, you can write and speak plain, forceful English, and steer clear of verbosity and the pretentious fluffiness that is death to the language. Many of the tests in Chapter 11 provide practice in substituting compendious words for long-winded expressions. (See also Sections 7.3–7.7.)

6.7 Literal and Figurative Uses of Language

Figurative use of language is a frequent, useful, colourful element of everyday speech and writing. We are not usually confused by it. When we hear that somebody has been 'spurred on', we do not suppose that a sharp instrument has been applied to his/her sides. We understand that he/she has been impelled to make additional efforts. If 'the books were cooked', we do not suppose that they were boiled in a saucepan or baked in an oven. We understand that the accounts have been falsified.

A common mistake is to employ language figuratively and to make nonsense of it by inserting the word *literally*. ('How did you feel when you heard that you had been selected?' 'Astonished! You could literally have knocked me down with a feather.')

Of course, you would not make that silly mistake, but many people do – and it's catching! The example illustrates too the danger of *cliché* inherent in many popular figurative expressions. (See Section 7.8.)

Tests of understanding frequently require you to distinguish between these two uses of language, for the passages set often include vivid and emotive figurative expressions. (See Section 6.8.) When summarising, any figurative expressions that are essential to the key points must be reworded as literal statements.

You are not as a rule questioned directly about *figures of speech*, but you should learn to recognise the following: alliteration; metaphor; paradox; onomatopoeia; personification; simile. They are in common use, and failure to recognise them causes misunderstanding of content and purpose. Figures of speech often play a major part in conveying the *nuances* of meaning which you must be able to detect in passages set as tests of understanding.

6.8 The Language of Fact and the Language of Feeling

Words may be used primarily to convey facts and ideas. They may be used primarily to communicate feelings or emotions. The former is described as a *referential* use of words. The latter is described as an *emotive* use of words.

- **Referential** use of language. Words are used as 'labels'. They name and describe things and their attributes. They are used factually and *objectively*. The writer (or speaker) says, in effect, 'I am using language to deal with things as they are.'
- **Emotive** use of language. Words are used to communicate feelings and emotional attitudes. They are used *subjectively*. The writer (or speaker) says, in effect, 'I am using language to communicate my feelings about these matters and I want to persuade you to share those feelings.'

113

Many words have both a denotation and a connotation. The *denotation* is the 'labelling function' of the word — what the word 'actually means' (to put it very crudely). The *connotation* is the feelings and emotions associated with the word — the 'emotional tones' that it carries with it. For example:

(i) They chose a *blue* car last time. (*denotation* of 'blue' uppermost)
(ii) We felt very *blue* when they left. (*connotation* of 'blue' uppermost)

Denotation is uppermost when words are used literally. Connotation is uppermost when words are used figuratively.

Referential language (stressing *denotation*) is the appropriate language for scientific, factual, practical and discursive writing.

Emotive language (stressing *connotation*) plays a large part in creative, persuasive, impressionistic writing.

Your recognition that language is being used in one or the other of these two ways helps you to determine the writers' intentions when you are studying passages set for understanding and response. Your own pieces of directed writing and composition are, of course, proof that you can (or cannot!) use words in ways that are suitable to a particular kind of writing. The explicit instruction 'Write in an appropriate style' is the key to successful directed writing. A composition the style of which is not appropriate to the kind of subject chosen falls at the first hurdle.

6.9 Idiomatic and Proverbial Expressions

An **idiom** is a form of expression (or of grammatical usage) peculiar to a particular language. For example, English idioms using the word *heart* include: 'a person/ cause after one's own heart'; 'with all one's heart'; 'from the bottom of one's heart'; 'break one's heart'; 'by heart'; 'go to one's heart'; 'in good heart'; 'with a heavy heart'; 'know by heart'; 'learn by heart'; 'lose heart'; 'lose one's heart'; 'not find it in one's heart to' . . . . And that is only a selection of 'heart idioms'.

Mastery of its idioms is a sure mark of proficiency in the use of a language. That is why it is so difficult to speak or write a foreign language 'like a native'. We may have the vocabulary we need and know the grammar, but the idioms often defeat us.

Mishandled idioms cost marks in an English examination and, although nobody can sit down to learn all the idioms of English just like that, you can prepare yourself for the examination by checking the accuracy of the idioms you hear and read *and* of those you habitually use. Careful listening and reading and the use of reference books (such as Roget's *Thesaurus* and Brewer's *Dictionary of Phrase and Fable*) will increase your range and fluency and help you to guard against blunders such as confusing 'lose heart' with 'lose one's heart' — an increasingly common mistake.

Proverbial expressions, like idioms, are part and parcel (idiom!) of everyday speech and frequently used in written English. Many are centuries old and some, with constant use, have degenerated into clichés (see Section 7.8). Many retain their freshness and vigour and the stock is continually renewed. Again, you have to rely on your sense of style to guide you when writing. Is the expression that you are about to use stale and overworked? (No self-respecting writer could use 'over the moon' or 'sick as a parrot'!) Can you find words *of your own* to say what *you* want to say? If so, use them.

114

However, you must acquaint yourself with the meaning of the commonest proverbs, any of which may be encountered in a passage set for understanding or summary. In answering those questions, you may be required to rewrite sentences containing idiomatic and proverbial expressions so that their sense is unchanged.

6.10   Good Writing

Chapter 7 discusses and illustrates the faults most commonly committed when using words. You will find that each offends against one or more of these basic rules of good writing:

- be plain;
- be direct;
- use no more words than are necessary;
- think hard to find the right word;
- use active verbs rather than passive verbs where you have a choice.

Your written English will reach the standard that the examiners expect if you make a consistent effort to apply those rules every time you write.

7 Misusing Words

The mistakes of style and vocabulary listed in this chapter are those most frequently made in written English.

Each mistake is defined and discussed in a separate section, but it is helpful to think about their causes before looking at each of them in turn. They all arise from one or more of these bad habits:

- carelessly or ignorantly using the wrong word;
- using more words than are needed;
- using pompous expressions to sound important;
- using stale, tired words and expressions;
- using language that does not fit the occasion.

Because they have common origins, the faults overlap. For example, writers who use more words than are needed will probably be guilty of tautology or circumlocution, or both at once. *Verbosity* (see Section 7.7) manifests itself in different ways, all of which break the rules of good writing.

7.1 Malapropisms

DEFINITION

A malapropism is a word used in mistake for one that resembles it, often resulting in an unintended comic effect; *always* resulting in nonsense.

EXAMPLES

(i) All newly elected members of the society must attend the *propitiation* ceremony to be held at 6 p.m. next Friday.
(ii) The interviewer lost his temper and accused the shifty politician of *invading* his questions.
(iii) As the excise duty has increased, so have deaths caused by drinking *implicitly* distilled spirits.

COMMENTS

The mistake is as old as language itself, but it takes its name from Mrs Malaprop, a character in R. B. Sheridan's play *The Rivals* (1775). One of her most famous 'malapropisms' neatly demonstrates the mistake: 'a nice derangement (*arrangement*) of epitaphs (*epithets*)'. Shakespeare's character Dogberry (*Much Ado About Nothing*) was a specialist in malapropisms nearly two hundred years earlier than Mrs Malaprop herself: 'You are thought to be the most *senseless* and fit man for the constable of the watch.'

7.2 Tautology

DEFINITION

Needlessly saying the same thing more than once in different words (*tauto-* = 'the same').

EXAMPLES

- (i) The guests arrived *in succession one after the other*.
- (ii) I have arranged to be called at 6 *a.m. in the morning*.
- (iii) Brown then bought out his partner and so became the *sole and only* proprietor of a *thriving* business *that was doing well*.

COMMENTS

Think hard about the sense and you will avoid tautologies. We all seem to have an itch to write (and say) more words than are needed, as if a plain statement is somehow not sufficient on its own. As a result, we use superfluous words which add nothing to the meaning but clog up the sense of what we want to say.

7.3 Circumlocution

DEFINITION

A roundabout way of speaking and writing.

EXAMPLES

- (i) Candidates who scored low marks in summary *in many cases* exceeded the word limit.
- (ii) Your application is *under active consideration* by the Board.
- (iii) Pensioners *received a disappointment in the shape of the fact that* their pensions were not increased.

COMMENTS

Spotlighted, the fault is so obvious that we wonder how we can ever commit it; but we all do. Each of those examples needs just a little thought to turn it into good English.

- (i) Candidates who scored low marks in summary often exceeded the word limit. (*Or* and *better*: Many candidates who scored low marks in summary exceeded the word limit.)
- (ii) Your application is being considered by the Board. (*Or* and *better*: The Board is considering your application.)
- (iii) Pensioners were disappointed because their pensions were not increased.

7.4 Pomposity

DEFINITION

Self-important and inflated language. Using out-of-the-way words and expressions to impress, and avoiding the shorter, simpler and more familiar terms that would express the same meaning. Pompous language conceals the sense — and it is often meant to. Jargon (see Section 7.5) is usually present.

EXAMPLES

    (i) The *counterproductive trends* in the industrial *production situation* are *escalating* to a *serious degree*.
    (ii) Candidates must *operate* within the *time parameters obtaining*.
    (iii) The *prolonged state of belligerency occasioned severe financial stresses. Governmental fiscal imposts* were increased *prior to its termination*.

COMMENTS

Circumlocution usually goes with a pompous choice of words (*to a serious degree* = 'seriously'). In themselves, there is nothing wrong with long words or words outside an everyday vocabulary; but there is no justification for far-fetched language when there are simple and familiar terms to do the job. The examples just given can be rewritten in plain, direct English, without changing the intended sense and with greatly increased clarity and force.

    (i) Industrial production is falling seriously.
    (ii) Candidates must keep to the time limit.
    (iii) The long war cost a lot of money. Taxes had to be raised before it ended.

Plain English is crisp and it means what it says. Pomposity is woolly and it often does not mean what it appears to say. The 'vogue words' of pompous people are loosely used. Examples are: *parameters*; *syndrome*; *ambivalent*; *liquidate*; *interface*; *approximate*; *optimum*; *orientate*; *viable*. All those words (and dozens more) are fashionable today. They *can* be used accurately and precisely, but only in appropriate contexts.

7.5 Jargon

DEFINITION

The use of technical terms in an inappropriate context. Technical terms are words and expressions that are used in particular arts, sciences, professions and occupations: there are technical terms in acting, for example, in physics, in psychology, in law, in medicine, in politics. In their appropriate contexts, they are accurate, intelligible, indispensable tools of communication. They become jargon *only* when they are transplanted. Each of the vogue words listed above has an important job to do on its home ground. For example, *syndrome* is a technical term in medicine; *parameter* in mathematics; *viable* in biology.

    Some technical terms have passed into general use without losing their accuracy and plain, honest dealing: *altering tack* (from sailing) is one such expression, used figuratively, as many of them are. The label 'jargon' (it means 'twittering'!) cannot be stuck on them.

Examples of and comments on jargon are included in the next section, which deals with a fault that is closely related to it.

7.6 Gobbledegook

DEFINITION

Pompous official writing, stuffed with the jargon of government departments: 'officialese'. Unfortunately, it has found its way out of the offices in which it first flourished and it is now one of the commonest faults in written English. The word *gobbledegook* is onomatopoeic, imitating the sound made by a turkey-cock.

EXAMPLES

(i) The district surveyor has arrived at the conclusion that the physical properties and configuration of the terrain of the site make the proposal to erect habitations thereon a proposition of dubious viability.

(ii) Throughout a long period of time extending over several years there have been considerable and recurring variations in personnel in the establishments of this manufacturing agglomeration.

(iii) It has been decided by the minister that the incidence of the levying of prescription charges under the new regulations shall remain under active consideration and that, pending a decision being formulated, the current practice shall apply to such classifications of exemptees as would have remained exempt had the new regulations not been promulgated.

COMMENTS

Many of the faults already discussed come together in those examples. Jargon and gobbledegook (the jargon of officialdom) are usually accompanied by tautology, circumlocutions and pomposity.

The meaning of (i) and (ii) can be expressed plainly and directly:

(i) The district surveyor has decided that the shape and surface of the site make it unsuitable for house building.

(ii) For several years, the number of workers in this group of factories has varied considerably.

It is not so easy to turn the third example into plain, sensible English. Either the writer did not know what he wanted to say or he did not want his readers to know. The meaning seems to be:

(iii) The minister is still considering how the new prescription charges will be levied. Until he makes a decision, people who were exempt under the old regulations will remain exempt.

7.7 Verbosity

Using more words than are needed. The symptoms of the disease include tautology, circumlocution and pomposity. Writers who use jargon and gobbledegook always suffer from verbosity and — be warned — they are highly infectious. We are all in danger of catching the sickness.

7.8 Cliché

DEFINITION

A cliché is an expression that has been used so often that it has lost its freshness and vigour. Some clichés have become so worn-out that they no longer add meaning. They have degenerated into verbal lumber, not worth the space that they take up.

EXAMPLES

(i) *To all intents and purposes* the government appears to have changed its policies without telling the electors.
(ii) As was only *right and proper*, the insurance company settled the claim *then and there*.
(iii) After so many disappointments, we cannot rationally hope that he will *turn over a new leaf* at his *time of life*.

COMMENTS

In (i) the cliché adds nothing to the meaning of the sentence. Rewrite: 'The government appears to have changed its policies without telling the electors.' What does *to all intents and purposes* say that *appears* does not?

In (ii) the cliché *right and proper* is not a tautology, though it sounds like one (*right* = 'correct' and *proper* = 'seemly'). But are the two senses needed? In this context the only relevant point is the legal correctness with which the insurance company behaved. The second cliché, *then and there*, means 'at once', 'promptly'. The clichés take up space without doing enough work to justify their presence.

Rewrite (iii): 'After so many disappointments, we cannot rationally hope that he will reform at his age.'

Clichés are usually verbose and they are *always* a sign of a stale mind. Whenever you are about to use a well-worn expression, stop. Then ask yourself, 'Do I need this formula? Can I find another – a more direct – way of putting my meaning in my own words?' Remember George Orwell's advice:

● cut out all prefabricated phrases.

7.9 Colloquialisms

DEFINITION

Expressions and grammatical forms used in familiar speech, but not appropriate in formal writing.

EXAMPLES

(i) 'Come on, Bill! We're going to be late.'
'Can't hurry. Breathless this morning.'
'You smoke too much.'
'I know. Shouldn't smoke at all, the doctor says.'
'Give it up, then.'
(ii) 'As I see it, there's a simple answer.'
'Show me.'

'Cut this para — this one. Begins, "Everyone has an active vocabulary and a passive vocabulary." Save six lines if we lost the last two sentences.'
'Yes, I see — but — hold on. Let's see — better — take it back. Whole para, I mean. Back to — yes that's it. Not happy about cutting it. There's a short page on proof 67 — see? Slot it in there — no damage done if we re-word connectives.'

COMMENTS

The following characteristics of colloquial English, illustrated in those two examples, are inappropriate in formal written English.

1. Free and easy expressions (*hold on*).
2. Contractions (*we're; there's; that's*).
3. Abbreviations (*para*).
4. Verbless sentences (*Breathless this morning*).
5. Omission of subjects, especially pronouns (*Save six lines . . .*).
6. Rapid leaping about from one topic to another (the second speaker's last utterances in (ii)).
7. Reliance on tones and gestures to fill out the meaning of the spoken words ('act out' the dialogue in (ii)).

Naturally, when you are writing dialogue (in a story composition, for example), colloquialisms are appropriate. Nobody will believe in your characters if they talk like a book.

7.10 Slang

DEFINITION

The *Concise Oxford Dictionary* defines slang as: 'words and phrases in common colloquial use, but generally considered in all or some of their senses to be outside of standard English'.

EXAMPLES

(i)   There's this *geezer* standing at the corner.
(ii) I gave him *the old one two*.
(iii) They *hopped it pretty smartish*.

COMMENTS

In Example (i) the slang word *geezer* is preceded by a characteristic construction of present-day slang: *There's this* . . . . In Example (iii), *pretty smartish* is also a slang construction. Such non-standard uses of grammar are often associated with slang vocabulary.

It is not always possible to make a clear distinction between colloquial English and slang. Slang is often, but by no means always, a feature of familiar speech. You would certainly use colloquial English in conversation with your grandmother or an old family friend, but you would probably not use slang; at least, not as frequently as you would use it in conversation with people of your own age.

It is helpful to think of language as being in 'levels of appropriateness'. Taking that view, *man* is the word for formal written English; *chap* for colloquial English; *bloke*, *guy*, *geezer* (or whatever word happens to be 'in') for slang.

Slang is a matter of fashion. Slang expressions originate in the specialised vocabularies of particular occupations, hobbies, social groups. (In this, slang resembles jargon.) These expressions are taken up by other users of English and are the 'in thing' for a time. Then they fall out of use and are forgotten. Today's slang is old-fashioned and unintelligible tomorrow.

It is wrong to use slang expressions in formal written English because: (a) their meaning may not be understood outside the comparatively small circle in which they happen to be used; (b) they go out of date very quickly; and (c) like jargon, they are 'prefabricated phrases', used by writers who are too lazy to find their own ways of expressing their own thoughts.

8 Correct Grammar

Faulty grammar in your written English will cost you marks. This chapter will help you to reach the grammatical standard required by the examiners. (You must also work through the follow-up exercises in Chapter 11.) It sets out the basic grammar that all candidates are expected both to know and to be able to make use of when writing. Then it lists and gives examples of all the common mistakes, supplying the corrections needed to turn them into good English. It is not a complete account of English grammar. Much information that would appear in a full study of the subject is deliberately omitted. It concentrates on the grammatical points that you can put to use to avoid some very common errors.

Candidates are not sufficiently aware that poor grammar is a frequent cause of failure in English examinations. A large vocabulary is important, but a knowledge of words alone is not enough. We may know all the words that we need to express a particular meaning, but unless we use those words grammatically, we cannot get their meaning across. If our handling of grammar is very poor indeed, we can hardly make ourselves understood at all; but *any* misuse of grammar is enough to slow communication down and cause misunderstanding. That is why your examiners require you to show them that you can write grammatical English.

Your ability to handle grammar correctly depends on your understanding of:

- the work that words do in sentences: words as *parts of speech*;
- the changes that must be made to word-forms according to the work that they are doing: *inflexions*;
- the grouping together and positioning of words in sentences: *syntax*.

8.1 Words as Parts of Speech

First, you must remember that:

- a word is a particular part of speech *by reason of the particular work that it does in a sentence*.

It is not useful to look at a word in isolation and say, 'This word is a noun'; but it helps our understanding of grammar to look at a word in a sentence and say, 'This word is doing the work of a noun in this sentence'.

The same word may do different work — and, therefore, function as a different part of speech — in different sentences. For example:

1. A child's *top* lay on the floor. (noun)
2. We shall easily *top* last year's results. (verb)
3. He seems to be their *top* man. (adjective)

There are *eight* parts of speech: nouns, pronouns, adjectives, verbs, adverbs, prepositions, conjunctions, interjections.

A **noun** is a word used in a sentence to name someone or something. For example: '*Jane* was sitting in that *chair*.' 'They all showed great *loyalty* to their *team*.'

A *common* noun names a member of or an item in a whole class of people or things. For example: 'It was a huge *book* of six hundred *pages*.' A common noun is the name *common to* all the members of or all the items in the class.

A *proper* noun names a particular person, place or thing. For example: '*Jean* is the best swimmer in *London*.' The name 'Jean' is *proper to* (belongs to) Jean. It distinguishes her from the others. The name 'London' is proper to one particular place. It distinguishes it from the others. Proper nouns begin with a capital letter.

An *abstract* noun names a quality or a state of mind or feeling. For example: 'Marks will be awarded for *accuracy* and *neatness*.' Abstract nouns name non-physical things: concepts that exist only in the mind: loyalty, honour, jealousy, anger, welfare.

A *collective* noun names a group or collection of people or things: *crew*, *team*, *library*, *flock* are words that are often used as collective nouns.

A **pronoun** is a word used in a sentence to stand for (or in place of) a noun. For example: 'The plate was so hot that *it* burnt the table.'

A *personal* pronoun stands for (or in place of) a person or thing. For example: 'Pass the ticket on to Robert if *you* don't want *it*.'

A *demonstrative* pronoun points to or at a person or a thing. For example: 'I like *these* but they would not be as useful as *those*.'

A *relative* pronoun relates to (refers to) a noun or pronoun used earlier in the sentence. That noun or pronoun is called its 'antecedent'. For example: 'My purse was in the bag *that* I left on the counter.' (The antecedent of *that* is 'bag'.)

An *interrogative* pronoun is used in some questions. For example: '*What* were you going to say?'

A pronoun of *number* or *quantity* indicates how many or how much. For example: 'Customers are restricted to *three* because we have *few* left.'

An **adjective** is a word used in a sentence to describe ('qualify') the person or thing named by a noun or a pronoun. For example: 'The *little* boy was used to crossing *busy* streets.'

A *descriptive* adjective qualifies a noun or a pronoun by describing its qualities. For example: 'Shall I wear my *green* dress?' A descriptive adjective may be separated from the noun or pronoun that it qualifies. For example: 'I think her dress was *green*.'

A *possessive* adjective indicates possession or ownership. For example: 'Was *her* dress green?'

A *demonstrative* adjective points to or at the noun or pronoun that it qualifies. For example: '*That* dress was hardly suitable for *this* occasion.'

A *relative* adjective introduces a subordinate (or dependent) clause (see Section 8.4) and links it to another clause. For example: 'We let them have *what* money we could spare.'

An *interrogative* adjective is used in some questions. For example: '*What* train did you catch?'

An adjective of *number* or *quantity* indicates how many or how much. For example: '*Few* customers showed *any* interest and we sold only *ten* books that day.'

(*Note:* Do not confuse adjectives with pronouns. An adjective is always used to qualify a noun or a pronoun. A pronoun always stands in place of a noun. For example: '*My* car [possessive adjective] is for sale and I want to put in a bid for *yours* [possessive pronoun].' 'Is *this* hat [demonstrative adjective] the right size?'

'No, but I think *that* [demonstrative pronoun] is.')

A **verb** is a word used in a sentence to indicate action or being. For example: 'We *ran* for the train but we *were* too late.'

Person and *number*. There are three persons and two numbers. For example:

	Singular	*Plural*
1st person	I laugh	we laugh
2nd person	you laugh	you laugh
3rd person	he/she/it laughs	they laugh

Tense. The time in which the action takes place or the state of being exists: present, past or future. For example: 'I ride' (present); 'I rode' (past); 'I shall ride' (future).

Voice. There are two voices: active and passive. For example:

Active	*Passive*
The mechanic repaired the car.	The car was repaired by the mechanic.
The expert is studying the evidence.	The evidence is being studied by the expert.

Transitive and *intransitive*. A verb is used transitively when it has an object. It is used intransitively when it does not have an object. For example:

Transitive	*Intransitive*
She sang an aria.	She sang.
The government is negotiating a new treaty.	The government is negotiating.
They fought a good fight.	They fought hard.

When a verb is used transitively, the action is carried across (*trans-*) from the subject of the verb to the object of the verb. Many verbs can be used both transitively and intransitively.

Finite and *non-finite* verbs. A finite verb has a subject. Because it has a subject, it is 'limited' (made *finite*) by having person, number and tense. A non-finite verb does not have a subject; therefore, it does not have person, number or tense. The non-finite forms of the verb are: the infinitive, the present participle, the past participle and the gerund.

The infinitive. The verb-form containing the word 'to'. For example: to walk; to read; to sing.

The present participle. The verb-form ending with *-ing* and functioning as an adjective. For example: 'This is a *teasing* problem.' The present participle is also used with the verb 'to be' to form the continuous ('imperfect') tenses of verbs. For example: 'We *were waiting* for the bus.'

The past participle. Like the present participle, it functions as an adjective, but it does not end with *-ing*. It takes many different forms. For example: 'A *beaten* and unhappy team flew home.' '*Bought* bread does not taste like home-*baked* loaves.' 'The election resulted in a *hung* parliament.' The past participle is also used to combine with auxiliary (helping) verbs to form the perfect (completed) tenses and the passive voice of verbs. For example: 'Those greedy children *have finished* the cake.' 'Their offices *were raided* last week.'

The gerund. Like the present participle, it is a verb-form ending with *-ing* but, whereas the present participle functions as an adjective, the gerund functions as a noun. For example:

The *dripping* tap kept us awake. (*dripping* is a present participle, functioning as an adjective qualifying the noun 'tap')

The steady *dripping* kept us awake. (*dripping* is a gerund, functioning as the noun subject of the verb 'kept')

Mood. The infinitive has already been noted. For example: '*To be asked* for my ticket again annoyed me.' The indicative is the 'mood' in which statements are made or questions are asked. For example: 'He *was* quite angry, *wasn't* he?' The imperative is the 'mood' in which orders are given or requests are made. For example: '*Go* away!' The subjunctive has few uses in modern English and, in any case, since most verbs have the same form for both the subjunctive and the indicative, the question of its use hardly arises. However, it is still correct to use the subjunctive mood of the verb 'to be' when expressing a wish or stating a condition that is very unlikely to be fulfilled. For example: 'If I *were* a millionaire, I would endow a research centre for peace studies.' 'She would still be champion if she *were* a few years younger.'

An **adverb** is a word used in a sentence to add to the meaning of ('modify') a verb, an adverb, or an adjective. For example: 'We did the journey *quickly*.' 'We travelled *quite* comfortably.' 'It was not a *very* crowded train.'

(*Note*: Adverbs often, but by no means always, end with *-ly*. You cannot safely identify a part of speech by its form. Its *function in the sentence* is the decisive factor.)

Simple adverbs may be classified as follows:

(a) Adverb of *time*. For example: 'They always arrive *late*.' (arrive *when*? – late)

(b) Adverb of *place*. For example: 'Stop *there*.' (stop *where*? – there)

(c) Adverb of *manner*. For example: 'He works *well*.' (works *how*? – well)

(d) Adverb of *quantity*, *extent or degree*. For example: 'I have eaten *enough*.' (eaten *how much*? – enough)

(e) Adverb of *number*. For example: 'We wrote *twice*.' (wrote *how often*? – twice)

Interrogative adverbs are used to ask questions. For example: '*When* are you going?' '*Why* are you leaving?'

Relative adverbs connect two clauses (see Section 8.4). They *relate* the clause that they introduce to a word in another clause which they modify. For example: 'May is the month *when* Paris looks its best.' (The relative adverb *when* joins the two clauses and it relates its own clause to and modifies the verb 'is'.)

A **preposition** is a 'relating' word. It introduces a phrase (see Section 8.3) that contains a noun or a pronoun. It relates that noun or pronoun to a word elsewhere in the sentence. For example: 'I backed the car *into* the garage.' (The preposition *into* relates the noun 'garage' to the verb 'backed'.) 'We chose the house *at* the end.' (The preposition *at* relates the noun 'end' to the noun 'house'.) Note that the preposition introduces a phrase: 'into the garage' functions as an adverb; 'at the end' functions as an adjective. The word *preposition* means 'placed before'. A preposition is always placed before a noun or a pronoun in the phrase that it introduces and it relates that noun or pronoun to another word. For example: 'There was a present *for* me.'

(*Note*: Many words can be used either as prepositions or as adverbs. For example: 'Leave the parcel *inside* the porch.' (The preposition *inside* relates the noun 'porch' to the verb 'leave'.) 'Leave the parcel *inside*.' (The adverb *inside* modifies the verb 'leave'.))

A **conjunction** is a joining word. It joins two separate items in a sentence. It may be used to join one word to another. For example: 'Toast *and* marmalade, please.' It may be used to join one phrase to another. For example: 'It is a bad journey by rail *or* by road.' It may be used to join one clause to another. For example: 'The old man left a lot of money *but* his son soon spent it.'

Co-ordinating conjunctions connect items that do the same work in the sentence. They are 'of equal standing'. In the three examples just given, the items are linked by a co-ordinating conjunction.

Subordinating conjunctions connect subordinate clauses to main clauses (see Section 8.4). For example: 'He went on working *although* he was tired.' 'The government lost support *because* it ran out of energy.'

An **interjection** is a word or a group of words 'thrown in' to a sentence to express a feeling (of surprise, boredom, tiredness, etc.). It has no grammatical connection with or function in the rest of the sentence. For example: '*Oh dear*, he is going to be late again.' '*Hello*! who's that?'

8.2 Inflexions

The grammar of some languages requires many changes of word-forms. For example, in German – a 'highly inflected' language – adjectives change their word-forms according to the person, gender, number and case of the nouns that they qualify. In this respect, English is an uncomplicated language. Adjectives do not change their forms. ('A *red* dress was hanging in the cupboard.' 'She always wore *red* dresses.')

Nevertheless, correct grammar demands some changes in word-forms, the chief of which occur in the use of:

1. *Personal pronouns*. For example: Kate and *I* were invited. They invited Kate and *me*.
2. *Verb-forms*. For example: The cause of many grammatical errors *is* [*not* 'are'] carelessly used inflexions.
3. Plural noun-forms. For example: *baby/babies*, but *donkey/donkeys*.
4. *Comparative and superlative word-forms*. For example: *sad/sadder/saddest*; *little/less/least*; *favourable/more favourable/most favourable*.

As you will see in Section 8.5, inflectional errors crop up time and time again.

8.3 Phrases and Sentences

Written English makes clear sense only when words are grouped together and positioned in sentences in grammatically correct ways. The rules that govern the arrangement of words in sentences are the rules of syntax. (*Syntax* = 'marshalling'; 'setting out in order'.)

(a) Phrases

- **A phrase** is a group of words that does not make *complete* sense.

1. in that photograph
2. sitting at the back
3. scorched by the sun

Each of those word groups makes some sense, but not complete sense. They are unfinished utterances.

(b) Sentences

- A **sentence** is a group of words that makes complete sense. It can stand on its own without the addition of other words. It is an *independent*, self-contained, finished utterance.

1. She smiled.
2. People could not hear.
3. The plants wilted.

Each of those word-groups makes an independent self-contained, *finished* utterance. It does not need additional words to make sense, although its meaning can be *expanded* by the addition of a phrase.

1. She smiled in that photograph.
2. People sitting at the back could not hear.
3. Scorched by the sun, the plants wilted.

(c) Subject and Predicate

A sentence makes complete sense because it contains two parts: a subject and a predicate.

- The **subject** of a sentence is the part that names (identifies or announces) the person, idea or thing about which the sentence is saying something.
- The **predicate** of a sentence is the part that says something about the subject.

Subject	*Predicate*
1. She	smiled.
2. People	could not hear.
3. The plants	wilted.

Every sentence must contain both of those parts. Take either away and it ceases to be a sentence, because it is no longer able to make an independent, self-contained, *finished* utterance.

(d) How Phrases Work

A phrase does the work of: an adjective *or* an adverb *or* a noun (see Section 8.1).

1. That chair *by the fireplace* is his. (The adjective-phrase qualifies the noun 'chair'.)
2. They have gone *on holiday*. (The adverb-phrase modifies the verb 'have gone'.)
3. He hoped *to win*. (The noun-phrase is the object of the verb 'hoped'. It answers the question *what*? They hoped *what*? – to win.)

Many of the common errors in written English are caused by incorrect positioning of phrases. If you are clear about the work that a particular phase is doing, you will position it correctly.

(e) Phrase Structures

Phrases are classified according to the work they do (adjective-phrase; adverb-phrase; noun-phrase) *and* according to their structures.

1. A *prepositional* phrase begins with a preposition.

EXAMPLES

(a) The crowd pressed *against the barriers*. (The prepositional phrase functions as an adverb modifying the verb 'pressed'.)
(b) A man *with a gun* was arrested. (The prepositional phrase functions as an adjective qualifying the noun 'man'.)

2. A *participial* phrase begins with a present participle or with a past participle.

EXAMPLES

(a) *Living in the country*, we were not used to crowds. (The participial phrase functions as an adjective qualifying the pronoun 'we'.)
(b) *Bought at a sale*, the car was a bargain. (The participial phrase functions as an adjective qualifying the noun 'car'.)

3. A *gerundive* phrase begins with a gerund.

EXAMPLES

(a) *Practising daily* perfected his skill. (The gerundive phrase functions as a noun. It is the subject of the verb 'perfected'.)
(b) She started *having nightmares*. (The gerundive phrase functions as a noun. It is the object of the verb 'started'.)

(*Note:* The gerund and the present participle both end with *-ing*, but they have different grammatical functions – and so do the phrases that they introduce. In the sentence 'Practising daily perfected his skill' the gerundive phrase functions as a noun. In the sentence 'Practising daily, he perfected his skill' *practising daily* functions as an adjective qualifying the pronoun 'he'. A gerundive phrase always functions as a noun. A participial phrase always functions as an adjective. This is far from being a mere quibble. Failure to recognise those two different functions is the cause of a great many errors in sentence construction.)

4. An *infinitive* phrase begins with an infinitive.

(a) *To sit and mope* is no answer to the problem. (The infinitive phrase functions as a noun. It is the subject of the verb 'is'.)

(b) They were ready *to go out*. (The infinitive phrase functions as an adverb modifying the adjective 'ready'.)

Accurate and fluent written English depends on correct structuring of phrases and their correct positioning in sentences.

8.4 Kinds of Sentences

(a) The Simple Sentence

In the subject of a sentence the most important word is the subject-word. In the predicate of a sentence the most important word is the verb. Provided that those two words are present, you have a sentence.

EXAMPLES

1. Stunned by explosions, fish rise to the surface of a river.
2. Having spent too long on comprehension, candidates often hurry their summaries, with disastrous consequences.

Subject	*Predicate*
1 Stunned by explosions, fish	rise to the surface of a river.
2 Having spent too long on comprehension, candidates	often hurry their summaries, with disastrous consequences.

Subject-word	*Verb*
1 fish	rise
2 candidates	hurry

Each of the original sentences can be stripped down to its two essential components (the verb and its subject-word) and *remain a sentence*: 'Fish swim.'/ 'Candidates hurry.'

The term *simple* does not refer to the length of the sentence or to its intellectual content. It is a grammatical term, referring solely to the structure of the sentence: a structure that is built on *one* finite verb.

The simple sentence is the bedrock construction on which the writing of good English rests. All the other kinds of sentences are based on the simple sentence. They extend its framework, but they do not alter its fundamental structure.

The simple sentence provides the backbone of written English and, as you will see in Section 8.5, many of the common errors arise because that backbone is broken; as happens when, for example, a writer splits a participial adjective-phrase away from the noun to which it refers, or separates a subject-word so far from its verb that he forgets to make them 'agree'.

(b) Clauses and Sentences

Many sentences contain *more than one* finite verb.

1. He *started* the car and *drove* down the street.
2. She *opened* her bag and *looked* in her purse, but it *was* empty.

There are two finite verbs in Example 1 and three finite verbs in Example 2. Put the same fact in different words: there are two *clauses* in Example 1 and three *clauses* in Example 2.

- A **clause** is a group of words containing a finite verb and forming *part of* a sentence.

(c) Main (or Independent) Clauses

Each of the clauses in Examples 1 and 2, above, can stand on its own and make complete sense without the help of the others.

1. He started the car./He drove down the street.
2. She opened her bag./She looked in her purse./It was empty.

Clauses of that kind are called *main* (or *independent*) clauses.

- A **main clause** makes a self-contained, *finished* utterance. It can stand alone without needing help from another clause.

(d) Subordinate (or Dependent) Clauses

Some clauses need help from other clauses to make complete sense. They cannot stand alone.

1. They rewarded the boy *who found the wallet*.
2. *When I feel tired*, I relax in the garden.
3. They were certain *that he would be elected*.

On their own, the italicised clauses cannot make complete sense. Clauses of that kind are subordinate (or dependent) clauses.

- A **subordinate clause** does not make a self-contained, finished utterance. It cannot stand alone. It needs help from the main clause.

Such a clause is *subordinate* because it is 'lower in rank' than a main clause. It is *dependent* because its meaning depends on a main clause.

Subordinate clauses function as: adjective-equivalents (Example 1, above); adverb-equivalents (Example 2, above); noun-equivalents (Example 3, above).

(e) Sentences: Simple; Complex; Double; Multiple

Classified by grammatical structure, there are four kinds of sentences. Here is a check-list.

Sentence class	Grammatical structure
1. Simple	*one* finite verb
2. Complex	*one* main clause AND *one* or *more* subordinate clauses
3. Double	*two* main clauses WITH or WITHOUT subordinate clauses
4. Multiple	more than two main clauses WITH or WITHOUT subordinate clauses

EXAMPLES

1. *Simple sentence (one finite verb)*   Finding their hotel comfortable and welcoming, the travellers decided to rest in Melbourne for a few more days before continuing their long journey.
2. *Complex sentence (one main clause with, in this example, two subordinate clauses)*   Because their hotel was comfortable and welcoming, the travellers decided that they would rest in Melbourne for a few more days before continuing their long journey.
3. *Double sentence (two main clauses without, in this example, subordinate clauses)*   Their hotel was comfortable and welcoming and the travellers decided to rest in Melbourne for a few more days before continuing their long journey.
4. *Double sentence (two main clauses with, in this example, one subordinate clause)*   Their hotel was comfortable and welcoming and the travellers, who had a long journey ahead, decided to rest in Melbourne for a few more days.
5. *Multiple sentence (in this example, three main clauses and no subordinate clauses)*   Their hotel was comfortable and welcoming and the travellers decided to rest in Melbourne for a few more days, but their long journey lay ahead.
6. *Multiple sentence (in this example, three main clauses with two subordinate clauses)*   Their hotel was comfortable and welcoming and the travellers decided to rest in Melbourne for a few more days but they knew that their journey, which was a long one, lay ahead.

The content of all six sentences is the same, but the simple sentence expresses it more directly and plainly than any of the others. Its greater effectiveness does not come solely from its verbal economy. It is, in fact, only one word shorter than the next most economical sentence (3), though nine words shorter than the wordiest (6). It is the best sentence because it is the most *sinewy*, all its parts held firmly together and in place. Even its nearest 'rival' (3) is looser ('. . . and . . . and . . .'). The rest are sprawling in comparison.

This is not to argue that a simple sentence is always the best. For some purposes and on some occasions, one of the other structures will be more suitable. What the comparison does prove is that good written English depends very greatly on the care and skill with which sentence structures are selected and handled.

8.5 Common Errors

(a) Errors in 'Agreement'

The verb must 'agree with' its subject in number and in person. This is the rule of *subject/verb concord*.

(i) *Faults Caused by 'Attraction'*

When the subject-word (noun or pronoun) is separated from its verb by nouns or pronouns of a different number, the verb may be 'attracted' to agree with a noun or a pronoun that is not its subject-word.

EXAMPLES

Wrong	*Right*
1. A crate of empty bottles were left at the back door.	A crate of empty bottles *was* left at the back door.
2. Recent technological developments of that long-known material, glass, has influenced industrial design.	Recent technological developments of that long-known material, glass, *have* influenced industrial design.
3. A new computerised system controlling the stock and despatch of thousands of spare parts were installed at the factory.	A new computerised system controlling the stock and despatch of thousands of spare parts *was* installed at the factory.

(ii) *Collective Noun Subjects and Their Verbs*

Treat a collective noun as a singular subject when the group or collection is thought of as a *whole* — as *one*. Treat it as a plural when the sense stresses that it comprises *separate members or items* and that they are being thought of as *individuals*.

Wrong	*Right*
1. The government have lost support.	The government *has* lost support.
2. My family have lived in this house for a hundred years.	My family *has* lived in this house for a hundred years.
3. The crew was inoculated against various tropical diseases.	The crew *were* inoculated against various tropical diseases.

This particular subject/verb problem spills over to pronouns and possessive adjectives referring to the collective noun subject. They must be made to agree with it. Be consistent and stick to the number you first settled on. A haphazard mixture of singulars and plurals is confusing.

Wrong	*Right*
1. The government is being harried by their opponents.	The government is being harried by *its* opponents.
2. The BBC has announced that	The BBC has announced that *it* will

they will not increase the fees that it has offered for racing coverage.	not increase the fees that *it* has offered for racing coverage.
3. After a poor season, the Midlands club informs our sports editor that their new manager has its full confidence.	After a poor season, the Midlands club informs our sports editor that *its* new manager has *its* full confidence.

(iii) *Relative Pronoun Subjects*

A relative pronoun is the subject of the verb in the subordinate clause that it introduces. The relative pronoun must agree with its antecedent, and the verb in the subordinate clause must agree with the relative pronoun.

Wrong	*Right*
1. This is one of the best books that has been published by this enterprising firm.	This is one of the best books [*plural antecedent of 'that'*] that *have* been published by this enterprising firm.
2. She is among those talented minor stars who has received consistently poor publicity.	She is among those talented minor stars [*plural antecedent of 'who'*] who *have* received consistently poor publicity.
3. Scholarship is still indebted to research into the derivations and meanings of English placenames that were pioneered by Sir Frank Stenton.	Scholarship is still indebted to research [*singular antecedent of 'that'*] into the derivations and meanings of English placenames that *was* pioneered by Sir Frank Stenton.

(iv) *Other Troublesome Pronoun Subjects*

Difficulties arise with these pronouns: *anybody, anyone, each, either, everybody, everyone, neither, none*. Generally, they are treated as singulars.

Wrong	*Right*
1. Anybody hoping to win a fortune on the pools are almost certain to be disappointed.	Anybody hoping to win a fortune on the pools *is* almost certain to be disappointed.
2. Neither of those proposals seem practical.	Neither of those proposals *seems* practical.
3. We do not impose decisions on our members, each of whom have a personal contract.	We do not impose decisions on our members, each of whom *has* a personal contract.

However, there are times when *none* is used in a plural sense to mean 'not any' rather than the clearly singular sense of 'not one'. The verb should then be plural. Most writers would prefer the latter of these versions: 'Although the box of eggs hit the floor from a considerable height, none was broken.'/'Although the box of eggs hit the floor from a considerable height, none were broken.'

The problem of the 'follow-up' pronouns and possessive adjectives is more acute. According to the rule, this sentence is correct; but is it sensible? 'When the victorious team arrived at the station, everybody rushed forward, shouting his head off in the excitement of the moment.' Surely 'shouting *their heads* off' would make better sense?

Again, the absence of 'common gender' personal pronouns and possessive adjectives makes for clumsiness and/or inaccuracy. The sentence 'Each UK citizen must show *his* passport at the barrier' is grammatically correct, but carries the nonsensical implication that all UK citizens are males! The 'official explanation' that, in such uses, 'he' means 'he or she' is pretty thin. Often *he and/or she* (*his and/or her*) will get us out of the difficulty, but repetition of the formula is clumsy. Often, plurals can perfectly well be substituted for singulars. Instead of 'Everyone wanting to pay by cheque must provide evidence of his identity', we can write 'People wanting . . . of their identity.' Here, as always, hard and clear thinking is needed.

(v) *'Either . . . or'/'neither . . . nor' Subjects*

The construction involves two separate subjects and one verb. When both subjects are of the same person and number there is no difficulty. 'Either Joan or Freda *is* certain to call.' 'Neither the children nor their grandparents *want* to go out.' When the two subjects are of different persons and/or number, the verb must agree with the *nearer* subject. 'Neither the pupils nor their teacher *welcomes* Monday morning.' 'Either one of my assistants or, in an emergency, I *am* available after closing hours.'

(vi) *Parenthesis in Subjects*

The punctuation of what appears to be a double (and, therefore, a plural) subject may throw all the stress onto the first part of the subject. The verb then agrees with it. 'Truth-telling, and all its attendant inconveniences, seldom *attracts* a politician.' 'The new weapon, with its technicians, *was* flown out in great secrecy.' The punctuation is all-important. Remove the parenthetical commas and the subject is clearly plural.

(vii) *Appositional Words in Subjects*

Words in apposition to the subject-word must not be allowed to break subject/verb concord.

Wrong	*Right*
1. The treasure-trove, coins, medals, precious stones, were sold.	The treasure-trove, coins, medals, precious stones, *was* sold.
2. Two wretched companies, the ill-fed and despairing residue of the rebel army, was captured.	Two wretched companies, the ill-fed and despairing residue of the rebel army, *were* captured.

(viii) *'It' as a 'Provisional' Subject*

Always singular, however 'attractive' the plurals that it may introduce. 'There seems little doubt that it *was* those blocked culverts that caused the flooding.'

(ix) *'Here' and 'there'*

Used as introductory adverbs, they are often mistaken for the subject of the verb.

Wrong	*Right*
1. Here, in remarkably good condition, is the chancel, the altar and the east window of this great ruin.	Here, in remarkably good condition, *are* the chancel, the altar and the east window of this great ruin.
2. After the quiet introduction, there follows energetic and near-dissonant passages of great power.	After the quiet introduction there *follow* energetic and near-dissonant passages of great power.

(b) Wrong Case

(i) *Nominative, Accusative, Genitive Cases*

1. *Nominative* case: the case of the subject-word.
2. *Accusative* (or *objective* case): the case of the object-word *and* of the noun or pronoun following ('governed by') a preposition.
3. *Genitive* case: the case of a 'possessing' word.

(ii) *Case in Nouns*

The genitive case is signalled by an apostrophe. (The rules are given in Chapter 9.) English nouns do not have special word-forms for the other cases. The commonest trouble spots in the use of genitive nouns are pinpointed and corrected in these examples.

Wrong	*Right*
1. The tomatoe's on that stall are too dear.	The *tomatoes* on that stall are too dear.
2. That boys' handwriting is illegible.	That *boy's* handwriting is illegible.
3. Victorian girl's clothes look very odd to us.	Victorian *girls'* clothes look very odd to us.
4. He was knocked out in the third round of the mens' competition.	He was knocked out in the third round of the *men's* competition.
5. Several of Dicken's novels have been filmed.	Several of *Dickens'* (or *Dickens's*) novels have been filmed.

(iii) *Personal Pronouns*

Nominative and accusative case forms are often misused.

Wrong	*Right*
1. They are making an exception of you and I.	They are making an exception of you and *me*.
2. It is a good crop in warm areas, but not practicable for we who garden in the north.	It is a good crop in warm areas, but not practicable for *us* who garden in the north.
3. This group – it includes Jane, Rosie and I – moves off after they.	This group – it includes Jane, Rosie and *me* – moves off after *them*.

(iv)   *Relative Pronouns: 'Who' (Nominative) and 'Whom' (Accusative)*

Wrong	*Right*
1. We have appointed a principal whom we think will give leadership.	We have appointed a principal *who* we think will give leadership.
2. We have appointed a principal who we think the staff will support.	We have appointed a principal *whom* we think the staff will support.
3. We have appointed a principal to who we think the staff will respond.	We have appointed a principal to *whom* we think the staff will respond.

(v)   **Personal Pronouns in Comparisons**

Note the difference between: (a) 'That firm is offering you a bigger salary than I.'/ (b) 'That firm is offering you a bigger salary than me.' The meaning of (a) is: 'That firm is offering you a bigger salary than I am offering you.' The meaning of (b) is: 'That firm is offering you a bigger salary than it is offering me.'

(vi)   **The Genitive Case of Personal Pronouns**

Never use an apostrophe to mark the genitive of personal pronouns. The correct word-forms are: *mine, yours, his, hers, its, ours, yours, theirs.*
(*Note:* it's is the contracted form of 'it is'.)

(c) Wrong verb-forms

(i)   **The Verbs 'to lay' and 'to lie'**

The verb 'to lay' must be used transitively. The verb 'to lie' must be used intransitively.

Wrong	*Right*
1. I was laying down when the door bell rang.	I was *lying* down when the door bell rang.
2. Lie the material on a flat surface.	*Lay* the material on a flat surface.
3. They have lain six courses of bricks.	They have *laid* six courses of bricks.

(ii)   **The Verbs 'to raise' and 'to rise'**

The verb 'to raise' must be used transitively. The verb 'to rise' must be used intransitively.

Wrong	*Right*
1. Rise the girder another foot.	*Raise* the girder another foot.
2. As the sun was raising, we rose the flag.	As the sun was *rising*, we *raised* the flag.

If you want an increase of pay, ask for a *rise* not a *raise*, or you may find yourself being hoisted off the floor!

(iii) *'May' and 'Can'*

They are 'defective verbs', so called because they lack the full range of tenses and forms. (For example, there is not an infinitive 'to may', nor is there a future simple tense, 'I shall can'!) The other defective verbs are: *must, ought, shall, will.*

May and *can* have different meanings. Correct usage is illustrated by these examples:

1. *May* I go out?
2. You *may*, if you *can* afford the time.
3. He *can* play a good game but his form is erratic.
4. He *may* play a good game but he must be calm.
5. The Act says that we *may* not import livestock without a licence.

(d) Phrases in the Wrong Places

This is a very common fault and one of the most serious that a writer can commit. Remember that a phrase does the work of an adjective *or* an adverb *or* a noun. (See Sections 8.3(d) and 8.3(e).) A phrase cannot do its proper work unless it is put in its right place in a sentence.

Wrong	*Right*
1. Old books are always in demand by collectors with coloured plates.	Old books with coloured plates are always in demand by collectors.
2. Rabbit wanted for a little boy with floppy ears.	Rabbit with floppy ears wanted for a little boy.
3. I remembered that I had not switched off the electric fire while running for the bus.	While running for the bus, I remembered that I had not switched off the electric fire.
4. Arriving at the ground late, the seats we wanted had been sold we found.	Arriving at the ground late, we found that the seats we wanted had been sold.
5. Alarmed by falling sales, millions were spent on advertising by the brewers.	Alarmed by falling sales, the brewers spent millions on advertising.

(e) Pronouns Used with Vague or Wrong Reference

A pronoun must always be seen to refer clearly and accurately to the noun (or noun-phrase) that is its antecedent. Woolly use of pronouns — particularly *this*, *that*, *these*, *those* and *it* — is a frequent cause of poor communication in writing.

For example: The team's record had not been inspiring despite a splendid month in mid-season. *This* was a cause for concern, but *it* should be remedied shortly, our reporter was told. *This* accounted for falling gates, but the setback was temporary and *it* was improving. Supporters, the club said, should bear *this* in mind when reading the results and forming an opinion. *These* would improve drastically if *it* was given time.

(f) **Sudden Shifts of Voice, Tense and Person**

Wrong	*Right*
1. Once the plumber had found the leak it was able to be repaired quickly by him.	Once the plumber had found the leak *he was able to repair it* quickly.
2. The examiners referred to poor handwriting, reporting that you had difficulty in reading many scripts.	The examiners referred to poor handwriting, reporting that *they* had difficulty in reading many scripts.
3. Unfortunately, many people were bored by the sermon and lose interest in the message.	Unfortunately, many people were bored by the sermon and *lost* interest in the message.

9 Punctuation

Correct punctuation plays a crucial part in the writing of clear English. The various marks are used to indicate:

1. **stop or pause** (full stop, question mark, exclamation mark, comma, semi-colon, dash);
2. **possession and omission** (apostrophe, ellipsis marks);
3. **direct speech or quotation** (inverted commas or quotation marks);
4. **apposition, bracketing, parenthesis** (pairs of commas, pairs of dashes, round brackets, square brackets);
5. **joining up** (hyphen).

9.1 Full Stop .

The full stop is used:
(a) *To mark the end of a statement sentence*
   This is its most important function. It is the sign that a self-contained utterance has been completed. It marks a finished, independent statement off from the one that follows. Every statement sentence must begin with a capital letter and end with a full stop. The full stop is also known as 'the period' because it 'puts a period to' a sentence (brings it to an end).
(b) *To mark an abbreviation*
   Oct. = October. Note the difference between an abbreviation (*Nov.* = November) and a contraction (*Dr* = D(octo)r). Most writers use a full stop to mark an abbreviation but not to mark a contraction. Many well-known and commonly used abbreviations (such as BBC) are not punctuated. Acronyms (NATO, UNESCO) are never punctuated.
(c) *To mark an omission (three full stops)*
   The three full stops marking an omission are called 'ellipsis marks'. When they occur at the end of a sentence, they are followed by a full stop. Study these examples:

   Read the sentence 'Good written English . . . clearly punctuated' and express its full meaning in your own words.

   Express the full meaning in your own words of the sentence beginning 'Good written English . . .'.

9.2 Question Mark ?

The question mark is used to *mark the end of a question sentence*. Do not use a full stop as well.

   Have you heard the news?

Do not use a question mark at the end of an indirect question.

I asked whether you had heard the news.

9.3 Exclamation Mark !

The exclamation mark is used to *mark the end of an exclamation, interjection or sharp command*. Do not use a full stop as well.

He's dropped it!
Oh dear! I shall be late.
Hand it over!

Use an exclamation mark only when strictly necessary. Do not try to add emphasis or to draw attention to the point that you are making by using this overworked punctuation mark.

9.4 Comma ,

The comma is used:
    (a) *To separate words used in a series or list*
        She bought tea, jam, milk and flour.
    (b) *To separate phrases used in a series*
        She walked quickly down the street, round the corner and into the main road.
    (c) *To separate clauses used in a series*
        She found the bus stop, waited a few minutes, got on the first bus and took an upstairs seat.

As a rule, when the last item in a series is joined on by *and* a comma is not used before the conjunction. (Conjunctions *join*, but commas *separate*.) However, the sense may sometimes require a final comma.

She bought tea, jam, milk, bread, and butter.

Do not put a comma after the last word in a list: always one comma fewer than the number of items.

Nuts, ginger, cloves are the ingredients. (3 items, 2 commas)

    (d) *In pairs, to mark off words in parenthesis*
        Some candidates, it was clear, had mis-read the question.
        He is upset, I know, but he will get over it.
    (e) *In pairs, to mark off words in apposition*
        Jones, the man responsible, is to be relied on.
        They sent their senior representative, the district inspector, the next day.
    (f) *To mark off the beginning of direct speech or quotation*
        The witness replied, 'I have no knowledge of that.'
        Look at the line beginning, 'Now the setting sun . . .'.

Remember that the presence or absence of a comma (or of a pair of commas) can change (or even destroy) the meaning of a sentence. For example, these two sentences are worded identically, but their meanings are different:

(i) The language questions, which are compulsory, must be answered on the special sheet provided. (*All* the language questions are compulsory.)

(ii) The language questions which are compulsory must be answered on the special sheet provided. (*Some* of the language questions are compulsory.)

Which of the two sentences is correctly punctuated depends on what the writer meant to say.

The use of a comma to separate main clauses is often a matter of choice. I chose to use a comma to separate the two main clauses in this sentence because I wanted to bring out a contrast:

These two sentences are worded identically, but their meanings are different.

It would not have been wrong to omit the comma after 'identically'.

Generally, a comma is not needed between two main clauses having the same subject.

They were nearly home when they ran out of fuel.

However, there will be occasions when a pause (marked by a comma) will add something to the sense or make it clearer.

They were nearly home and they were confident of winning, when they ran out of fuel.

Most writers would argue for the comma in that sentence.

9.5 Semi-colon ;

The semi-colon is used:

(a) *To separate items in a list when the items themselves contain commas*

Accessories for this model include: supplementary lenses, ranging from 28 mm to 400 mm; dedicated electronic flash; filters, both for colour and black-and-white film; an aluminium-framed hold-all.

(b) *To separate clauses the sense of which would be weakened if they were split off into a new sentence.*

When we started, we hoped to complete the cataloguing in six months; but, after a year, we had not made much progress.

Baffled by the absence of clues, the investigators were looking for a new lead; they suspected that one might have been overlooked in the initial confusion.

9.6 Colon :

The colon is used:

(a) *To introduce a list*

The following items will be sold on Tuesday: livestock, hay, implements, gates and fencing.

(b) *To introduce quotation or lengthy items of direct speech*

Keats wrote: 'A thing of beauty is a joy for ever'; and critics have been arguing about its meaning ever since.

The precise words in the agreement are: 'We shall waive our customary practice in your case and free you from the obligation to maintain the paths.'

(c) *To mark a dramatic break between two main clauses*

Man proposes: God disposes.

They cannot win: we cannot lose.

We do not know: we have faith.

(d) *To introduce a clause that explains or expands on a statement made in an earlier clause*

The seedlings are in a bad way: there has been no rain for a month.

I received a rebate from the Inland Revenue: a great surprise.

9.7 Apostrophe '

The apostrophe is used:

(a) *To mark the genitive case of a noun*

(i) Singular noun: add 's

book The book's pages were defaced.

(ii) Plural noun ending with *s*: add '

books The books' previous owner was at the sale.

fairies The fairies' wings came off in the amateur pantomime.

Remember: It is the number of the genitive (possessing) noun that matters, not the number of the possessed noun. Compare: 'Those are my boy's books.'/'He played for the boys' under-11 team.'

(iii) Plural noun not ending with *s*: add 's

men Use the men's entrance.

mice There are mice's nests in the attic.

(iv) Proper noun ending with *s*: add ' *or* 's

Marks Marks' (or Marks's) bowling has improved.

Dickens Which of Dickens' (or Dickens's) novels have you read?

Generally, add 's; but you may think that 'Ulysses' bow' *sounds* better than 'Ulysses's bow'. Either word-form is correct.

(v) When two (or more) proper nouns share the ownership, mark the one nearer (or nearest) to the 'possessed' noun.

Pete and Dud's comic act delighted us.

(b) *To mark the omission of a letter or letters*

They can't (cannot) pay.

He'll (He will) write soon.

Ten o'clock (of the clock).

9.8 Inverted Commas ' ' " "

Inverted commas are also called 'quotation marks' or 'speech marks'. Either single marks ' ' or double marks " " may be used. Inverted commas are used:

(a) *In direct speech to indicate the words actually spoken*

'I can hear a noise in the basement,' Bill said.

Bill said, 'I can hear a noise in the basement.'

'I can hear a noise,' Bill said, 'in the basement.'

Note that *only* the words actually spoken are enclosed in the quotation marks.

(b) *In quotations within quotations*

The policeman asked Bill, 'Did you say, "I heard a noise in the basement"?'

Note: In that example double quotation marks were used inside single quotation marks. It is also correct to use single marks inside double.

The policeman asked Bill, "Did you say, 'I heard a noise in the basement'?"

Note: The question mark was included with the words actually spoken by the policeman, who was asking Bill a question. Bill's quoted words did not include a question mark, since they took the form of a statement not a question.

(c) *To indicate the title of a film, book, play, poem, newspaper*

Have you seen 'Star Wars'?

Do you read 'The Trumpet'?

I learnt Keats's poem 'Ode to Autumn' by heart.

(*Note:* Titles are sometimes underlined or italicised instead of being enclosed within quotation marks: There is an excellent account in *Racing Times*.)

Remember that quotation marks are never used in reported speech (nor are question marks).

Direct speech   Their lawyers asked, 'Are you ready to sign the contract?'

Reported speech   Their lawyers enquired whether we were ready to sign the contract.

9.9   Dash —

The dash is used:

(a) *As a pause mark before an explanation*

They sold their heirlooms — furniture, pictures, books.

(b) *To separate a 'summing up' from the items preceding it*

The gearbox, transmission, suspension — all constitute a revolutionary design concept.

(*Note:* Be on your guard. The dash is often overworked. *Never* use it as a substitute for a full stop or a comma.)

9.10   Round Brackets ( )

Round brackets are used:

(a) *To enclose additional information or explanations*

Hardy's long life (1840–1928) spanned the reigns of three monarchs.

(b) *To enclose apposition or parenthesis*

After his death, his impoverished widow sold his finest painting (the portrait of Sir Digby Wood) to a scoundrelly dealer for £25.

A pair of dashes may be used for this purpose instead of round brackets. Both dashes and brackets should be reserved for occasions when a pair of commas does not provide a strong enough effect.

9.11 Square Brackets [ ]

Square brackets are used to *indicate that a word or words included in quoted matter are not part of the original material.*

Johnson answered, 'I have no doubt that they [the poems of Ossian] are forgeries.'

9.12 Hyphen -

The hyphen is used:

(a) *To join up two (or more) words that are regarded as a compound word*

mother-in-law; *twenty-two*; *self-contained*

Many expressions begin as hyphened words and lose the hyphen with continued use: *sea-plane/seaplane*; *look-out/lookout*.

Remember that the presence or absence of a hyphen can change the meaning of a word.

(i) They hope to recover that valuable chair.
(ii) They hope to re-cover that valuable chair.

(b) *To indicate that an unfinished word at the end of a line is completed at the beginning of the next line*

The scientists are still looking for the answer.

Remember that the unfinished word must be split at the end of a syllable and that the hyphen must be placed at the end of the line, not at the beginning of the next.

10 Spelling

10.1 Self-help

English spelling does present some difficulties, but not nearly so many as people like to believe when they are excusing themselves for being bad spellers. The main causes of bad spelling are inattention and laziness — not the problems inherent in English orthography. Tackle your spelling difficulties on the lines suggested here and you will reach the required standard by the time you take your examination.

(a) Visualise and Syllabise

Pay attention to the look of words as you read and when you use your dictionary: *observe* their spelling. Look at and remember their *syllables*; not all of which may be sounded in their correct pronunciation, but all of which are present in their correct spelling (*vet/er/in/ary*). Look at and remember *silent letters*, too. Some seem to be silent because they are not pronounced in sloppy speech (Feb*r*uary; arc*t*ic). Some *are* silent because they are not pronounced in correct speech (de*b*t; vic*tua*ller).

(b) Prefixes and Suffixes

The commonest of all spelling errors occur at word joints, where a prefix is affixed at the beginning of a word or a suffix is affixed at the end (see Section 6.4). There is no excuse for misspelling (mi*s* + *s*pelling) 'disappoint' (di*s* + appoint), 'dissatisfy' (di*s* + *s*atisfy) or 'keenness' (kee*n* + *n*ess), to give just a few examples of the kind of words that are frequently the cause of lost marks.

(c) Pinpoint Your Mistakes

When you misspell a word, you do not get all of it wrong. You make the mistake at a particular point. Look it up. Write it out, underlining your trouble spot(s) (to*b*acco; accommodation; pa*r*a*ll*el). Learn it.

(d) Donkey Work

There is only one way to get better at spelling: work at it. The advice I am giving will help you to approach spelling intelligently, but it cannot remove the hard labour.

1. Resolve not to repeat your mistakes.
2. Make a list of the words you get wrong — and *learn* them.
3. Invent your own ways of avoiding your besetting errors. I used to have trouble with *mantelpiece*. I put it right by working out this *mnemonic*: 'You

don't put a mant*le* on a mant*el*piece'. It may sound silly to you, but it cured me of misspelling *mantelpiece*.

4. Face the fact that you will simply have to memorise the correct spelling of some words by repeating it over and over again. It is a long time now since I went wrong with 'ono-mato-p-o-e-i-a' (= *onomatopeia*); but it took hard work to fix it in my memory. I did it partly by the syllables, partly by individual letters — and mostly by sheer determination to get it right.

10.2 Trouble Spots

Study these examples. Whenever you misspell a word in one of these categories, add it to the list and learn it.

(a) *Silent-letter words*
   silent *b:* bomb, climb, lamb
   silent *g:* design, gnash, sign
   silent *k:* knife, knob, knuckle
   silent *p:* pneumonia, psychic, receipt
   silent *w:* wrap, wrestle, wrist

(b) *Words containing au*
   auction, gauge, somersault

(c) *Words containing ua*
   equal, qualify, quay

(d) *Words spelt with gh*
   silent *gh:* bough, fought, thorough
   gh = f: coughing, laughter, trough
   gh = g: ghastly, ghetto, ghost

(e) *Words spelt with ph*
   beginning ph: pheasant, physical, physics
   ending ph: autograph, paragraph, triumph
   containing ph: emphatic, nephew, symphony

(f) *Words spelt with ch*
   ch = k: aching, chemist, scheme
   'soft' ch: bachelor, machinery, which

(g) *Words spelt with tch*
   butcher, match, wretch

(h) *Double-letter words*
   bb: abbreviate, rabbit, rubbish
   cc: accelerate, according, occur
   dd: address, muddle, sudden
   ff: afford, paraffin, toffee
   gg: aggravate, luggage, suggest
   ll: collision, excellent, pillar
   mm: command, common, grammar
   nn: beginning, channel, tyranny
   pp: apparent, appoint, support
   rr: barrel, carriage, quarrel
   ss: dismiss, harassed, profession
   tt: attitude, lettuce, mattress

10.3 Word Groups

Grouping words by their beginnings or endings is a useful way of remembering how to spell them. Bear these classifications in mind and add to the examples provided.

(a) *Beginning des-*
describe, deserve, destroy

(b) *Beginning dis-*
disastrous, discipline, dissolve

(c) *Ending -ance or -ant*
assistance, nuisance, tenant

(d) *Ending -ence or -ent*
absence, present, prominence

(e) *Ending -al*
educational, horizontal, municipal

(f) *Ending -el*
chapel, chisel, parcel

(g) *Ending -le*
axle, muscle, vehicle

(h) *Ending -sion*
collision, occasion, transmission

(i) *Ending -tion*
ambition, partition, volition

(j) *Ending -ar*
calendar, irregular, similar

(k) *Ending -er*
cylinder, traveller, surrender

(l) *Ending -or*
corridor, governor, interior

(m) *Ending -our*
colour, harbour, vigour

(*Note:* When a noun ending with *-our* adds *-ous* (to form an adjective), *u* is dropped from *-our*.
glamour *but* glamorous
humour *but* humorous
vigour *but* vigorous)

10.4 Common Confusables

Homophones and near-homophones (see Section 6.5) are often confused. Take care when using the words in this list.

accept/except; access/excess; affect/effect; allusion/illusion; altar/alter; ascent/assent; capital/capitol; choose/chose; clothes/cloth; coarse/course; complement/compliment; conscience/conscious; council/counsel; descent/decent; desert/dessert; dairy/diary; dual/duel; dyeing/dying; formally/formerly; later/latter; lead/led; loose/lose; peace/piece; personal/personnel; principal/principle; quiet/quite; respectfully/respectively; stationary/stationery; their/there; to/too/two; weather/whether

10.5 Some Spelling Rules

Some of the traditional spelling rules are complicated and riddled with exceptions. The donkey work recommended earlier in this chapter yields much better results. However, there are a few comparatively simple rules to which there are not many exceptions.

(a) Rule 1

The prefix/suffix rule (see Section 10.1(b)). Never add or subtract a letter at the 'joint' in a word.

EXAMPLES

disservice, misunderstand, underrate

(b) Rule 2

With *suc(c), ex* and *pro*, double *e* must go. By applying that rule, you can remember how to spell prec*e*ding and proc*ee*ding and similar words.

EXAMPLES

exceed, succeed, proceed (N.B.: procedure)
concede, precede, recede

(c) Rule 3

i before *e* when the sound is *e*, except after *c*.

EXAMPLES (The sound is 'e')

ie achieve, grief, piece
ei conceit, deceive, receive

EXCEPTION

seize breaks the rule: *e* sound; no *c*; but *ei*

EXAMPLES (The sound is not 'e')

ie cried, fierce, friend
ei eight, rein, their

(d) Rule 4

When a word ends with *e* and you add to it, drop the *e* when the addition begins with a vowel or *y*.

acquire/acquiring; bone/bony; hate/hating

(*Note:* Words ending with *ce* or *ge* keep the *e* when the addition is *able* or *ous*: courage/courageous; notice/noticeable.)

(e) Rule 5

When a word ends with *e* and you add to it, keep the *e* when the addition begins with a consonant.

EXAMPLES

advance/advancement; hate/hateful; like/likewise

EXCEPTIONS

argue/argument; awe/awful; due/duly; true/truly

(f) Rule 6

Most words ending with a single consonant double that consonant when an addition beginning with a vowel is made.

EXAMPLES

blot/blotting/blotted; mat/matting/matted
begin/beginning; transmit/transmitted; propel/propelling
refer/referring; signal/signalled; travel/traveller

EXCEPTIONS

develop/developing/developed
limit/limiting/limited
profit/profiting/profited

(g) Rule 7

When *full* is joined to another word, it loses one *l*.

EXAMPLES

boast + full = boastful
fear + full = fearful

(h) Rule 8

When *full* is joined to another word ending with double *l*, both words lose one *l*.

full + fill = fulfil (*but* fulfilled)
skill + full = skilful (*but* skilfully)
will + full = wilful (*but* wilfully)

(i) Rule 9

When a word ends with double *l*, it loses one *l* when it is joined to another word.

EXAMPLES

all + so = also
well + fare = welfare

(j) Rule 10

Words ending with *our* drop the *u* when *ous* is added.

EXAMPLES

humour/humorous; valour/valorous; vigour/vigorous

(k) Rules for Plurals

1. Most words add *s*: lamp/lamps.
2. Most words ending with *o* add *es*: tomato/tomatoes.
   Exceptions: cuckoo/cuckoos; piano/pianos; solo/solos; studio/studios.
3. Words ending with *consonant* + *y* change the *y* into *i* and add *es*: memory/memories; lady/ladies.
4. Words ending with *vowel* + *y* keep the *y* and add *s*: donkey/donkeys; toy/toys.
5. Words ending with *f* or *fe* change the *f* or *fe* into *v* and add *es*: calf/calves; half/halves; loaf/loaves.
   Exception: roof/roofs.
6. A few words change their vowels: foot/feet; goose/geese; tooth/teeth; man/men; mouse/mice.
7. A very few make no change: deer/deer; salmon/salmon; sheep/sheep.

11 Work Out Problems: Language, Understanding, Summary

The problems in this chapter test: vocabulary, style, usage (including grammar), understanding, summary, punctuation and spelling. Answers are provided on pages 168–170, but do not look at the answer to a problem until you have written out your own solution. Use your dictionary and revise the relevant section (or sections) of this book while you are working out each problem and studying the answer.

PROBLEM 1 (answers on page 168)

Form the negative of each of the following words by adding a prefix: confirmed, defensible, honourable, logical, proper, rational.

PROBLEM 2 (answers on page 168)

For each of the following words write down a homophone. Then use each of the homophones that you have supplied in a sentence (six sentences in all) to show that you understand its meaning and use: beech, birth, maize, stake, taught, vale.

PROBLEM 3 (answers on page 168)

Part of each of the sentences in this question is underlined. The underlined part is repeated after the letter **A** (printed below the sentence). After the letters **B** and **C** two other versions of the underlined part are given. By writing down the appropriate letter (**A, B** or **C**), indicate which of the three versions would be the best English in the context of the sentence.

  1 The north face of a wall generally suits shade-loving <u>plants, the plants may not like the cold however.</u>
    A plants, the plants may not like the cold however.

B plants, however the plants may not like the cold.

C plants; the plants, however, may not like the cold.

2 An unemployed person, the report shows, is <u>spending less than half on food than the weekly sum</u> spent by those in employment.

    A spending less than half on food than the weekly sum

    B spending on food less than half the weekly sum

    C spending less than half on food as compared with the weekly sum

3 Some diesel cars are <u>as fast as petrol-engined cars</u> of the same capacity and far more economical with fuel.

    A as fast as petrol-engined cars

    B equally as fast as petrol-engined cars

    C as equally fast as petrol-engined cars

4 We are hardly surprised <u>nowadays</u> when a popular newspaper, hungry for circulation, announces that there are fortunes to be won in its latest lucky dip.

    A nowadays

    B in this day and age

    C currently

5 The candidate assured the voters that he would spend <u>the majority</u> of his time on parliamentary business.

    A the majority

    B the maximum amount

    C most

6 Seeing my old friend again after so many years, <u>he seemed very fit.</u>

    A he seemed very fit.

    B I thought he seemed very fit.

    C he struck me as seeming very fit.

7 The promoters of this entertainment must be either lacking in all sense of artistry <u>or they are shamelessly exploiting</u> their simple-minded audiences.

    A or they are shamelessly exploiting

    B if not shamelessly exploiting

    C or shamelessly exploiting

8 Ten minutes before the final whistle, United's careful tactics <u>literally came unstuck</u>.

    A literally came unstuck.

    B came unstuck.

    C definitely came unstuck.

9 Both my son and my daughter did well in the examination but his career, unlike <u>hers</u>, lay in science.

    A hers

    B hers'

    C her's

10 If the new vaccine can be perfected, <u>hopefully this disease will be conquered</u>.

    A hopefully this disease will be conquered.

    B this disease will – hopefully – be conquered.

    C it may be hoped that this disease will be conquered.

PROBLEM 4 (answers on page 168)

Rewrite the following sentence in reported speech, using each of the given introductions in turn (three sentences in all):

Do you always go to the seaside for your holidays?

    A Jane will ask me . . .
    B I have asked Jane . . .
    C Jane asked her aunt . . .

PROBLEM 5 (answers on page 168)

Rewrite the following passage in reported speech:
    'I can't understand what's wrong with my new saw,' said Mr Brown. 'It's so blunt, it wouldn't cut butter.'
    'There's nothing wrong with it, Dad,' replied his seven-year-old son Tommy. 'I know, because I cut through a big nail with it only yesterday.'

PROBLEM 6 (answers on page 168)

Bodily labour is of two kinds: either that which a man submits to for his livelihood or that which he undergoes for his pleasure. The latter of them generally changes the name of labour for that of exercise, but differs only from ordinary labour as it rises from another motive.
    A country life abounds in both these kinds of labour and, for that reason, gives a man a greater stock of health, and consequently a fuller enjoyment of himself than any other way of life.

---

1 Supply a suitable short title for the passage.
2 Make clear in your own words the distinction drawn between exercise and labour.
3 Make clear in your own words the three stages of the argument in the second paragraph by which the writer seeks to prove the superiority of a country life.

PROBLEM 7 (answers on page 169)

Fill each gap in the following sentences with a word that, in the context, is of opposite meaning to the italicised word.

1 Although most of the characters in this novel are *fictitious*, some . . . persons are introduced.
2 The . . . vegetation of the upper slopes was now replaced by the *prolific* growth of the plains.
3 The *natural* charm and simple dignity of the old king were in sharp contrast to the . . . manner and foppish airs of his son.
4 In less than six months, the financier sank from the *zenith* to the . . . of his fortunes.
5 The *clumsiness* of the clown, his partner in the double act, heightened our appreciation of the juggler's . . . .

Some of the following sentences are examples of good usage; others are faulty. Each of the faulty sentences contains an error of one of the kinds indicated by **B, C, D, E** below.

A No error.
B Wrong choice of word — i.e. mistaken use of a word for one that it resembles.
  Example: We could not except their invitation.
C Lack of agreement (subject/verb or noun/pronoun).
  Examples: A packet of chocolates were given to each child.
       A person can only do their best.
D Incorrect punctuation.
  Example: Fan belt, distributor, sparking-plugs, were carefully checked.
E Unattached or wrongly attached phrases.
  Examples: They enjoyed their hot drinks, cold after a swim.
       Crossing the street, the church is a fine spectacle.

If a sentence contains no error of the kind **B, C, D** or **E**, mark it **A**; otherwise mark it with the letter corresponding to the kind of error it contains.

1 He designed a remarkable engine and being air-cooled he was able to cut production costs.
2 They promised the electors less interference and fewer taxes.
3 One of Europe's most imminent scientists then addressed the meeting.
4 Red Rum was one of the finest racehorses that has ever been seen.
5 People, who are over 65, qualify for age-relief under present tax regulations.
6 An editor's decision to publish or not to publish a scandalous story depends on what his criteria are.
7 After 1900, the merit of Hardy's poetry was widely recognised, but formally he was better known for his novels.
8 Labouring in heavy seas, the trawler put out distress signals at midnight.
9 Keeping up with fashion, the old furniture was sent to auction and replaced by modern pieces.
10 With those qualifications, you could try to become a journalist; alternately, you could train as a librarian.

Which of the two sentences in each of the following pairs more accurately conveys the sense intended?

1(a) I had a letter from my father, who was staying in London.
1(b) I had a letter from my father who was staying in London.
2(a) Visitors are requested not to give the animals food, which will harm them.
2(b) Visitors are requested not to give the animals food which will harm them.
3(a) My experience has been that horses, which are mealy-muzzled, run well.
3(b) My experience has been that horses which are mealy-muzzled run well.

PROBLEM 10 (answers on page 169)

Bring each of these sentences into line with good English usage. Make as few changes as possible and do not alter the intended sense.

1 All students do not learn German.
2 The reason why he was not elected to the committee was because he made such a bad speech.
3 Cowering under the bridge, an enemy patrol saw the bedraggled and frightened fugitive.
4 Walking is perhaps the best form of relaxation for, unlike golf, fishing or motoring, no elaborate and expensive equipment is required.
5 In recent years, sales have proved conclusively that customers prefer automatic than twin-tub washers.

PROBLEM 11 (answers on page 169)

Select the appropriate letter from the list below to indicate which of these sentences are grammatically correct.

1 His alibi was good.
2 The criteria was questionable.
3 The ensemble was playing at the Wigmore Hall.
4 The parenthesis was marked off with commas.
5 The phenomena was thoroughly investigated.
   A 1 and 2 only
   B 2 and 3 only
   C 3 and 5 only
   D 1, 3 and 4 only
   E 2, 4 and 5 only

PROBLEM 12 (answers on page 169)

Select the appropriate letter to indicate the correct meaning of each of these words.

1 mortuary is: A brickwork
              B a keen sense of disappointment
              C a building in which dead bodies are kept for a time
              D a deadening sensation in the limbs
2 plummet is: A a small plum
              B a sounding-line
              C graphite
              D a nestling's feather
3 ossification is: A being snubbed
              B becoming stupid
              C over-eating
              D turning (or being turned) into bone
4 proselytise is: A to demonstrate angrily
              B to turn verse into prose
              C to make converts
              D to take precedence

5 subjugate is: **A** to strangle
                    B to conquer
                    C to name the inflexions of a verb
                    D to delegate authority

PROBLEM 13 (answers on page 169)

Read this passage carefully and then answer the questions.

In our time it is broadly true that political writing is bad writing. Where it is not true, it will generally be found that the writer is some kind of rebel, expressing his private opinions, and not a 'party line'. Orthodoxy, of whatever colour, seems to demand a lifeless, imitative style. The political dialects
5   to be found in pamphlets, leading articles, manifestos, White Papers and the speeches of Under-Secretaries do, of course, vary from party to party, but they are all alike in that one almost never finds in them a fresh, vivid, home-made turn of speech. When one watches some tired hack on the platform mechanically repeating the familiar phrases — *bestial atrocities, iron heel,*
10 *blood-stained tyranny, free peoples of the world, stand shoulder to shoulder* — one often has the curious feeling that one is not watching a live human being but some kind of dummy: a feeling which suddenly becomes stronger at moments when the light catches the speaker's spectacles and turns them into blank discs which seem to have no eyes behind them. And this is not
15 altogether fanciful. A speaker who uses that kind of phraseology has gone some distance towards turning himself into a machine. The appropriate noises are coming out of his larynx, but his brain is not involved as it would be if he were choosing his words for himself. If the speech he is making is one that he is accustomed to make over and over again, he may be almost unconscious of
20 what he is saying, as one is when one utters the responses in church. And this reduced state of consciousness, if not indispensable, is at any rate favourable to political conformity.

---

1   As used in the passage, 'Orthodoxy, of whatever colour' (lines 3–4) means much the same as
    A any style of writing
    B religious belief of any kind
    C conformity with the accepted beliefs of any political party
    D emotive expressions of the right or the left
2   The writer asserts in lines 4–8 that
    A dialects hamper politicians
    B the political speeches of Under-Secretaries are more vivid than pamphlets, leading articles and manifestos
    C the various parties differ widely in their propaganda
    D the language of political speeches and writing is stale, ready-made stuff
3   The 'tired hack on the platform' (line 8) is
    A a weary rebel
    B a partly defaced slogan behind the speaker
    C part of the public address system
    D a politician mouthing platitudes
4   The suggestion in lines 12–14 is that
    A the speaker's eyesight is poor
    B the speaker is dehumanised

157

C the speaker lacks political insight

D the speaker is not the centre of attention

5 The phrase 'that kind of phraseology' (line 15) refers to

A the 'private opinions' mentioned earlier

B expressions such as those in italics

C home-made turns of speech

D the responses made in church services

6 The writer is highly critical of the political language 'of our time' for all but one of the following reasons; which one?

A It is repetitive.

B It is not the product of hard thought.

C It increases party differences.

D It reflects a lowered level of political awareness.

PROBLEM 14 (answers on page 169)

Study this passage carefully and then answer the questions.

There are many striking similarities between English and German. Some of the most commonly used words in the two languages look alike and sound similar: *Gras* = grass; *Korn* = corn; *Haus* = house; *bringen* = to bring; *hart* = hard; *gut* = good. These are but a very few of many possible examples. Philologists have proved that many English and German words which no longer look or sound similar, and which now have very different meanings, go back to a common origin. In grammar, too, the languages share certain characteristics, notably in the formation of comparatives and superlatives, the conjugation of verbs, and the genitive case. The evidence that the two tongues derive from the same source is overwhelming; but it is equally true that they have developed along very different lines, as anyone who is in a position to contrast the complications of German grammar with the simplicity of English grammar will readily agree.

---

1 In not more than 10 words, provide a suitable title for the passage.

2 Identify three points mentioned in the passage that are used to prove a common origin for the two languages.

3 Which of those points serves to bring out both their similarities and their differences?

4 Summarise the passage in not more than 40 of your own words.

PROBLEM 15 (answers on page 170)

Rewrite the following sentences in plain, direct English. Do not change the meaning.

1 It is regretted that your claim, which has been under active consideration, cannot be accepted by the District Assessor.

2 In the majority of cases, it was possible for students to be found placements operative within the period of time elapsing between the conclusion of the summer term and the commencement of the September session.

3 If it is decided that your application for admission to this course has been successful, you will receive notification on or before 1 November.

4 For a period of several years after the cessation of hostilities, the availability of new cars to the consumer was adversely conditioned by the supply situa-

tion then obtaining, and a severe shortage developed in relation to the considerable demand experienced.

5 In my mind it is much to be deplored that the Council has thought fit not to give an affirmative response to the proposal to refurbish the seating accommodation in the concert hall on the grounds of self-imposed financial constraints.

PROBLEM 16 (answers on page 170)

Write out the following, supplying the correct punctuation.

1 The students buses were unloading at 9 oclock.
2 Its necessary said the teacher to use punctuation youll confuse your readers if you dont.
3 The childrens enthusiasm increased as the conjuror performed trick after trick reaching a climax when a white rabbits head emerged from a top hat.
4 The builder said that he could paint the metalwork but stresses and strains were engineers problems he couldnt be expected to be responsible for the structures strength.
5 I very much doubt said Tom whether you fully understand the message I want you to deliver to Fred I certainly do replied Jack you want me to tell him that the practice will be on Thursday this week thats just the point exclaimed Tom Thursday next week not Thursday this week its on Wednesday as usual this week is it yes Ive said so twice already perhaps youd better give him the message yourself perhaps I had

PROBLEM 17 (answers on page 170)

Select the correct word to fill the gaps in these sentences.

1 He was the kind of leader . . . everybody admires. (who/whom)
2 I am sure he is the man . . . we saw at the bus stop yesterday. (who/whom)
3 If the experienced players cannot understand the new rules, what hope is there for . . . beginners? (we/us)
4 The cause underlying these recurrent disagreements, which are dangerous in present circumstances, . . . for international action. (call/calls)
5 Nobody . . . enter the keep . . . obtaining written permission. (can/may; unless/without)
6 He will, I know, be grateful if you . . . help him to raise money for this project. (could/can)
7 The plot of the play centres . . . intricate personal relationships. (round/on)
8 The inquest exonerated the nurse . . . blame; congratulated her, in fact, on a . . . decision (from/against; couragous/courageous)
9 Candidates must not enter the examination room more than 15 minutes before the paper is due to begin . . . leave before it is due to end. (or/nor)
10 If that . . . a knock at the door, it was probably the postman. (were/was)

PROBLEM 18 (answers on page 170)

At some of the numbered points in the passage below, the usual marks of punctuation have been omitted. The punctuation marks omitted are of the following kinds: comma, semi-colon, colon, full stop followed by capital letter. At some of the points numbered, on the other hand, none of those marks should be used, as it would be superfluous or even contrary to the sense of the passage. Indicate by

159

one of the letters **A** to **E** which mark of punctuation, if any, you would use at each of the places numbered, as follows:

A no mark of punctuation
B comma
C semi-colon
D colon
E full stop followed by capital letter

Three possible explanations of the accident were put forward (1) a worn tyre, unnoticed at the time because of the many (2) radical changes in maintenance procedures at the garage (3) inadequate lubrication of the gearbox (4) and the fracture of a vacuum pipe (5) on which smoothly progressive braking depended (6) each of these theories was investigated (7) none provided a satisfactory explanation (8) in view of these findings (9) we may never know the cause of a most unusual accident (10) which cost lives and money (11) unless (12) that is (13) some quite remarkable (14) and unsuspected evidence is eventually uncovered.

PROBLEM 19 (answers on page 170)

With one exception, each of the following sentences uses two expressions where one would suffice. Which sentence does *not*?

1 When the lights changed to green, the learner-driver reversed at a brisk pace back into the front of the car behind.
2 The government made great use of its argument that most of the electors would find it more preferable to pay less in taxes rather than to have increased pay.
3 You could use inferior materials, but the job would not last and it would be only marginally cheaper.
4 As expected, Betty won in the final, being a very strong forehand player and relatively superior to Celia at the net.
5 We called at the hotel in Birmingham at which, so the local news led us to believe, the touring team intended to stay at when they left London.

PROBLEM 20 (answers on page 170)

Read the following passage and then answer the questions.

The letter, which was signed by several of the disaffected soldiers, painted in gloomy colours the miseries of their condition, accused the two commanders of being the authors of this, and called on the higher authorities to intervene by sending a vessel to take them from that desolate spot while some of them might still be found surviving the horrors of their confinement. The letter concluded with a paragraph in which the two commanders were stigmatised as partners in a slaughterhouse: one being employed to drive in the cattle for the other to butcher.

---

1 Give the meaning of the following expressions as they are used in the passage: (a) disaffected; (b) painted in gloomy colours; (c) the authors of this; (d) be found surviving the horrors of their confinement; (e) stigmatised.
2 Without using figurative language, reword the soldiers' description of their commanders.

Answers

3.9 WORK OUT 2, pages 66–69

1. In the first paragraph the writer lists these problems: careless dropping of litter; deliberate dumping of refuse and worn-out cars; frequent hooliganism; damaged trees; broken fences; fire lighting; sheep-worrying by ill-trained dogs; disturbance of grazing animals on common land. Each of those problems is caused by deliberate or negligent misconduct. People do what they should not do (drop litter, light fires, and so on) or they fail to do what they should do (keep their dogs under control, close gates, and so on). In every case, somebody's action or inaction results in damage.

The problem described in the second paragraph is caused by sheer weight of numbers. People are not misbehaving either deliberately or negligently. They are not to blame. It is their very presence that causes the trouble. Just by so many of them being there all at once the visitors damage what they have come to seek.

2. The vegetation is worn away by the incessant passage of feet in the peak period for visitors. If that pressure is not lessened for a time during the growing season, the ground cover cannot renew itself. Then, as people continue to walk over the bare land, the soil is eroded. The effects of this on the life cycle of plants and animals are extremely serious.

That is what is meant by 'erosion'. It is the National Trust's worst problem, because it requires remedies that are either difficult or unpleasant to apply. Some of them, in fact, are in conflict with the Trust's open access ideal. Whereas the other problems can be tackled successfully though expensively by increasing the number of wardens, erosion can be tackled only by reducing the number of visitors to the most threatened areas. Temporary closure of endangered estates may be necessary, though it is not Trust policy to close any of its properties. The best hope lies in persuading people to visit estates that are not overcrowded, instead of making for the most popular places. If persuasion fails, then some form of rationing will have to be introduced, though the Trust would be most reluctant to do that. However, if the number of visitors continues to increase, then the Trust will have to control daily admission to its most threatened estates, either by charging or by refusing to allow more than a given number to enter at any one time.

3. At first, I thought I was going to have to wade through a mass of facts and figures. However, the figures provided in the first paragraph are just a quick, factual introduction to the problems. Even there, the writer manages to make his subject sound interesting by using arresting words such as 'dumping' and 'nightmare' and by making plain, easy to follow statements such as 'damage trees, break fences and start fires'.

Of course, I had to follow the passage closely and think hard about its meaning. Some of the words, such as 'ecology' 'regeneration' and 'erosion', puzzled me at first, but I realised he had to use those terms and I found that I could work out their meaning from their context.

Again, there are some long sentences (such as the one beginning 'Apart from closure . . .'), but I got at their meaning by reading them slowly and carefully. I don't think they are any longer than they had to be. The ideas he is expressing are quite complicated, and because he made me see that they mattered, I was interested enough to want to pay attention to them. In any case, he uses plenty of short, crisp sentences in between the longer ones. For example, the two short sentences at the end of the fourth paragraph bring an important stage of his explanation to an end very clearly and directly.

I think it was the vividness of many of the expressions that did most to keep me interested and to help me to understand the importance of the subject. Describing the rationing proposals, he says, 'The brake could be applied . . .'. That is language that anybody can understand at once. It is a very simple, everyday way of making things clear.

The whole situation came alive for me when I was hovering high up with 'an airman or a buzzard' and watching some of the estates 'stir like anthills' while others were as silent and empty as they were in Saxon times. I can carry that picture in my mind, and it sums up most of what he wanted me to learn from this passage.

I think this is a good piece of writing, for it certainly got me interested in the National Trust's problems and helped me to understand how difficult they are to solve.

4. Welcome to Ryemoor! You are anxious to start your walk, so I won't keep you long. There are just a few things I want to say to help you to enjoy your day.

You are going to pass through some wild and difficult country, so read your maps carefully and keep an eye on the compass. Check your packs before you start. Make sure you've got your waterproof clothing and your emergency rations. The weather can change very quickly up here. Mist and rain sweep across the fells without much warning.

On your way to the high ground, you will pass through farmland. Please stick to the waymarked routes. Don't climb over fences. Look for stiles and gates, and remember to close the gates after you.

I see that two of you have brought your dogs. Keep them on their leads as you pass through the farms. Don't let them off when you are in open country unless they are well-trained. Please don't let them disturb the sheep and cattle grazing on the common land above the valley.

Please don't damage trees and hedges to get wood for fires or for any other purpose. There's a big fire risk, so lighting fires is forbidden. And I need hardly ask you not to drop litter. Country lovers like you know that the proper place for litter is their pocket or their pack.

Forgive me for preaching, but it's become necessary to remind everyone — even experienced walkers like you — of these simple but very important rules. This beautiful landscape belongs to us all. The National Trust holds it *in trust* — for you and all our other visitors.

I do hope you'll enjoy your walk. I have enjoyed meeting you and welcoming you to Ryemoor.

3.10 WORK OUT 3, pages 69-73

1. The quarrel is caused by Freeman's refusal to design a yellow costume for Fiammetta to wear in *Carmen* unless he is allowed to change all the other costumes and scenery. He points out that such major alterations would delay the opening night by about two months.

Having failed to bully him into submission, Fiammetta tries flattery and then, at her hotel, attempts to seduce him into agreement. Freeman, who is keenly aware of her beauty, tells her that he is very ready to take her kisses but they won't persuade him to change his mind.

Furious in defeat, she says that no honourable man would behave as he is doing. He is quite unmoved by her appeal to a conventional code which, he says, has no meaning for him. He has fought his way up from nothing and he has no sentimental illusions to handicap him.

This provokes another angry outburst. Fiammetta says that she also has clawed her way out of the gutter. She claims that they are two of a kind and that she is just as ruthless as he is. But Freeman is not convinced. He still thinks she wants the dress, not him. His belief that she is trying to trick him makes him lose his temper at last, and they face each other in deadlocked fury.

Then, simultaneously, they see the absurdity of their confrontation, and they begin to laugh at themselves and each other. Still refusing her a yellow dress, which she says she no longer cares about, Freeman puts his arms round her, promising to design a new scarlet dress worthy of the brilliant spirit of this 'gutter-snipe', as he lovingly calls her.

2. Fiammetta and Freeman both work in opera, her talents as a singer matched by his as a designer. They are both extremely strong characters, fond of and used to getting their own way and not particularly scrupulous about the methods they use. By their own accounts, they both started life with no advantages except their own abilities and powerful personalities. They both have a ruthless will to succeed which, together with great artistic gifts, has taken them to the top of their chosen careers. Both have marked sex appeal and no conventional scruples about using it to their own advantage.

Fiammetta is the more colourful personality of the two. Her physical beauty and flamboyant behaviour make her the centre of attention on and off the stage. She can — and does — manipulate people. Her rages frighten them, her disdain freezes them, her charm wins them over. She chooses her weapons with deliberate calculation to suit the occasion and the adversary.

Yet we learn from this episode that Freeman is the stronger of the two. Against his quiet, controlled, concentrated power she fights in vain. Only once does he lose his temper while she storms and sneers and persuades. He does not let her see how powerfully she attracts him until the battle is won. With none of her showy brilliance, he has a steely quality she lacks. He is older, more experienced, and an even cleverer tactician than she is.

3. I did enjoy reading this passage because I got involved with these two striking characters. I don't think I much approved of either of them. I didn't take sides, but I was very interested to see who won. I felt that I knew them both, so I found their quarrel exciting. It was amusing, too, to see them trying to outwit each other, and the fact that in the end they both saw the funny side of themselves made me like them better than I did at first.

Any story-teller who can hold a reader's attention as Phyllis Bentley does here must be very skilful. She places her characters in a world that may not be at all familiar to many of her readers, yet she brings them and it alive at once.

The opening description of Fiammetta has so much colour and life that I knew what a spellbinder she must be. It was as if she walked into a room in which I was sitting, waiting for her to appear. I think that was what got me involved in the story from the very beginning.

It is a very cleverly written piece of description, not just because of the vivid details of Fiammetta's voice and looks and clothes, but also because it made me feel that I was looking at her with Freeman's eyes. I experienced the impact she made on him. One very skilful touch ('grey or violet? Freeman never knew') took me right into the developing situation and made me understand the power of her attraction for him.

By this time, I was so interested that I had no difficulty in taking in the background details of their quarrel, and I understood how unreasonable Fiammetta was being in wanting to sing Carmen's role in a yellow dress.

I'd also realised how strong Freeman is. He smiles as he plays his trump card and explains that the opening night would have to be postponed if he agreed to her request. And from then on, Fiammetta can't rattle him. He keeps cool and he seems to know what her next move is going to be before she makes it. So although there is a lot of rising and falling tension as they battle it out, I suspected that he would win. I noticed too that when he does 'plunge into rage', she has already weakened her position fatally by letting her feelings for him become apparent.

I enjoyed this piece of writing so much that I'd like to read the rest of the book. I got so interested in these two remarkable people that I'd like to know what happens to them in the end. However long or short their relationship turns out to be, I'm quite sure that it will never be an easy one — and I'm quite sure that it will never be a dull one.

3.11 WORK OUT 4, pages 73–81

1. Queenie was taken ill on Sunday 4 July. When Adrian arrived, she was in bed, looking awful without her make-up, which, for once, she was too distressed to bother about. She described the sharp pains in her chest, but the doctor had not been sent for, because she was afraid of doctors.

When Adrian's mother came, she realised that Queenie was very ill. She sent for an ambulance, and before it arrived Queenie's mind began to wander. She started talking about the past as if she was still living in it. However, once she was in the ambulance, she remembered her rouge and refused to leave home until Adrian took it to her. Two hours later, Adrian's mother rang from the hospital to say that Queenie's 'turn' had been diagnosed as a stroke and she would have to stay in hospital for a long time.

On 29 July Adrian visited her in hospital. Unable to speak intelligibly, she was very thin and so changed that he would not have recognised her without her rouge.

In mid-September, by which time she was at home again, her speech was still impaired, though her facial expressions conveyed her feelings and thoughts quite clearly.

By 7 November, although she still could not speak properly, she was making some progress. Adrian had considerable success that day in his attempts to teach her to speak again.

2. There is no doubt that Adrian Mole cares for the rather trying old couple whom he had befriended. He bolts his meal and rushes round to see them when Bert telephones for help. He makes an effort to go to see them when he doesn't really want to go — 'Took a deep breath and went to see Bert and Queenie today'. He pays a lot of attention to their needs and habits, and he understands how to interpret their behaviour. For example, when he sees that the television is switched off, he realises that something serious has happened.

He gives them very practical help. When Queenie has her 'turn', he makes a cup of tea, feeds the dog, and makes Bert one of his favourite sandwiches. He does housework for them.

Adrian is worried about Queenie, and he takes a lot of trouble to comfort her when she is taken ill and to help her to learn to speak again afterwards. He recognises the problems that age brings and he sees how vulnerable Bert and Queenie are — their fear of losing each other, and Bert's worry about the possibility of being turned out of his bungalow. In the hospital ward, although he is embarrassed by Queenie's speech defects and by the antics of the other elderly patients, he feels deep sympathy for people who are living in the past, because 'their present is dead horrible'.

At the same time, he sees how comical Bert and Queenie sometimes are. Bert's reference to a woman of 78 as 'my girl' at once touches and amuses him. So does the fact that, while holding Queenie's hand, Bert addresses her as a 'daft old bat'. Queenie's shout 'Fetch me pot of rouge, I'm not going until I've got me rouge' is recorded in his diary, but he understands how much her 'warpaint' means to her and he makes sure she gets it.

Nor is he blind to the fact that both of them, especially Bert, impose on him, even though they are fond of him. He notes with some bitterness their unjust accusation that he has neglected them while he's been 'gadding about'. He resents being ordered to clean up before the home help comes, though he sees the funny side of Bert's selfish demand.

It is far from an easy relationship for a boy 'aged 13¾' to sustain. They often jar on him. For example, Bert's verbal sparring with Adrian's mother strikes him as uncouth, especially as he knows they like each other.

Yet, if he is frequently irritated by them, he is often amused and touched. Above all, he cares enough about them to go on helping them. However unrewarding his friendship with them may sometimes seem to be, Adrian Mole has a genuine affection for Queenie and Bert.

3. From the outside, the Old Ladies' Home seems unwelcoming, even hostile. 'Prickly dark shrubs' and a 'heavy door' give it a grim appearance, and its white-washed brick walls reflecting 'the winter sunlight like a block of ice' strike a chill into the visitor's heart.

Inside, the nurse at the reception desk seems cold and forbidding, with her 'white uniform' and her 'close-cut hair'. The bulging linoleum gives way under the stranger's feet, and a musty smell 'like the interior of a clock' suggests all kinds of nameless horrors. Behind a range of cell-like doors, a strange noise 'like a sheep bleating' is at first the only sign of life. Then, in one of the cramped, overcrowded rooms, two old women are waiting. One — her lopsided face twisted in a fearful grin — jerks the door open. The other lies silent on the bed wearing a cap and shrouded in a counterpane. To their young visitor they seem grotesque and terrifying in their dreadful 'cave'. The bare floor smells of damp, and even the wicker chair she holds on to feels wet and rotten. The cold and the darkness press in upon her. She is trapped in a thieves' den, and she is convinced that they are going to murder her.

4.

Saturday 3 February

Terrible 'Campfire Visit' to old women's 'Home' — 'Prison'? — 'Madhouse'? Scared out of my wits for three miserable credit points — if I ever get them!

Cold, hostile building, guarded with dark, thorny shrubs and a heavy door. Shining like a block of ice with the sun on its whitewash.

Took a pot plant for whoever it was I was supposed to be visiting. The nurse — white uniform, close-cropped hair, and grim as a prison wardress — told me its name, but it meant no more to me than the anonymous old woman I'd got to give it to.

She led me towards a battery of closed doors, walking quite steadily over an uneven floor that seemed to be giving way under my feet. I felt as if I'd go through it at any moment.

Everything silent as the grave. Then, from behind one of the doors, a noise like a bleating sheep. It turned out to be an old woman clearing her throat. That did it! The nurse decided to put me in there. She banged on the door. The horrible noise went on and on, and I wanted to run. Then an old crone with a lopsided face — trying to smile? — tugged the door open bit by bit. That dreadful nurse shoved me in — and left me to it.

I couldn't say anything. The old woman went on 'smiling' and waiting. There was another — even older — lying on a bed, wearing a cap and shrouded in a counterpane. A corpse? I never knew. The one by the door snatched my hat off and dragged me right in with her other claw. The door shut behind me — and she said, 'MY, MY, MY' just like some hideous apparition in a horror film.

The room was crammed with furniture and reeked of damp. I held on to the back of a chair. Ugh! It felt wet and rotten. The terrible little cave got colder and darker. I couldn't see or hear. I just knew they were going to kill me. Rob me first, then murder me.

Somehow, I got the door open – looking back, I realise they didn't try to stop me – and I bolted. I nearly broke my neck on that awful lino. The nurse yelled something at me as I shot past her desk, but I didn't stop to find out what she wanted.

I left the plant in the old women's room. As a matter of fact, it fell out of my hand when I grabbed the chair. I think the pot smashed on the floor. As for the credit points, somehow I don't think I'll get them – not when the nurse's report comes in.

5. People of my age often say they want 'respect' from the young. I don't. 'Respectful' behaviour is cold and distant. It's polite, of course, and that's better than rudeness, but there's nothing about it to warm the heart. I want friendship, and I think it is possible to build a genuine friendship even when one person is old and the other is young.

That is why I should like to meet Adrian Mole. I feel that he and I would get on together. I'm afraid I don't feel like that about Marian. She is utterly unlike him – but I'll give you my impressions of her later.

Adrian has imagination. He can put himself in another person's place. That would make it easy for me to put myself in his. There would be a strong sympathy between us, despite the age gap.

He is a sensitive boy – sensitive to the views and feelings and needs of others. I like his practical good sense. He takes trouble with people and is a real help to them. He sees the funny side of things too, although he has a rather endearing, almost 'old-fashioned' seriousness of outlook and expression. He would be an amusing and likeable companion.

I hope the benefits of our relationship would not be all on my side. I'd welcome his help in little practical ways, but I certainly wouldn't exploit him as those two do at times. He is generous in helping others, but I feel he needs help too. I believe I could give him help – if only by listening to him, letting him tell me about his hopes.

Marian is an altogether different kind of person. She is self-centred. She visits the Home simply because it is part of her 'Campfire' training and she intends to get credit points for doing so. She has made no attempt to prepare herself for the visit. She takes the pot plant because it is the expected – the conventional – thing to do. Admittedly, nobody seems to have given her any preparatory guidance, but she herself has seen no need for it.

She is unimaginative and cold about people, however fanciful she is about the 'horrors' of her experience. Her way of talking about the old people she is supposed to be taking an interest in shows how little she cares about them or wants to understand their situation – 'I have asked to pay a visit to *some* old lady' and 'any of them will *do*'. To her, they are objects, not people.

She had a frightening experience, of course, and I do feel a bit sorry for her. But she did nothing to try to discover what her visit to such a place might be like. She didn't realise beforehand that there would be *people* inside those white-washed walls. She is thoughtless and insensitive.

I can best sum up my attitude to these two young people by saying that Marian has none of Adrian's maturity of imagination. Whereas I'd be glad to be in his company, I'd be very uncomfortable in hers – as I'm sure she would be in mine. We'd have very little to say to each other, and I'm sure she wouldn't make any effort to get to know me. Other people, especially older people, don't interest Marian.

1

STUDENTS' GRANTS: AN INTRODUCTION

Approach the local education authority in good time. Eligibility is determined by: the nature of the course; a three-year UK residency; no previous grant. Mandatory grants must be paid to students accepted for degree courses. Discretionary grants may be paid for other courses. Grants for tuition, examination fees and union contributions are paid direct to the educational institution. Travel costs and maintenance are paid to the student. Above the minimum grant, maintenance depends on student and parental income. Mature or disabled students receive special grants. Social security in term is restricted to single parents and handicapped people.

98 words

2

WHY MINORITY OPINIONS MUST BE PROTECTED AND ENCOURAGED

Both a conservative and a radical party are essential to political health because the standpoint of each corrects the errors of its opposite and each exerts a restraining influence on the other. The complete triumph of one would suppress the truth represented by the other, for truth is not the monopoly of one point of view and the continuing struggle between embattled opposites is a necessary condition of betterment. It follows that minority opinions embody an aspect of truth and that minorities should be not merely tolerated but protected and encouraged. Political truth is so complex that the utmost freedom must be afforded to all opinions. Whenever a minority – however small – differs from the rest of mankind, its voice must be heard. Even if the received opinion is correct, it is likely that its opponents have something valuable to say and truth itself would suffer if they were silenced.

149 words

3

LIFE IS DANGEROUS IN A NOISY WORLD

Noise kills and injures – and we are at risk every day. At 0 db (db = *decibel*), it can just be heard. At about 180 db, it is fatal. Danger begins at 65–86 db, the noise level near a motorway. Above that, prolonged exposure deafens and enfeebles. A quick dose of 150 db (low-flying jets near an airport) inflicts agony and may wreck ears. Daily noises are in the damage band: motor mowers or revving bikes (110 db); 'hard rock' (115 db); pneumatic drills (130 db); even food mixers (100 db at 2–4 feet).

Defend your house against noise. Operate useful but noisy appliances away from the living area and stand them on padding. Keep radios and television down to safe levels. Repel outside noises with trees, shrubs, walls and fences. Quell those that penetrate with carpets, curtains, and big floor and wall furniture.

Agreed, we can't banish all noise, nor should we try. Liberation from domestic drudgery and Shanks's pony are worth a decibel or two. And noises *can* delight — a baby's crying, a roaring exhaust, throbbing 'pop', nature's music. Total silence means death. But so does unrestricted noise!

192 words

PROBLEM 1 (page 152)

unconfirmed, indefensible, dishonourable, illogical, improper, irrational

PROBLEM 2 (page 152)

beach, berth, maze, steak, taut, veil
1 A sandy beach is a great asset to a holiday resort.
2 The yacht was at its berth near the old quay.
3 No visitor had ever succeeded in finding the way out of the maze, which was formed of high yew hedges.
4 Traditionally, large, juicy steaks have been the principal diet of boxers and rowing-men.
5 They pulled hard on the slack mooring rope until it was taut.
6 Her features were hidden by a veil of black lace.

PROBLEM 3 (pages 152 and 153)

1 C.   2 B.   3 A.   4 A.   5 C.   6 B.   7 C.   8 B.   9 A.   10 C.

PROBLEM 4 (page 154)

A Jane will ask me if I always go to the seaside for my holidays.
B I have asked Jane if she always goes to the seaside for her holidays.
C Jane asked her aunt if she always went to the seaside for her holidays.

PROBLEM 5 (page 154)

Mr Brown said that he could not understand what was wrong with his new saw, which was so blunt that it would not cut butter. His seven-year-old son Tommy replied that he knew that there was nothing wrong with the saw because, only the day before, he had cut through a big nail with it.

PROBLEM 6 (page 154)

1 A Country Life: Healthiest and Best.
2 Labour is the physical work undergone for a living; but exercise is the physical work undertaken for pleasure.
3 The first stage of the argument states that both kinds of labour are plentiful in a country life. The second stage claims that better health follows from that. The third stage concludes that, as a result, a country life provides greater pleasure derived from enhanced self-fulfilment.

PROBLEM 7 (page 154)

   1 historical.   2 sparse.   3 artificial.   4 nadir.   5 dexterity.

PROBLEM 8 (page 155)

   1 E.   2 A.   3 B.   4 C.   5 D.   6 A.   7 B.   8 A.   9 E.   10 B.

PROBLEM 9 (page 155)

   1(a).   2(b).   3(b).

PROBLEM 10 (page 156)

1 Not all students learn German.
2 The reason he was not elected to the committee was that he made a bad speech.
3 An enemy patrol saw the bedraggled and frightened fugitive cowering under the bridge.
4 Walking is perhaps the best form of relaxation for, unlike golf, fishing or motoring, it does not require elaborate and expensive equipment.
5 In recent years, sales have proved conclusively that customers prefer automatic to twin-tub washers.

PROBLEM 11 (page 156)

   D

PROBLEM 12 (pages 156 and 157)

   1 C.   2 B.   3 D.   4 C.   5 B.

PROBLEM 13 (pages 157 and 158)

   1 C.   2 D.   3 D.   4 B.   5 B.   6 C.

PROBLEM 14 (page 158)

1 The similarities and the differences between English and German. (*9 words*)
2 (i) Many of their most frequently used words look and sound alike. (ii) Many other words have a common origin. (iii) They have similarities of grammar.
3 The grammatical evidence.
4 The similarities between and shared origins of many English and German words, together with some grammatical affinities, prove the kinship of the two languages. Nevertheless, they have moved far apart, as their contrasting grammars show.

35 words

1 Your claim has been considered carefully, but the District Assessor is sorry to say that he cannot accept it.
2 Placements for the summer vacation were found for most students.
3 You will be told by 1 November if you have been accepted for this course.
4 For several years after the war ended, fewer cars were made than there were customers for them.
5 I deplore the Council's decision not to spend money on new seats for the concert hall.

PROBLEM 16 (page 159)

1 The students' buses were unloading at 9 o'clock.
2 'It's necessary,' said the teacher, 'to use punctuation. You'll confuse your readers if you don't.'
3 The children's enthusiasm increased as the conjuror performed trick after trick, reaching a climax when a white rabbit's head emerged from a top hat.
4 The builder said that he could paint the metalwork, but stresses and strains were engineers' problems; he couldn't be expected to be responsible for the structure's strength.
5 'I very much doubt,' said Tom, 'whether you fully understand the message I want you to deliver to Fred.'
'I certainly do,' replied Jack. 'You want me to tell him that the practice will be on Thursday this week.'
'That's just the point!' exclaimed Tom. 'Thursday next week, not Thursday this week. It's on Wednesday, as usual, this week.'
'Is it?'
'Yes. I've said so, twice, already.'
'Perhaps you'd better give him the message yourself.'
'Perhaps I had!'

PROBLEM 17 (page 159)

1 whom. 2 whom. 3 us. 4 calls. 5 may; without. 6 can. 7 on. 8 from; courageous. 9 or. 10 was.

PROBLEM 18 (pages 159 and 160)

1 D. 2 A. 3 C. 4 C. 5 A. 6 E. 7 E. 8 E. 9 B. 10 A. 11 C. 12 B. 13 B. 14 A.

PROBLEM 19 (page 160)

Sentence 3.

PROBLEM 20 (page 160)

1 (a) disloyal; (b) described in depressing words; (c) responsible for their situation; (d) be still alive despite their suffering in prison; (e) described in abusive terms.

2 Their commanders inflicted casualties mercilessly upon them; one driving them into the killing ground where the other slew them.

Index*

*Page numbers in *italic* type refer to worked examples.